Lyric & Spirit

Lyric & Spirit

Selected Essays
1996–2008

Hank Lazer

OMNIDAWN PUBLISHING
RICHMOND, CALIFORNIA

Cover art by Grisha Bruskin:
Nota Bene A, 2006, Oil on linen, 21 x 62 inches;
Nota Bene B, 2006, Oil on linen, 21 x 62 inches;
Nota Bene D, 2006, Oil on linen, 21 x 62 inches.
Courtesy of Mr. Grisha Bruskin and Meyerovich Gallery,
San Francisco, California (www.meyerovich.com).

Book cover and interior design by Ken Keegan.

Offset printed in the United States on archival, acid-free recycled paper
by Thomson-Shore, Inc., Dexter, Michigan

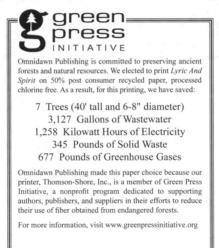

Omnidawn Publishing is committed to preserving ancient
forests and natural resources. We elected to print *Lyric And
Spirit* on 50% post consumer recycled paper, processed
chlorine free. As a result, for this printing, we have saved:

7 Trees (40' tall and 6-8" diameter)
3,127 Gallons of Wastewater
1,258 Kilowatt Hours of Electricity
345 Pounds of Solid Waste
677 Pounds of Greenhouse Gases

Omnidawn Publishing made this paper choice because our
printer, Thomson-Shore, Inc., is a member of Green Press
Initiative, a nonprofit program dedicated to supporting
authors, publishers, and suppliers in their efforts to reduce
their use of fiber obtained from endangered forests.

For more information, visit www.greenpressinitiative.org

Library of Congress Catalog-in-Publication Data

Lazer, Hank.
    Lyric & spirit : selected essays, 1996-2008 / Hank Lazer.
        p. cm.
    ISBN-13: 978-1-890650-32-2 (pbk. : alk. paper)
    I. Title: Lyric and spirit. II. Title.
    PS3562.A984L97 2008
    814'.54--dc22

                                        2007052474

Published by Omnidawn Publishing, Richmond, California
www.omnidawn.com   (510) 237-5472   (800) 792-4957
        10 9 8 7 6 5 4 3 2 1
        ISBN: 978-1-890650-32-2

Acknowledgments

Thanks to the following editors, journals, and occasions—each crucial in the writing of these essays.

"The Lyric Valuables: Soundings, Questions & Examples" was initially presented as a talk (in an abridged form) at the Northeastern Modern Languages Association meeting in 1996, and subsequently published in *Modern Language Studies*, Vol. 27, No. 2 (Spring 1997): 25–50, in a still somewhat abridged form.

"Vatic Scat": Jazz and the Poetry of Robert Creeley and Nathaniel Mackey" first appeared in *River City: A Journal of Contemporary Culture* 17.2 (Summer 1997): 100–108. (Thanks to editor Paul Naylor)

"Lyricism of the Swerve: The Poetry of Rae Armantrout" appeared first in *A Wild Salience: The Writing of Rae Armantrout*. Ed. Tom Beckett, with Bobbie West and Robert Drake. Cleveland: Burning Press, 1999: 131–154, and then, somewhat revised, in *American Woman Poets in the 21st Century*. Eds. Claudia Rankine and Juliana Spahr. Middletown, Connecticut: Wesleyan University Press, 2002: 27–52.

"The Early 1950s and the Laboratory of the Short Line" was first presented (in an abridged form) at the June 1996 National Poetry Foundation conference "American Poetry in the 1950s." The essay has not previously been published.

"Nice Work If You Can Get It: John Taggart's *Pastorelles*" first appeared in *Talisman: A Journal of Contemporary Poetry and Poetics* #28/29 (Winter 2005): 115–123. (Thanks to Ed Foster)

"Q&A Poetics" has not previously been published.

"Thinking / Singing and the Metaphysics of Sound" was first presented (in an abridged form) at the AWP Conference in Austin, Texas, in March 2006. (Thanks to Elisabeth Frost and to Cynthia Hogue) This essay has not previously been published.

"Returns: Innovative Poetry and Questions of 'Spirit'" first appeared (in a considerably abridged form) in *Facture* 2 (2001): 125–152. (Thanks to Paul Naylor)

"Sacred Forgery and the Grounds of Poetic Archaeology: Armand Schwerner's *The Tablets*" first appeared in *Chicago Review* 46.1 (2000): 142–154.

"The Art & Architecture of Holding Open: The Radical Yes of *Architectural Body*" first appeared in *Interfaces: Image Texte Language* Vol. 1 No. 21/22 (December 2003): 31–40. (Thanks to Arakawa and Madeline Gins)

"Meeting in the Book: Rosmarie Waldrop's *Lavish Absence: Recalling and Rereading Edmond Jabès*" first appeared in *Jacket #23* (August 2003). (Thanks to John Tranter)

"Poetry and Myth: The Scene of Writing, Thinking as Such" first appeared in *Mythosphere: A Journal for Image, Myth, and Symbol* 1.4 (1999): 403–414. (Thanks to William Doty)

"Force, Vector, or Pressure: The Phenomena of that Relationship" (An Interview with Chris Mansel) appears on Chris Mansel's blog and has not otherwise been published. (Thanks to Chris Mansel)

"Reflections on *The Wisdom Anthology of North American Buddhist Poetry*" has appeared in *Talisman: A Journal of Contemporary Poetry and Poetics* #32/33 (Summer/Fall 2006): 4–17 (thanks to Ed Foster), and in *Revista Canaria de Estudio Ingleses* 52 (abril 2006): 23–34 (thanks to Manuel Brito), and was presented as a talk at La Laguna University, Canary Islands, May 2006 (thanks to Matilde Martín and Manuel Brito).

Contents

To Jane

— Critical in every sense

Introduction

It has been twelve years since I have collected a group of my essays for publication as a book. When I last assembled my critical writing, the results was, to my surprise, a two volume collection of essays, *Opposing Poetries* (Northwestern University Press, 1996), with one volume focusing on Issues and Institutions (and thus a great deal on the sociology and politics of poetry's institutional life) and the other on a series of extended readings of specific books and authors. Over the past twelve years, I have continued to publish essays and reviews, to give papers at conferences, and to present guest lectures on and off campus. For the present collection, I have culled through a much larger collection of critical essays to make manifest, with, I hope, some depth and coherence, two abiding issues that have occupied my interest for somewhat more than the past twelve years.

These dual focal points—lyric, lyricism, and musicality (even the beauty of sound), and spirit, or how to find new ways to write a poetry that engages spiritual experience without resorting to a tired or merely received rhetoric and formulation—have been abiding preoccupations of mine in poetry and critical prose. Perhaps that is one of the defining oddities of my approach to reading and writing: to experience poetry and critical prose as part of a single ongoing process of thinking and exploring. Thus, the writing of the critical essays on lyric/lyricism coincides with and grows out of the poetry of *Days* (written in 1994–95, and published by Lavender Ink in 2002, and referred to in a concluding note as a kind of laboratory for the lyric). The writing on spirit exists in partnership with the heuristic work of *The New Spirit* (written in 1999, and published by Singing Horse Press in 2005), and the more recent series of poems, *Portions* (2001–2006). My sense and practice of poetry and criticism as inseparable and overlapping has been a commitment of mine from the beginning of my writing life in the early 1970s, was a position staked out in *Opposing Poetries*, and, to a large degree, was essential to my initial sense of kinship with a range of Language poets in the 1980s and 1990s.

The essays in *Lyric & Spirit* identify two major topics that may also mark ruptures or flashpoints or locations of productive discomfort *within* contemporary experimental poetic practice. One aspect of that discomfort is with an experimental poetry lineage, for example, that includes poets such as Robert Duncan, Jerome Rothenberg, Paul Celan, and Emily Dickinson, while many contemporary innovative poets have a deep suspicion of the mythic or shamanic or theological underpinnings of such writing. Similarly, lyric or lyrical as a synonym for beautiful sounds or for a pleasing musicality may bring about a similarly aversive response, all the while embracing an exemplary listening to the melopoeia of Pound, some Stein, Williams, Stevens, and others. Through these inter-related essays, I wish to explore the nature and sources of this uneasiness, and to present examples of new modes of and approaches to writing lyric and spirit. The uneasiness that I am alleging does not occur merely at a theoretical or arm's length distance but is also part of my own experience as a poet, as my writing re-inhabits the domains of lyric and spirit, and as my affiliations as a poet depart from more conventionally recognizable forms of the experimental.

Both sections of *Lyric & Spirit* begin with a lengthy essay which sets the terms, concepts, and primary examples for the rest of the section. The essays here collected represent a wide range of approaches, from somewhat traditionally scholarly approaches to more obviously talk/lecture pieces to reviews to interviews and self-interrogation (or a mock interview). Most of the essays have been published in journals (online and in print), though several of the essays appear here for the first time or appear here in substantially expanded versions (based on the initial composition which was simply too long for journal publication). While I might wish to apologize for a few instances where a key concept or passage gets repeated in two or three places, I don't think it will be too harmful for the reader to sound out or think through some of these locales more than once. In fact, a deliberate choice in *Lyric & Spirit* is to offer extended close readings (and listenings) of specific poems, passages, and poets' work so that the very specificity and nuanced differences of the more general terms "lyric" and "spirit" can be demonstrated. I have updated some references in the essays—particularly when a newer, better edition of a primary text became available—but I have not done so throughout the collection. For better or for worse, as with the writing of poetry, I consider the essay as a temporary and intense habitation for a realm of thinking that is contingent, temporary, and immediately part of a process of thinking that does not arrive at absolute conclusions. I find it very difficult to re-enter these dwelling places in such a way that beneficial revision becomes a possibility. During the weeks or months of initial composition, plenty of revision and re-writing went on. But years later, I find that my thinking has changed substantially enough to make re-entry, except as a reader, not advisable.

While the range of writing that you are about to enter into is (I hope) somewhat informed by reading in philosophy and critical theory—reading that I do because I find it pleasurable—I have tried throughout to be accessible and approachable. It is my hope that *Lyric & Spirit* will be of value to a range of poets (and non-poet-readers), inspiring other pieces of writing and other iterations in an ongoing conversation. I hope as well that this book will stimulate conversation about the relative centrality to innovative poetry of the terms lyric and spirit. I know that in my own writing, I reached a point where I could no longer imagine continuing the writing without a thorough going re-investment in these terms. To do otherwise would have been to throw the baby out with the bath water. I think that that is one of the virtues or pressures of aging: at a certain point in one's life (and in one's writing life), finitude becomes all too apparent, and one must decide what is truly worth doing, or attempting to do. It is in that spirit that this book is compiled.

(January 2008)
Tuscaloosa, Alabama

Lyric

The Lyric Valuables:
Soundings, Questions, & Examples

I would like to give some considered thought to what George Oppen called the "lyric valuables."[1] Specifically, I am interested in several related issues: lyric (or lyrical) in relation to what? that is, what are the changing contexts of the lyrical in contemporary poetry? what modes of music or musicality are crucial to the lyrical (as opposed to a lyrical intensity that results from a concentrated image making—i.e., my interest is thus in, to borrow Pound's categories, *melopoeia* rather than *logopoeia* or *phanopoeia*)? how does contemporary poetry participate in changing the nature of what we hear as "beautiful" in poetry?

Also, I am interested in considering Stein's comments in "Composition as Explanation" where she describes the rather sudden shift from outlaw to classic, the almost instantaneous shift in our perception of the ugly and the beautiful. This latter area of inquiry seems to me to be principally pedagogical and phenomenological in nature. In teaching, we are often faced with a situation where we hope to alter or expand the aesthetics of our students. We ask them to learn ways to read and enjoy poetries that, initially, strike them as "ugly," "crazy," "arbitrary," "random," and so on. In effect, we are asking them (and ourselves, through our own continued explorations as readers) to read and to hear differently. Increasingly, I have been struck by the fraudulent nature of such schooling. I have begun to tell my students not to confuse the classroom experience with their broader education in poetry. When considering the "lyric valuables," what is the problem with school? The time frame. To experience a conversion on demand, within a fifteen week period, or, more likely within a week or two, is unreasonable. To read and to hear differently may take what amounts to a paradigm shift, a fundamental

---

1 First delivered as a talk in 1996 and then published in 1997, this version of the essay represents a significant expansion of the 1997 publication.

reconsideration on the part of the reader of what constitutes the meaningful and the beautiful.

Stein, in 1926 in "Composition as Explanation," laments the absence of listeners and readers and contemporaries: "it is so very much more exciting and satisfactory for everybody if one can have contemporaries, if all one's contemporaries could be one's contemporaries" (496). In part, she may be seen to cast blame on the reader: "If every one were not so indolent they would realize that beauty is beauty even when it is irritating and stimulating not only when it is accepted and classic" (497). But Stein laments equally the rapidity of that shift in perception: "the creator of the new composition in the arts is an outlaw until he is a classic there is hardly a moment in between and it is really too bad very much too bad" and "There is not an interval. For a very long time everybody refuses and then almost without a pause almost everybody accepts. In the history of the refused in the arts and literature the rapidity of the change is always startling" (496). Perhaps a change in taste does occur as an about-face; but Stein's version in "Composition as Explanation" of that turnabout omits the events of the time in between, the time as preparation, perhaps unseen and unknown, for a shift in aesthetics. But perhaps Stein's earlier perspective in *The Making of Americans* is more to the point, or the lack of a point. Perhaps a gradualness is more truthful to our own extended reading experience, our own extended change in taste. For each of us, there will be certain poets whose work initially sounds jarring, unpleasant, irrelevant, and ugly. Such an experience, for adventurous listeners, may be fairly commonplace in music—the later compositions of John Coltrane, for example, or pieces by Terry Riley or Carla Bley or Lou Harrison—work that initially sounds like noise that later comes to have a distinct beauty to it. In poetry, that experience might come from reading work by John Ashbery or Gertrude Stein or Charles Bernstein or John Cage. Did the change in perception occur all at once? The change in perception may have been remarked upon all at once, but the change itself occurred over time in a perhaps imperceptible gradualness that makes an account of it impossible.

Is a pure lyricism any longer credible? Such a question can be asked partly from the perspective of Adorno's assertion that poetry (or lyrical poetry?) after Auschwitz is impossible, that the beauty put forward in such poetry no longer bears an ethical or credible relationship to a century of mass atrocities. To question whether a lyricism is any longer possible may also stem from an intense desire to create a "new realism." Thus perhaps in our time the more credible instances of the "lyric valuables" occur in a broader context, less segregated, less precious, less isolated, more in a dialectical relationship (as in Lyn Hejinian's *My Life*) to surrounding modes of language and expression. At another extreme, one suggested by John Cage's work, one might ask is it possible to produce a writing that is thoroughly anti-lyrical (an absolute minimalism?) that nonetheless remains interesting, that nonetheless compels attention and rewards relistening?

And, even before I begin to propose examples allegedly worthy of consideration, does my selection and advocacy of a passage of poetry as "beautiful" amount to anything more than a personal liking? Is the outcome merely my effort to convince you to assent to this declaration of beauty?

A descriptive taxonomy of contemporary lyricisms might be a fine goal. But the lyricisms I am listening to are resistant; they depend, in part, on their sounding out a thinking that departs from the customary. We might then seek to be immersed in a variety of musical priorities, an integral: lower limit quickly shifting musics (as in Clark Coolidge's poetry), upper limit an almost impreceptibly slowly changing music (as in Theodore Enslin's work).

> Ed Foster: What is it in your own work that determines the order of the words—a simulation of musical structures, musical cadences, qualities in syntax, the course of the idea ...
>
> Theodore Enslin: Certainly it is not primarily to state an idea. The development of the language, the cadence of the language, the musical cadence—those things.... I am more or less at sea when I begin. I know pretty well where I want to go, even

though I'm not sure whether I can get there. My hope is always that the sense of the thing becomes clear both to me and,
if it's going to be saved, to anybody else—will be clear not in
the sense of making an idea: That can be, yes—I'm not ruling
it out, but it is not my primary concern. After this happens
with many (good people, too) as a poem builds toward some
kind of climax, you get this memorable line, and that freezes
my blood. I hate it, that memorable line, that whole…Well,
maybe it's important to some people. It's not to me. (33–34)

We might consider too the way that Zukofsky's poetics of the early
1930s (in "An Objective") remain pertinent as they continue to be
worked out in newly emerging lyricisms. One of Zukofsky's definitions
is "A poem: a context associated with 'musical' shape, musical with
quotation marks since it is not of notes as music, but of words more
variable than variables, and used outside as well as within the context
with communicative reference" (16). Zukofsky continues, "The order
of all poetry is to approach a state of music wherein the ideas present
themselves sensuously and intelligently and are of no predatory intention" (18). As in the thirteenth section of Enslin's "Autumnal Rime":

Of the clocks sounds timing hesitance sounding
is between vibration ear and touch the finger
springing coil release to find resounding
not a sound   a hesitance of clocks   of larks
an exultation   tock the blow a hammer sounds
the finger touch a tier of sounds in scale
resounding between the touch   the timing sounds
of clocks this hesitance   ear and touch vibration
release between a spring   the hesitance of ear
resounding clocks   between the ear and touch
the hesitance of clocks   the timing hesitance
to coil vibration to release the clock
sounds timing   blow of hammer tock
of larks and exultation   sounds sounds
ears and touch   sounding clocks   clocks sounding
to release the sound in flight
an exaltation (49)

I would also like to contextualize my current consideration of the lyric valuables within a range of fairly recent critical projects. Over the past twenty years, many poets and critics, particularly those who are partisan to a more innovative poetics, have successfully critiqued and called into question the premises of the personal lyric in American poetry. A partial listing would acknowledge the work of Charles Altieri, Marjorie Perloff, Charles Bernstein, Jed Rasula, and Donald Hall, as each assisting in the burial of the mainstream personal lyric, as pointing out the extraordinary limitations of such writing. More recently, a younger generation of poets have begun to wonder about the renewal of two possibilities *within* an avant-garde poetic practice. Specifically, there has been considerable discussion of the place of the lyric and of spirituality *within* an innovative poetic practice. A partial listing would include the essays of Mark Wallace, Leonard Schwartz, Susan Schultz, Patrick Phillips, Susan Smith Nash, and the editors of the magazine *apex of the M* as raising these concerns. It is alleged that the work of older poets associated with the Language poetry movement has somehow repressed certain poetic resources in the realm of the lyrical and spiritual. It is my own opinion that such an assertion has more to do with the difficulties of poetic succession than with any truthful observation about the nature of an earlier generation of innovative poets. Again, a partial listing of more established innovative poets whose work most definitely engages issues of lyricism and spirituality would include Susan Howe, Lyn Hejinian, Theodore Enslin, John Taggart, Rachel Blau DuPlessis, Kathleen Fraser, bpNichol, Charles Bernstein, and Nathaniel Mackey. Thus, in part, in this essay I wish to sound some examples of lyricisms *within* ongoing innovative poetries. For there is truly no need to import or add what is already present.

But recent thinking about the lyric raises other issues as well. From rather different perspectives, Mark Wallace and the editors of *apex of the M*, are interested in the lyric's possibilities for address. For Wallace in "On the Lyric as Experimental Possibility," the lyric may be a fit resource for newly imagined and newly constructed poetic hybrids:

It always remains possible to test the value of a form again, to see what use might be made in the present moment of its historically determinable characteristics, or to alter, recombine, or change those characteristics to redefine the possibilities of that form in the present moment. One interesting possibility, for instance, would be to combine elements historically thought of as belonging to one sort of poetic form with elements of another form, thus distorting both forms to create new hybrids.(1)

And one can certainly argue that such combinations have been central to the efforts of many twentieth-century poets. Wallace's specific interest in the lyric, though, has to do with its imagined possibilities for clarity or immediacy of address:

Historically, one primary difference between the lyric and other forms of western poetry has been the nature of address. The lyric often speaks to another person (in some cases perhaps a group of persons) very specifically, rather than addressing the 'world in general' as does epic poetry or the modern American 'poem with history[.]'…I am interested in the way the lyric suggests that address needs to be understood as specific, however troubling the specific address of specific lyric poems may be. I am crucially interested in the question of who might hear me, and who, in turn, I might possibly hear. (2)

Wallace concludes, "the sense of lyric I am suggesting presents a mode of world address that is potentially more useful than a more generalized, public address that speaks at (and therefore past) everyone" (10).

Similarly, the editors (Lew Daly, Alan Gilbert, Kristin Prevallet, and Pam Rehm) of *the apex of the M* [2] establish a critical relationship to Language poets and other more established modes of experi-

---

2 From 1994 – 1997, *apex of the M* published six issues. They have ceased publication, but copies of issues #4 – 6 are available at the time of this printing. See the web site for current information: http://epc.buffalo. edu/mags/apex/.

mentation in poetry by re-emphasizing the social element of poetic communication. In "State of the Art," the opening statement for the first issue of the magazine (#1, Spring 1994, pp. 5–7), the editors announce that they

> are interested in a radical transparency of language that is ultimately objectless, that allows for the non-linguistic, and finds the basis for its *address* in a relationship with others that is not a making of the other into a theme or an object to be possessed, is not a losing of oneself in another, and is certainly not a violent confrontation with the other that first and foremost endeavors to alienate individuals from the very possibility of dialogue and therefore responsibility (emphasis mine, 5).

The editors are critical of poetry that is "so insistently non-dialogical and so assuredly self-referential"; they seek instead a poetry which would be a "reembodiment in a loving dialogue" (7). The opening statement for the second issue of the magazine begins to make clear what the terms might be for a newly imagined "Good" in poetry. Their emphasis is indeed on the social, on dialogue, on communicability, and the newly introduced transcendental term becomes "context," as the editors seek a poetry and

> a language built upon an acknowledgment of context as well as an acknowledgment of others that neither effaces nor assimilates them. Much of the avant-garde work of recent years exhibits an almost stupefied preoccupation with mediacy, method, and condition of signs, etc.: what have become the new transcendental categories of our time. … More liberating than alienation and exclusion of the reader by a blind priority given to signs is language written from solicitude. (5–6)

The editors conclude that "context must dominate language to the extent to which existence is dominated by injustice" (7). Interestingly, though, the specific context of the magazine's own circumstances of production—its specific social and institutional context—do not get explored or exposed. Thus, much of the criticism made of an immediately prior (and ongoing) avant-garde by the editors has been susceptible to interpretation as, in part, an anxiety of poetic succession. I believe that such an explanation is pertinent, but that it does not negate the merit of certain specific critiques offered by the editors. For example, their criticism of irony and ironizing is worth serious consideration:

> In the face of atrocity, poetics should be less concerned with the free-play of the signifier and the reading subject than with the possibilities of justice for and vindication of the subjected. Poetry's madness leads to love. Anguish and the ecstatic, not play and the ironic, are the tears in the fabric of ideology. Irony and play completely depend upon the continued existence of that toward which they are ironic and playful. Anguish and the ecstatic allow for the entrance of context, while also allowing a more obscure movement to replace our own. (6)

But, as the examples of Ashbery, Bernstein, Silliman, and Perelman show, irony may also involve compassion, engagement, and, perhaps, in Kenneth Burke's term, a comic frame of acceptance.

The editors of *apex of the M*, in their desire for a more direct relationship between poetic practice and social intervention, clearly are not repeating a mainstream poetic desire for poems with political subject matter. The editors seems well aware of claims such as Adorno's that "among the links that mediate art and society, subject matter is the most superficial and fallible one" (AT, 326). Adorno claims that "the unresolved antagonisms of reality reappear in art in the guise of immanent problems of artistic form. This, and not the deliberate injection of objective moments or social content, defines art's relation to society" (8). For Adorno, art offers an embodiment of resistance: "Art will live on only as long as it has the power to resist society. If it refuses to objectify itself, it becomes a commodity. What it contributes to society is not some directly communicable content but something more mediate, i.e. resistance" (321). But the power and disturbance of such resistance—and, as I am arguing, new modes of lyricism constitute important sites of such resistance—is not a fixed event. The initially irritating, the once radical work of art is involved in a journey of aesthetic reception, is on an exodus of familiarization and appropriation. Adorno continues, "What is social about art is not its political stance, but its immanent dynamic in opposition to society.... If any social function can be ascribed to art at all, it is the function to have no function" (322). But the editors of *apex of the M* are currently being taught a disruptive, resistant poetics by poets holding endowed chairs of literature, and their magazine itself is institutionally funded. While these facts in and of themselves do not negate the force of the poetry being produced, they do mark a significantly different institutional location for the acts of resistance and carry with them different complications for imitation, conformity, and reproduction. As explanations and mediating structures assist in the domestication and institutionalization of new poetries, a certain disruptive force begins to be dissipated. Such worries, implicit in the tone of the editors' opening remarks to the first two issues of their magazine, merit serious attention, perhaps in conjunction with Adorno's conclusion that "the socially critical dimensions of art works are those that hurt, those that bring to light (through the medium of expression and in historically determinate ways) what is wrong with present social conditions" (337). The strategic problem for avant-garde artists today is to steer a course between the two poles of ineffectiveness which Adorno delineates: "In its relation to society art finds itself in a dilemma today. If it lets go of autonomy it sells out to the established order, whereas if it tries to stay strictly within its autonomous confines it becomes equally co-optable, living a harmless life in its appointed niche" (337).

In "'Called Null or Called Vocative': A Fate of the Contemporary Lyric," Susan Schultz, like Wallace and the editors of *apex of the M*, suggests new and renewing possibilities for the lyric. But where Schultz's writing is most helpful is in delineating the currently conflicted views of the lyric:

> My title, from Michael Palmer's "Letter 3," makes apt shorthand for recent debates about the lyric. On the one hand, mainstream poets from Rita Dove to Galway Kinnell to Sharon Olds and back again believe in the voice of the "I" and center their poetics on it. On the other, language

writers such as Charles Bernstein have happily written epi-
taphs for the lyric "I" over the past two decades, arguing
that the personal pronoun is more a theatrical pose than a
defensible position.

   Voice, according to Bernstein, is a possibility but should
hardly be considered an end. Marjorie Perloff, for her part,
has written about ways in which the lyric has been ruptured
productively and used as a vehicle for narratives, however
fractured. In short, proponents of what Alfred Corn termed
"the other tradition" (what some still call the avant-garde)
approach the lyric with utmost suspicion. (70)

The flashpoint for debates over the value and currency of the lyric,
then, turns out to be what Schultz (by way of critic Shelley Sunn
Wong) calls the "dubious identity politics" of an I-based lyric (70).
Schultz, thus, is sympathetic to the kind of radical surgery advocated
by Adorno: "The utopia anticipated by artistic form is the idea that
things at long last ought to come into their own. Another way of
putting this is to call for the abolition of the spell of selfhood hith-
erto promoted by the subject" (AT, 195) Schultz, though, does not
want to do away with the lyric; instead, she argues for the possibility
of a "voiceless lyric":

> If lyric is to remain a possibility in contemporary poetry, it
> must adapt to, and answer, these formidable critiques. Lyric
> poets (because there are always such) must find ways in
> which to accommodate the lyric to the actual world, where
> voice does not denote mastery so much as conflict, identity
> so much as its confusions and contradictions. I want to sug-
> gest that one of the possibilities for contemporary poetry is
> what might be called, paradoxically, the "voiceless lyric," or
> a lyrical poem from which the "I" had been excised…. For
> now, let me say that the unvoiced lyric acknowledges antihu-
> manist critiques of the unitary self, while retaining a belief in
> the significant silences and spiritual and erotic desires tradi-
> tionally expressed in lyric poems. (70–71)

Schultz cites recent successful examples of the lyric in Charles Bernstein's *Dark City* (1994), a success made possible by Bernstein's critique of the lyric: "...a moment akin to Nixon's 'opening' of China; Nixon got away with that one because he'd destroyed Alger Hiss. Bernstein gets away with his lyric because he's spent the bulk of his career attempting to destroy our (hypothetical) desire to value *New Yorker* poems" (79). Schultz concludes that "the twenty-first-century lyric will be, of necessity, found in combination with other genres, joined in the coproduction of ruptures at once mimetic of the world and, potentially, capable of transforming small moments of it. We can return to the lyric, in its old sense, only sometimes, and then after long forays into the animal soup of the actual world" (79).

My own thinking about the lyric gives greater emphasis to the possible disruptiveness and fundamental importance of *melopoeia* itself. From my perspective, most evaluations of the lyric, including Wallace's, the editors of *apex of the M*, and Schultz's, move too rapidly to signification, "meaning," subject matter, and address, without dwelling long enough with the specific odd music of newly emergent lyricisms.

But is it enough merely to "dwell" with these alleged lyricisms? What must be done with a specific musical registration in language? What are modes of *ethical* explanatory engagement with the particularities—the opacity and percussive qualities—of current lyricisms?

⸻

As a prelude to more extended discussions, we might first listen to several examples of shifting percussive lyricisms in the work of Clark Coolidge, poet and jazz drummer:

On the Way

Wristed courses on the nod
fat mornings, the road tools
for spacious opens on the witness delves
and patch it, iron its lights, and in ember
wire the tiny christ its interstitial
ghostage (*Odes of Roba*, 18)

On Walking

Broad strokes across the left hats
the night the day came up in slats
setting a plaza where the sketch could be told
in enthusiasm silence the brown walls
and nearly collided fates, greets
I put off my feet till
nodule still bell hour
the fact matter (*Odes of Roba*, 57)

In these brief poems by Coolidge, the way of going is both enabled and blocked by the sudden shifts in syntactical direction. We are brought to a halt in the clatter of colliding words and syllables, the coagulating slow sounds of *still bell hour* followed by the seeming summary of what has happened, *the fact matter*, the increasingly dense music of the passage itself reaching a limit.

———

    At present, we can begin to see the emergence of a lyricism based not on a univocal intensification but upon a shifting of discourses, as in the writings of Harryette Mullen, Ron Silliman, and Charles Bernstein. In fact, the rapidity of shifting discourses begins to constitute its own metric; lyricism may inhere in the direction- (or discourse-) shifting as a mode of exhilaration (and acceleration), something analogous to the fluid change of direction of much of Thelonious Monk's musical compositions (particularly "Thelonious," "In Walked Bud," "Evidence," "Epistrophy," "Skippy," "Bright Mississippi," and most especially in Monk's solo recordings). It is possible now to incorporate philosophical or abstract language into the realm of the lyrical, to savor the collision and collusion of different discourses within a single poem. Or, as Lyn Hejinian asserts in *My Life*, "'we can no longer ignore ideology, it has become an important lyrical language'" (113). As I argue *Opposing Poetries* (Volume 2: *Readings*), it is possible to create, as Charles Bernstein has, a kind of clotted jumbly lyricism. In *Dark City* (1994), in "Heart in My Eye," Bernstein writes,

> —or hate
> the boom-shebang effect
> fostered at time
>
> interlock, station flayed by
> inoperable hampers, obsequious
> swoops, as pulp bumps
> plop, thingamawhoseit buffle
>
> joint, glassed in gradually
> gestures of gerrymand
> origin, jitters jocose oblong— (114)

Bernstein is increasingly drawn to the odd demotic word such as "boomshebang" (or, as elsewhere in the same poem, "higglety pigglety" and "slumpy"). He has established a well-developed ear for a peculiar dissonance in word-sounds, a kind of deliberately clotted, awkward, technical language that has its own percussive music. I dare say that no one else is writing lines such as "voids convivial handtray intubation" (*Dark City*, 114), and that no one else is as attuned to such a peculiar music.

In our time, there is a profoundly important argument on behalf of the stammer, the stutter, the garbled statement as having its own particular beauty, a beauty that lies significantly outside the modes of regulated language and of language used for decidedly manipulative (political and commercial) ends. Here, the work of Nathaniel Mackey, both his poetry and criticism, is crucial. In "Alphabet of Ahtt," Mackey begins,

> Anagrammic scramble. Scourge
>   of sound. Under its brunt
> plugged ears unload...
>   Tight squeeze
> toward a sweatless heaven.
>   Anagrammatic tath. Anagrammatic
>   that...

Shucked husk. Severed
rope tossed upward. Not
knowing why but reaching
elsewhere,
edgy. Not without hope though
how were we to take it as
they yelled out, "Nathtess's melismatic
ttah"?
Not knowing why, we looked straight
ahead, shrugged our shoulders,
popped out fingers, we could dig it,
"what's next?"   (*School of Udhra*, 43)

In *Discrepant Engagement*, Mackey points to Victor Zuckerkandl
who offers "'a musical concept of the external world,' something he
also calls 'a critique of our concept of reality from the point of view
of music'" (232). For Mackey, who draws heavily on blues and jazz
traditions, "part of the genius of black music is the room it allows for
a telling 'inarticulacy,' a feature consistent with its critique of a predatory coherence, a cannibalistic 'plan of living,' and the articulacy
that upholds it" (252 – 253). Thus, in his criticism and in his poetry,
Mackey argues for the way "Brathwaite helps impeded speech find
its voice, the way Thelonious Monk makes hesitation eloquent or the
way a scat singer makes inarticulacy speak" (274).

   Perhaps better than any other poet/critic of the present, Mackey
expresses the significance of the disruptive lyricisms which I am attending to in this essay. For Mackey, such musicalities have an important anti-foundational aspect to them. He terms an attachment
to such music "discrepant engagement":

   It is an expression coined in reference to practices that, in
   the interest of opening presumably closed order of identity
   and signification, accent fissure, fracture, incongruity, the
   rickety, imperfect fit between word and world. Such practices highlight—indeed inhabit—discrepancy, engage rather
   than seek to ignore it. Recalling the derivation of the word
   discrepant from a root meaning "to rattle, creak," I relate discrepant engagement to the name the Dogon of West Africa

give their weaving block, the base on which the loom they
weave upon sits. They call it the "creaking of the word." It
is the noise upon which the word is based, the discrepant
foundation of all coherence and articulation … [.] In its anti-
foundational acknowledgment of founding noise, discrepant
engagement sings "base," voicing reminders of the axiomatic
exclusions upon which positings of identity and meaning
depend. (19)

As Mackey argues in a talk he gave at the Jack Kerouac School, such
singing involves "a tearing of the voice, a crippling of the voice that
paradoxically is also enabling" ("Cante Moro," 85). It involves an
anti-foundationalism that Mackey also hears in the blues:

> One of the striking things about the blues tradition is the
> way the instrument becomes that other, alternate voice.
> Everyone talks about the speechlike qualities of the instru-
> ments as they're played in African-American music. Built
> into that is some kind of dissatisfaction with—if not critique
> of—the limits of conventionally articulate speech, verbal
> speech. One of the reasons the music so often goes over into
> nonspeech—moaning, humming, shouts, nonsense lyrics,
> scat—is to say, among other things, that the realm of con-
> ventionally articulate speech is not sufficient for saying what
> needs to be said. We're often making that same assertion in
> poetry. ("Cante Moro," 86)

Mackey's poetry, his particular lyricism, a jazz-Black Mountain hybrid of considerable signficance, plays the music of the stuttering
mis-step, the heuristics of a nearly beyond sense:

> Tautologic
>   drift in which once more what spoke
>   of speaking spoke of speaking.
> Made us wonder would it ever do
>   differently, all but undone to've
>   been so insisted on,
>   anagrammatic

ythm, anagrammatic myth…

Autistic.

Spat a bitter truth. Maybe misled but
if so so be it. Palimpsestic

stagger

anagrammatic

scat   (*Udhra*, 43–44)

Interestingly, Mackey's musicality sounds its edge of sense-making within a play of *print*, of the anagram and the palimpsest, the layering of sound noted in the multidirectioned play of the written word.

———

Must the lyrical exist necessarily in contrast with the spoken? What then of David Antin's talk-poems? Is there a lyricism that occurs "naturally" in speech? Must we, in a poetry reading, be able to distinguish between the introductory or prefatory remarks of the poet and the poem itself? Is the lyrical dependent then on an artificial quality, an act of framing (by means of a different cadence, a different voice, a different mode of performance) that has something of the precious in it?

———

Is it not possible that all poets, the writings of all poets, participate in a kind of lyricism? That no writing would or could be uniformly interesting (or uninteresting), and/or that the reading practices of the reader activate a lyricism? That, in Oppen's phrase "the lyric valuables," what is at issue is a preference for an intensification, a noticing (or making) of value based on some perception of difference. I read your many pages of writing, and some passages strike me as beautiful, as of particular interest, and the term "lyrical" is one way I have of identifying and beginning to discuss that beauty.

Edgar Allen Poe, perhaps, had sought a steady-state beauty. Many mainstream lyric poems seek nearly the same: a confined terrain of medium beauty succeeded by, ahh, some closing passage of greater beauty. The lyricism to which I am attending is contextualized much differently and presents a greater tolerance of other writing in proximity with the beautiful.

Is the lyrical then some kind of "success" that the poet has with language? I think of Oppen's remarks in "Of Being Numerous," of making poetry out of one human language. Is the language itself not lyrical? Consider John Cage's remarks: "music / never stops it is we who turn away" and "waiting for a bus / we're present at a concert / suddenly we stand on a work of art the pavement" (*X*, 140). Is it ever possible to locate "the lyric valuables" apart from the perceiver's mode of attention, the context and education of that attention?

Because I declare a particular passage to be an example of "the lyric valuables," is it so? Is it merely the force of the rhetoric I employ that might make it so? Is the truthfulness of such a declaration merely a function of my ability to point out (fairly traditonal elements of) definable musicality, such as assonance and consonance and off-rhyme?

Is it possible to talk about "the lyric valuables" in a way that acknowledges the dimension of time, that begins with the premise that a piece of writing is not one single thing, that as Stein points out (though principally in a register of lament) there is a change in attitude, that there is a trajectory no matter how sudden from the ugly to the beautiful, from outlaw to classic? Even though there is perhaps a pivotal turning of attitude, is there not also, perhaps paradoxically and simultaneously a lyricism of gradualness such as Stein herself explores in *The Making of Americans*? Is the movement from the ugly to the beautiful not also a process of assimilation, of domestication, of a removal of difficulty? Is there not also great value in "difficulties that stay difficult"? Consider Plath (in "Daddy"), "it stuck in a barb wire snare, / ich ich ich ich, / I could hardly speak," making, even as it sticks, a pleasant or at least recognizable melody. When then does cognition become RE-cognition, and is that the making of the ugly into the beautiful? I read Susan Howe for quite some time befuddled, and then (cf. Helen Vendler on Ashbery, though Vendler it seems to me is talking principally about her perception of the sporadic occurrence of meaning and meaningfulness, which is another metric), ah-ha, I find a passage that is "beautiful,"

> we that were wood
> when that a wide wood was

In a physical Universe playing with

words

Bark be my limbs my hair be leaf

Bride be my bow my lyre my quiver (*The Europe of Trusts*, 17)

and I begin to feel at home in her work. Who or what has been do-
mesticated? Has the text? Have I? Have I not merely learned to impose my pre-existing ear upon an Other text? Have I not merely re-
assured myself of my adequate preparation to read and to listen and
to sound out Howe's poetry? Have I not lost sight of what bothered
me? Is a perception of "the lyric valuables" not inevitably tied to an
act of devaluing, of discarding what is not a lyric valuable? Consider
Ron Silliman's modular sentences as a democratic assault on such
acts of discrimination. But, by virtue of finitude, won't any act of
writing be such a discrimination?

     Consider quotation, like anthologizing, as inevitably an act of ly-
ricizing. Choose, then, an example from bpNichol's *The Martyrology*.
How is such extraction inevitably a falsification? Consider the same
problem in quoting from Hejinian's *My Life*. The latter is a work
where the author is conscious of this precise problem; she puts the
issue on display in the very form of the chapters, the quotation or
superscription, which has part of its existence in RE-cognition in the
text, in modulation too.

     Would it make any sense to study, to put forward examples for
careful study, of the NON-lyrical, of the unvaluable? Wouldn't attention endow that writing with some special qualities?

     Why have I decided that questioning is the appropriately
oblique angle necessary for approaching "the lyric valuables"?

———

     Let us move, then, into some extended specific considerations,
some instances, perhaps, of "the lyric valuables." First, some passages
from Lyn Hejinian's *The Cell*. Roughly in the middle of this book, a
series of poems without titles, poems with dates that present them-

selves as a kind of unfolding meditation on a series of related issues, a poem begins

> The person thinks by being
> > aloud
> That is the relationship of
> > music to poetry
> A single body whose function
> > is to represent the queen
> Which things are seen
> An emphasis on a medium
> > bares what is assumed
> Arrhythmic, then immortal
> All the mortalities merge in
> > the definition of "rhythm" (116)

Hejinian's passage leaves us at a remove from lyricism *per se*, offering instead a musing about some constituent elements of *poesis*. Yes, "the person thinks by being aloud," and a mode of lyricism for our time is the *sound* of that thinking, a kind of analytic lyric, a manifestation of thinking (of poetic thinking, if there is a such a distinguishable entity) not so much by means of an overriding summarizable thought (the past tense of thinking), but the sound of thinking in process, an oddly elusive, shifting, darting, the offering up of a complex rhythm (including arrhythmia) akin to the jazz rhythms of Monk and others. It is, thus, an incarnation that supports Hejinian's premise "So reality is a process not an identity" (105). Such a lyricism directs us to "a grouping below the eyes / In breast, in time" (116). Hejinian's poem then dips into that mode of irregular but recognizable lyricism of sound:

> It is repetitive to be
> > exceeding and effaced
> The landscape brightly backlit (childhood)
> > is the false loss
> The rocks and the stalks
> > are sharp
> Even the waters, or the

> light splashing back
Sand comes back at the
> examiner
Sound—the trajectory of plenitude (116)

In sounding Hejinian's poem, I would like simultaneously to propose an element of recognition of its lyricism and to acknowledge
the inadequacy of my recognition (particularly as some essential or
comprehensive element of the lyrical). If we listen carefully to the
previous passage, we hear a fairly conventional and recognizable lyricism in the irregular but pleasing deployment of assonance: *effaced
/ landscape*; *false / loss / rocks / stalks / waters*; *splashing / back / sand /
back / examiner*. This kind of musicality may indeed be *an* element
of a current (and historically persistent) lyricism. Such musicality
would be somewhat remarkable for its recontextualization of the
beautiful. But, as Hejinian and others are aware, there is also a certain inevitable nostalgia to that particular (admittedly hard to pin
down) lyricism:

> One thing that I think
> about melody is the ordinary
> coincidence
> Anything that repeats must be
> a childhood to affect you (94)

It is a lyricism from childhood, from an earlier time of poetry, a kind
of craft that in many mainstream personal lyrics reaches a monoto-
nous dead end in a kind of segregated beauty that seems childish,
seems a craft that has become restrictive. There is, though, in "rough-
er" texts, a quality of assurance, a comforting if somewhat retro
beauty in such passages. For Hejinian, they may account, in part,
for her ability as a poet to cross over, to appeal to often segregated or
disparate poetry audiences. Poets and readers from different commu-
nities can identify and appreciate this mode of lyricism:

> I carry my thoughts in
> an ocular bucket
> Space accumulates in a far

<pre>
        larger tub
It is late at night
        and sultry in the heavy
        oval (22)
</pre>

But in keeping with my earlier quotations from Stein, I am more
interested in the temporal procession in which a "new" mode of the
beautiful begins to appear. The examples (principally) of assonance
(in the just quoted passage, the dual sound melodies of *bucket* / *tub*
/ *sultry* and *space* / *accumulates* / *late*, set off against the percussion
section of *carry* / *ocular* / *bucket* / *accumulates*) are more accurately
the recontextualization of already known beauty, of already accomplished musicality, and thus constitute a kind of nostalgia. Such
nostalgia can, in fact, become a principle of composition, as in John
Ashbery's work where much of the lyricism is old sounding, a kind
of revived late nineteenth-century lyricism whose recurrence and
disappearance constitute a kind of odd metric. Hejinian, it seems
to me, remains self-conscious of this nostalgic variety of lyricism, a
beauty which she indulges in and loves though resists as a habit inadequate to the more pressing heuristic demands of *poesis*. The poem I
have been quoting ends:

<pre>
    The examiner is discretely cavorting
        to itself
    There is no sane availability
        of the harsh sound in
        its wake
    The gradual efficiency in its
        dream
                December 9, 1987 (117)
</pre>

Even the date at the end of the poem alerts us to the temporary
incarnation of such a process in which the "person thinks by being aloud" (though the poem, as a written text, exists at the border
between the written and the spoken, even if, in writing, it asserts a
primacy of the "aloud"). The specific development of a new musicality in Hejinian's poetry I would begin to locate in a kind of lyricism of abstraction. I would hasten to note that such a development

seems to me to be distinctly a community effort not an individual
enterprise. I have argued elsewhere (in *Opposing Poetries*, volume 2:
Readings) for the particular nature of such a polysyllabic lyricism in
Charles Bernstein's work. I would argue that such a newly developing lyricism is at once communal and individual, carrying forward
simultaneously the group activity of educating one another to an
emerging possibility (heard in the work of many practitioners) yet
drafted in passages that (over time and through refinement) become
somewhat idiosyncratic and individualistic. In Hejinian's *The Cell*,
the ending of the poem quoted suggests such lyrical polysyllabic abstraction, but there are other passages more to the point:

> Thinking in its gripping microtude
> That genital
> An independence anticipates the mind
>   reader
> The sampling and lamentation of
>   the contemporary (118)
> . . .
> A portrait of a person
>   idealized in its porosity
> The drop of its voluptuary
>   patrol (84)

How does it come to pass that we learn to hear differently, that
our hearing changes, tht we develop a capacity to attune to once-off-
putting-now-engaging verbal compositions? For such a turn, Kuhn's
notion of a paradigm shift is far too definite, too dramatic a turning of the ear's weathervane. And is it possible to hear as "beautiful"
what remains jarring, to attend to that early phase of beauty which
Stein advocated, "that beauty is beauty even when it is irritating,"
without eventually domesticating or familiarizing (to the point of
simple comfort, expectation, even habit) the cacophonous and newly
emerging modes of lyricism? And how do we begin to discern which
irritations, which cacophonies, will eventually prove sufficiently

engaging to dance with us in that narrative of thinking-attunement wherein we eventually learn them to be beautiful?

Is any and every assault on already familiar forms of beauty not finally recuperable as a new mode of beauty foreordained to a similar cycle of replacement? Perhaps we should think of the half-life of beauty, or the half-life of ugliness? Thus we might salute the peculiarly persistent ugly-beautiful musicality of Stein, Dickinson, and Zukofsky?

———

The beginning of *My Life* situates us within a dialectical tension or torsion, a thinking of the lyrical which also carries with it elements of self-awareness and self-criticism, a lyricism in dialog with its mixture of indulgence and refusal:

> *A pause, a rose*   A moment yellow, just as four years later
> *something on paper*   when my father returned home from the
> war, the moment of greeting him, as he
> stood at the bottom of the stairs, younger,
> thinner than when he had left, was
> purple—though moments are no longer
> so colored. Somewhere, in the background, rooms share a
> pattern of small roses. Pretty is as pretty does. In certain
> families, the meaning of necessity is at one with the senti-
> ment of pre-necessity. The better things were gathered in a
> pen. (7)

The superscription itself constitutes a lyrical concentration. As the chapter extends for its full forty-five sentences, the superscription or caption continues to speak its truncated occurrence. It has its own completeness, a verbal equivalent of the stars on an American flag. The superscription, in this instance, enacts an instance of the momentary, heading up a passage where the status and nature of the "moment" is a momentary concern. The color-ized moments—yellow, purple—within their extended sentence (another version of the momentary) are restrained by the current understanding that in spite of the way moments *once* seemed to have color, the more mature

belief would be that "moments are no longer colored so." A black-
and-white Joe Friday factual consciousness, an unheightened realism,
an anti-lyricism of sorts. Though at such a moment of sensibleness,
one must still admit "*roses*," a rose still being a rose, even if *sub rosa*,
subordinated to "*a pattern*" "*somewhere, in the background.*" Must
the lyrical pander in order to be lyrical? "Pretty is as pretty does."
Must a writer believe in his or her own intelligent selectivity? Not all
things are gathered in a pen. "The better things." Which are the better things? Which are the most beautiful things? Which things sound
the best? Is "the best" the principal substance of the poem, or is "the
best," of necessity, a rose, something pretty, a moment? Wouldn't the
principal substance of any extended poem, of necessity, be lots and
lots of the less than best? And those best moments, "the lyric valuables," must their value be tied to scarcity, float as stars in sky or field
of bars, appear as an italicized superscription:

> *A pause, a rose*
> *something on paper*

Within the superscription itself there is a flatness of statement contrasting with the off-rhyme of *pause* and *rose*, but before such a lyrical melody be taken too seriously or monologically, the melody gets
deflated with the deliberately flat *something on paper*. Is the lyrical
the moment of greeting? Is the war elsewhere and the poem a different domain? Was the war for him a pause? A rose? One side of the
poem says, "*The plush must be worn away.*" The rose recurs, a homeomorph, as a wart on an uncle's nose, "*a little puddle.*" "*But a word is
bottomless.*" All the more reason that to harness the word to a lyrical
moment of intensified expression contains its own shortsightedness
within the process itself. "*Perhaps initially, even before one can talk,
restlessness is already conventional, establishing the incoherent border
which will later separate events from experience.*" Is there a recognizable border, a way the poem has of demarcating and framing events
which the poem nominates as "experience"? Wouldn't the lyrical
valuables stem from the drawing of such borders? "That *morning
this morning.*" The particular, by the precision of its inevitable difference, is the substance of the valuable. The paradox that Cage too
immerses us in, is that *every* particular is of interest. Not merely

Shakespeare's "things are neither good nor bad but thinking makes them so," the same holds for interest, the same holds for intensity and intensification. What is a fit material for the lyrical? Potentially anything. (See, for example, the way Donald Barthelme in *Snow White* reverses perspective and creates a humorous lyricism constructed upon the rhetorical filler of phrases such as "you know" and "you might say.") Though finitude may be the principal requirement. For George Oppen, at once mythically flashy and self-accusing: "the shipwreck of the singular." Hejinian ends her first chapter's meditation by saying, by writing, "*the overtones are a denser shadow in the room characterized by its habitual readiness, a form of charged waiting, a perpetual attendance, of which I was thinking when I began the paragraph, 'So much of childhood is spent in a manner of waiting.'*" Doesn't the waiting, then, (as in much of Ashbery's poetry) deserve considerable attention? Hejinian's sentences allow waiting into them. They, each, are a morning, this and that, in which by the supple variability of kinds of sentences, difference and particularity become their own irregular metric, capable of a clipped, aphoristic, didactic, or extended and self-cancelling beauty, and other forms of beauty not named here. These, then, are some of the ways time feels. In *My Life*, Hejinian's versions of the lyrical give us a feel, a sounding, resounding, for time and the shifting modes of consciousness we experience in time and as time.

The lyrical, then, bears with it the danger of being too lyrical, of being merely pretty, of making too great a concession to already familiar musicalities of language. There is an inevitability that the lyrical involves an element of isolation, of a heightening of some effect, and in that gesture lies the excellence (as difference) of the lyric *valuables* and their inherent falseness, the inescapably rhetorical nature of the lyric as a manipulation. As an aside, it seems to me that the peculiar lyricism of John Taggart's work is of immense value precisely as an *extended* lyricism, a minimalist lyricism, founded on an unabashed spirituality, that depends on a prolonged modulation of the moment by means of a serial modification of key phrases. (See, for example, "That This May Be," "Very Slow," "In True Night," "The Rothko

Chapel Poem," and "Marvin Gaye Suite" in *Loop* [Los Angeles: Sun
& Moon, 1991], as well as the more recent long poem "Excursion.")

In Oppen's first book, *Discrete Series* (1934), before he ceased
writing poetry for nearly thirty years, we find

> People everywhere, time and the work
>   pauseless:
> One moves between reading and re-reading,
> The shape is a moment. (CP, 11)

Inevitably then "a pause, a rose, / something on paper"? The lyrical
depends upon breaking, temporarily, the relationship of the part to
the whole, of heightening the importance of the moment, of giving
the moment an engaging shape, in spite of the fact that surrounding
the lyric valuables will be a being that is pauseless. For an intellectu-
ally engaged poet such as Oppen, the lyrical involves the emotion of
a mind aroused, consciousness moved to serious attentiveness:

> The virtue of the mind
>
> Is that emotion
>
> Which causes
> To see. (CP, 87)

But Oppen's lyrical intelligence owns up to its somewhat opposed, or
apposed, recognition: "' Powerless to affect / The intensity of what is'"
(CP, 92). That is: *what is* already provides adequate intensity (a realization crucial as well to John Cage's writing, music, and painting).

In *The Materials* (1962) we find "From Disaster":

> Ultimately the air
> Is bare sunlight where must be found
> The lyric valuables. From disaster
>
> Shipwreck, whole families crawled
> To the tenements, and there

Survived by what morality
Of hope

Which for the sons
Ends its metaphysic
In small lawns of home. (CP, 29)

The poem suggests that those valuables are to be found in the air, in bare sunlight, a clear and clarifying sound in proximity to "disaster." From disaster, after the intervening gap of the (stanza) break, comes shipwreck. Is the shipwreck that valuable item that comes from disaster, or is the shipwreck a continuation of that disaster? As families crawl upon the wrecked raft of tenement survival, goaded along like Williams' "pure products," surviving by a distorted hope they cling to, they hold to a kind of debased lyrical isolation: the finely clipped small lawns of the privatized (American capitalist) valuables. Are these, with the grave steady cadence, the heavy feet of small lawns of home, playing off of the delicate and highly traditional echoic ear of *Which for the sons / ends its metaphysic / In*, the lyric valuables, in sound or in substance? Or, is that small lawn a continuation of the disaster? Perhaps all this stems from the first word of the poem, "ultimately." A particularly American inevitability? Nonetheless, "the lyric valuables" remain as a possibility.

In fact, the particularly lyrical signature of Oppen's work may come in his ethical refusal of singularity:

Obsessed, bewildered,

By the shipwreck
Of the singular

We have chosen the meaning
Of being numerous. (CP, 151)

Poetry, though, as a medium, and poets in that medium, have a tough time resisting an impulse toward intensification, as if that impulse were an absolute identification with the properties of the medium. Yes, as Cage has it, the sounds outside the school of music are equally an instance of music. And there is an intensification of consciousness, a new attuning to the world about one, that goes with that thought. At its extreme, toward which Cage's thought moves only asymptotically, is the negation once and for all of the necessity to make art, since artfulness, like music, is already existent every- where. (Again, "'Powerless to affect / The intensity of what is.'") For Oppen, the lure toward that intensification, seemingly inseparable from *poesis* (and in a culture that does not value those lyric valuables, the poem being outside the dominant cultural modes of valuation), has pernicious political consequences:

> 'Whether, as the intensity of seeing increases, one's distance
>   from Them, the people, does not also increase'
> I know, of course I know, I can enter no other place
>   (CP, 152)

In the distance of only eighteen lines, the poet who has just pro- claimed the choice "of being numerous" acknowledges his work as the work of *one* who works in one particular language precinct:

> Yet I am one of those who from nothing but man's way of
>   thought and one of his dialects and what has happened
> Have made poetry (CP, 152)

He is one *of those*, thus beginning a social engagement, a group be- ing. Even his admission of intensity as increasing "one's distance from Them, the people," occurs in social interchange, for Oppen is quoting another, Rachel Blau DuPlessis, her question to him in a let- ter. The achievement of singularity in poetry is certainly a paradox in a medium made from so socially generated a thing as language. In a sense, a poet makes speak a common possession, a thing possessed by no one person: language, a particular dialect or precinct of its capac- ity and our capacity for meaning-making, for melody. A poet sounds it out; in reading it resounds. For Oppen, the siren of singularity may be, dangerously, the metaphysical equivalent of the small lawns:

> To dream of that beach
> For the sake of an instant in the eyes,

The absolute singular

The unearthly bonds
Of the singular

Which is the bright light of shipwreck (CP, 152)

For Oppen, that dialectical tension (between the whole and the part, between a desire for inclusiveness and for a clear focal point, between multiplicity and singularity) manifests itself as competing desires and declarations. On the one hand,

> It is difficult now to speak of poetry—
>
> about those who have recognized the range of choice or those who have lived within the life they were born to—. It is not precisely a question of profundity but a different order of experience. One would have to tell what happens in a life, what choices present themselves, what the world is for us, what happens in time, what thought is in the course of a life and therefore what art is, and the isolation of the actual

and on this hand, Oppen is speaking of a potentially infinite inclusiveness, a vast context within which one might offer an instance of the isolated actuality; but on the other hand, Oppen remains drawn to a kind of singularity, toward a perspective that resolves the many:

> One must not come to feel that he has a thousand threads
>   in his hands
> He must somehow see the one thing (168)

In fact, this tension *is* the fundamental energy present in *Of Being Numerous*, a tension made credible and engaging precisely because of Oppen's impassioned (and ethically engaged) ambivalence. His more "knowing" statements, his wise self-counsel, speak against singularity: "Surely infiniteness is the most evident thing in the world" (174). But in his quest for an ethical and metaphysical clarity, Oppen again and again is drawn toward the singular as a lyrical intensification.

In *Primitive* (1978), Oppen's final book, he is still wondering about the substance of the poem. In "The Poem," the question of the poem's fundamental matter opens the poem:

> how shall I light
> this room that measures years

In part, one answer has to do with lyricism's tendency toward epiphany, toward light and enlightenment, toward a visionary apotheosis:

> to save the commonplace save myself Tyger
> Tyger still burning in me burning
> in the night sky burning
> in us the light
>
> in the room it was all
> part of the wars
> of things brilliance
> of things
>
> in the appalling
> seas language
>
> lives and wakes us together
> out of sleep the poem
> opens its dazzling whispering hands (14)

Here, the poet's emphasis is on light, what I have identified with a lure toward intensification which I see as an essential aspect of lyricism. Here, I also find Oppen speaking and singing against himself, writing a poetry of dense juxtaposition where the musicality—not enumerated in this poem's obsession with light rather than breath or voice—insists on its audibility in the double sounding of "seas" and "seize" (language, particularly the lyric valuables as a seizure, as a suddenness in language) and in the guiding force of the sibilant warS, thingS, brillianCe, SeaS, liveS, wakeS, Sleep, openS, daZ-Zling, whiSpering, handS. While the poem's argument points toward the light, the saying of the poem engages us in an unremarked other

location for the poem, in music, in sound, and thus perhaps excuses
the seemingly silly last line of the poem, explaining why perhaps the
hands are "whispering." The poem, though, is a conceptual space, a
room, Italian *stanza*, a space within which essentials can occur. For
Oppen, especially in the last poems, that space is also the site for an
invocation, an invitation to some mode of otherness. Thus, in the
last poem of *Primitive*, "Till Other Voices Wake Us," Oppen ends
with a corrective of Eliot (whose "Prufrock" ended, in the poetics
of isolation and alienation, with the lament of a speaker called out
of art's reverie, "till human voices wake us, AND we drown") and a
summoning of otherness. Here, though, the light of that otherness,
arising out of a listing of plurals, becomes fundamentally a music:

> series empirical
> series all force
> in events the myriad
>
> lights have entered
> us it is a music more powerful
>
> than music
>
> till other voices wake
> us or we drown   (*Primitive*, 30–31)

For Oppen, the hope is for a poetry that does not deny singularity,
the exceptional, the intensified, that writes honestly that lyrical witness, but that nonetheless is in dialog with "other voices," with the
plural human enterprise, which stands as enlightening corrective to
the potential shipwreck of the singular.

In his letters, Oppen reflects on this music. In 1960, Oppen,
referring to how to read Zukofsky's "*A*," advises his half-sister June:
"Just read — just let the music, meaning poetic music, not actually sound, take care of it" (37). In 1964, writing to William Bronk,
Oppen's test of poetry sounds a bit like Emily Dickinson's quest for
poems that explode the top of her head: "when I read a poem and
am unable to speak for several minutes thereafter, and read the poem
twenty times and find that I cannot control my voice —I regard it

as a good poem" (104). In 1969, advising Jane Cooper on how she
might proceed toward her next book, Oppen offers one of his most
extended meditations on the music of poetry:

> I was puzzled by your asking about music. But now I feel
> that music is the problem, the problem of the *next* book, the
> problem of the way *on* there seem to me cadences that trap
> you, as if an obligation Whereas music! the passion of music,
> the passionate needs of the music itself, the nerve to put a
> full stop, the nerve to break off   Maybe I mean not cour-
> age but fear which must not be denied by the music: to
> respond to the wildness of the world, the wildness of time,
> the wildness, therefore, of oneself —   I don't mean that I
> haven't heard and felt the heart of your poems: speech and
> the saying of one's name that breaks the houses of silence
> Really, the contrary: to use silence, not to be caught up in
> a cadence, obliged to a cadence   ?   Which would leave
> form, music, as that which makes the poem graspable, the
> music itself, and every note, for the sake also of the *thing*
> grasped   But above all, and most amply, the silences:
> the breaking of rhythmic obligations. (199)

Oppen's own late work constitutes one significant exploration of
that blank space and silence as a key compositional element for the
poem, one key resident of that "room" which is the poem. To my ear
and eye, Robert Creeley's poetry (particularly in its cadence, in its
brilliant use of hesitation and shift in direction) and Larry Eigner's
poetry (particularly in its deployment on the page) constitute two
of the more noteworthy adventurings into that music that respects
and partners silence. To take the term *music* more literally, it would
be difficult to consider the resources of silence without careful attention to the music of Thelonious Monk (an important influence on
Creeley, who tells us repeatedly that his attention to jazz, not to poetic models, gave him his fundamental sense of rhythmic and aural
possibilities for his poetry).

But a particular music, one strand of the "lyric valuables,"
emerging in our time is what I think of as a kind of "dense music," a
musicality dependent not on a stretching by means of silence, but a

cadence based on the close bonding of similar sounds and a rapidity of shifts in discourse-direction.

⁓

The terms "music" and "musicality," which I have been using in relation to contemporary lyric valuables, are themselves suspect labels. As Don Byrd (in an essay on Zukofsky's poetry) points out,

> Since the seventeenth century, even most of the innumerable poems entitled "Song," to say nothing of the more elaborate analogies between poetic and musical forms, are references *to* music, not music as such. I can think of only a few instances in which it is not clear that the poet is talking, and the reader is being asked to imagine that he is singing or playing the harmonium. (178)

Even so, we could then begin to discuss the musical possibilities of speech, which, after all, would follow rather precisely Zukofsky's famous integral in "*A*"-12, where he defines his poetics as "An integral / Lower limit speech / Upper limit music" (138). Or, another way of thinking about the lyric is as the site of dialectical tension over two divergent views of music: the identification of poetry and musical is (merely) metaphorical vs. an insistence on the sounds of words themselves as constituting a specific music. As we enact those musics, as we read and mouth the poems, we participate physically in the rhythms and sounds peculiar to a given time of thinking. As any survey of the beautiful in poetry will show, the pulse and twist of that thinking has a changing ring to it.

⁓

It is time, now, to make clear that, in fact, I am not nor have I been talking about *the lyric*. I suppose unspoken in this essay is the assumption that, of course, the personal lyric is dead. If not dead, for the most part uninteresting as a *current* activity. The short personal lyric, as many have noted, coincidental with the institutionalization of "creative writing" and the rapid metastasis of the workshop, became utterly formulaic, casting in doubt the very sincerity of the sincerely expressed personal lyric. The acts of intensification and the necessary closure by way of epiphany, once rampant, became, when seen as a kind of period piece, inseparable from governing forms and rhetorics (each of which had been suppressed, since the critical and creative faculties had been institutionally segregated, with the poetic/ creative being declared "natural" and "spontaneous"). No, I am not writing, then, actually about the lyric. I am, then, thinking about something a bit different, a more amorphous unit of expression: *lyricism*. This lyricism, which may in part be a mode of recontextual- izing some elements of the personal lyric and the voice lyric, has an indeterminate metric of appearance.

There is, for example, the exceedingly dense music of bpNich- ol's *The Martyrology*, though any excerpting of it, in a manner similar to Hejinian's captions in *My Life*, becomes a miniaturiza- tion or an anthologizing which is most definitely at odds with the nearly boundless larger writing project. To isolate a portion of *The Martyrology* as an instance of lyricism both honors the intensity evoked by and embodied in the text and disengages it from the sur- rounding and different discourses that make possible, cooperatively, the very musicality that is being displayed in isolation. There is, then, no typical passage of *The Martyrology*. There are, though, pas- sages of a high and playful lyricism:

4

an infinite statement. a finite statement. a statement of infancy. a fine line state line. a finger of stalemate. a feeling a saint meant ointment.

tremble.

a region religion
reigns in. a returning. turning return the lover. the retrospect of relationships always returning. the burning of the urge. the surge forward in animal being inside us. the catatosis van del reeba rebus suburbs of our imagination. last church of the lurching word worked weird in our heads.

(passages from "Scraptures: 7th Sequence" [1967] in *gIFTS: The Martyrology Book[s]7&*, unpaginated)

Here, the overt spirituality, the overtly religious terminology, marks the return, the repossession, of a lyricism. Though the density of Nichol's music dislodges (while lodging in its music) the very argument that begins to be proclaimed. By cognate sounds the poem mounts its logic of association: *infinite, finite, infancy, fine line*, or *region religion reigns in*. The poem becomes then that *last church of the lurching word worked weird in our head*. And the tune, a Dr. Seuss on acid, a Thelonious Monk stone sober mucking around the trinkle tinkle tunes, becomes the argument:

3

> liturgical turge dirge dinta krak kree fintab latlina santa danka schoen
> fane sa paws claws le foret. my love coo lamna mandreen sont vallejo.
>   oh valleys and hills lie open ingkra sintle
> list la list cistern turning down.
>   je ne sais pas madam. je ne sais pas mademoiselle.
> je ne sais pas l'amour mirroring mes yeux meilleur my urging for you.

Part of the ecstasy of lyricism is the dissolution of the poem into its own constituent musicality. For Nichol, that holy scrapture is *liturgical turge dirge*, a polyvocal multilingual *amour mirroring*, which, in the manner of the most traditional of lyrics, addresses that transcendent *you* toward which the poem approximates, seizes, that is, sees its way, sounding it out: *mes yeux meilleur urging for you*. Or, as the prior section ends

> and the lovers
>   loafers, low firs, old frrrs, la lovers, la lrrrs.

It is, then, a music of particular density, a high bonding of similar sound to similar sound, the lyricism being inseparable from the particularized torquing and twisting of sounds in their displayed mixture of echo and difference. I call this, as I imagine Louis Zukofsky might have, in a yiddish accent, *dense music*. In Nichol's work, the dense music nearly always carries with it a quality of glee, a foolishness, a joyous gratitude for the occurrence of the music, that it is. For Zukofsky, the music is more chiselled by scalpel, made from finely tuned turnings within a single discourse, as in "Songs of Degrees," which begins

> Hear, her
> Clear
> Mirror,
> Care
> His error.
> In her
> Care
> Is clear (*All*, 151–152)

and works many minutely nuanced variations on that opening. (For a lucid, carefully sounded reading of "Songs of Degrees," see John Taggart's "Louis Zukofsky: Songs of Degrees," in *Songs of Degrees: Essays on Contemporary Poetry and Poetics*, University of Alabama Press, 1994, pp. 82–113.) A more contemporary *dense music* may be found in Harryette Mullen's poems, a lyricism dependent on doing the switches, on quickly shifting discourses, what might be called a discourse dancing. Mullen (in *Muse & Drudge*, 1995) might begin one page with

> sauce squandering sassy cook
> took a gander bumped a pinch of goose
> skinned quadroon cotillion filled
> uptown ballroom with squalid quadrille (53)

a fairly conventional if vernacular/demotic deployment of a clotted dense lyricism, but then she will shift into a more punningly self-conscious musical musing in the next stanza:

> don't eat no crow, don't you know
> ain't studying about taking low
> if I do not care for chitterlings
> 'tain't nobody's pidgin

Mullen's poetry offers a postmodern exhilarating fast-paced roller-coaster ride of quickly shifting but continually melodic discourses:

rose is off the bloomers
storm in the womb
an old broom scatters
shotgun rumor

hip chicks ad glib
flip the script
spinning distichs
tighter than Dick's hatband (66)

Hers is a sensible and sensuous musical excess of punning pastiche in an eighty page book that maintains this dizzying, pleasing music of the packed four-line stanza:

fixing her lips to sing
hip strutters ditty bop
hand-me-down dance of ample
style stance and substance

black-eyed pearl
around the world girl
somebody's anybody's
yo-yo fulani

occult iconic crow
solo mysterioso
flying way out
on the other side of far (40)

It is toward that "other side of far" that lyric valuables will continue to be cast, continuing to strut a hand-me-down dance of inherited musics, torqued and twisted, written, spoken, sung in poems whose ugliness is an ungainly beauty, a disruptive cacophony on the unaccountable way to becoming a familiar beauty.

It might make sense, then, to think of the lyric in crisis. But surely that sense of crisis may be one of the lyric's most accustomed soils for growth, and thus nothing peculiar to our moment. Perhaps then if we return to current considerations of the lyric, we can begin to see the points of fracture, the site of particularly apparent inconsistencies of conception. Of critics of contemporary poetry, Helen Vendler is most identified with a loyalty to the capacities and beauties of the lyric. While Theodore Weiss' essay-review, "Reviewing the Reviewer," an examination of Vendler's *Soul Says: On Recent Poetry* (1995), presents a more general consideration of her affinities and limitations, Weiss repeatedly attends to Vendler's orientation to the lyric, claiming that "she naturally gravitates to the lyric" (37). He points to a review by Vendler in which she remarks that she is "wedded to the lyric as a form" (37). What interests me is Vendler's implicit and explicit definition of that form. What Weiss sees as essential to Vendler's version of the good is a self-mirroring poetry: "what she is after is ... the poem that is 'a mirror of my feelings.' Or 'the voice of the soul itself'" (37). As Weiss correctly claims, for Vendler the "lyrical must be introspective" (40).

For Vendler, then, the lyric is linked to a personal voice, to a singularity of expression, and to a poetry rooted in a well-wrought mode of personal expression. Seamus Heaney, for example, is praised by Vendler for *not* succumbing to a broadly social and political poetry. As Weiss argues, Vendler admires Heaney because "he stresses not society, but self. Like her, he requires 'singularity' and the 'individuated life in the arts.' She calls these characteristics the 'heroic virtue'; only it can 'convey the strict morality of the imaginative effort toward aesthetic embodiment'" (43). Similarly, Vendler's praise of Adrienne Rich is tied to the recuperative powers of individual expression, of the lyrical over the social. Initially, Vendler admired Rich because the critic felt, with Rich's first book, that Rich "was writing down my own life." As an aside, I would add that that is precisely why I and many others who take genuine pleasure in more innovative poetries do *not* finally hold Vendler's pantheon of lyric poets in such high esteem. I most definitely feel that they are *not* writing down my life; I feel, instead, that they are opting for a conservative, narrowly professionalized, nostalgic, outmoded rhetoric of self-expressiveness that has somehow managed to evade the more interesting modes of representation in poetry of the past one hundred years, more interesting modes that *do* feel more truthful and accurate.

Vendler attempts to create a version of the lyric that is transcendental and ahistorical:

> If the normal home of selfhood is the novel, which ideally allows many aspects of the self, under several forms, to expatiate and take on substance, then the normal home of "soul" is the lyric, where the human being becomes a set of warring passions independent of time and space. It is generally thought that the lyric is the genre of "here" and "now," and it is true that these index words govern the lyric moment. But insofar as the typical lyric exists only in the here and now, it exists nowhere, since life as it is lived is always bracketed with a there and a then. Selves come with history; souls are independent of time and space.... The lyric is the gesture of immortality and freedom; the novel is the gesture of the historical and of the spatial. (5)

But of course "soul" too has a history; it is not a transcendental category apart from time, the contingent, the material, and the social. "Soul" too is a socially and culturally mediated act of imagination. (And, one wonders, how can Vendler, a Stevens scholar, forget so thoroughly the notion of supreme fictions?) Clearly, the specific music, the sound and pulse and pace of the lyric all *do* change; they mark, in their participation in the narrative of from outlaw to classic, rather precisely their particular historical moment. For Vendler, the reason for being of the lyric is that it is the ideal form for "revealing the inner life" (6). She claims that "everything said in a poem was a metaphor for something in my inner life, and I learned about future possibilities within my inner life from the poetry I read with such eagerness" (3). But her entire category of "the inner life" is one that arises in boldface in an era of confessional poetry. I would rather situate the lyric in a broader heuristic domain, as a site for many kinds of thinkings, as the sounding out of new modes of expressiveness, as a musicality not governed by personal psychology nor thematized consolations.

Or, to offer a more radical critique of Vendler's identifica-
tion-as-praise, consider Adorno's conclusion that "to those who
obsessively relate art works only to themselves, the avenue of lived
experience is closed, except in the false form of a surrogate manipu-
lated by culture" (AT, 348). I believe that Vendler's version of the
lyric is not capable of an adequate representation of contemporary
reality. Or, as Mark Wallace (in the previously cited essay on the
lyric) suggests, "the concept of 'make it new' seems useful to the
extent that it suggests that works of literature should be as complex
as their times" (2). Correctly, Weiss locates Vendler's narrowing of
the lyrical Good in her inability to absorb, enjoy, or understand
the challenges of Modernist poetry (except as practiced by Wallace
Stevens?). Weiss understands that there are many other goals than a
lyrical introspection:

> And such a case was made by a much larger poet [than
> Jeffers] Vendler has little sympathy for. Pound despised self-
> absorption, the passivity of the narcissistic. So his turn to
> the Asiatic, to imagism, to objects and objectivity. Similarly
> Eliot with his belief in the impersonal, Williams and a host
> of poets that followed him and that Vendler ignores. For she
> was led into poetry by Lowell, Berryman, and others of their
> generation, as by Plath and Ginsberg; these, most of them,
> admired their great predecessors but, by the demands of
> their lives, recoiled from them into the lyrical or the confes-
> sional. (40)

But Vendler again and again shows that she takes the side of the
lyrical/personal. She can admire Rich's poetry precisely because her
poems, "for all their epic wish to generalize the social whole ... are
both limited by, and enhanced by, their essentially first-person lyric
status" (Vendler, 223). Weiss adds, if a poet is a genuine one [for
Vendler], "the lyrical must break through" (43). The Good, for
Vendler, remains the tidy order of a rather traditional lyric (or less
tidy forms rescued by the appearance of the saving lyric). She worries
that with "the expansion of the poetic line visible in both Rich and
Graham (and in other contemporary poets, from Ginsberg to Wright
and Ashbery) means that many poems are coming to resemble cloud

chambers full of colliding protons rather than well-wrought urns"
(Vendler, 240). While Vendler can begin to praise Jorie Graham
for "freeing lyric from its perennial labyrinth of the single voice"
(240)—and Vendler's narrow reading habits can be infuriating,
for shouldn't Vendler know that such a process of freeing is being
achieved, *has been achieved*, by a range of poets that Vendler seems
unable to read: Charles Bernstein, Susan Howe, Nathaniel Mackey,
Harryette Mullen, bpNichol, Jack Foley, or, earlier, Pound, Olson,
Zukofsky, even Eliot—Vendler feels compelled to pull back and reassert the defining power of the more segregated lyric: "For Graham it
is only by chronicling accurately and punctually one's individual fate
that one can, in lyric, 'do' history" (248).

Vendler's touch of anxiety about possible new directions in lyricism, as well as her knee-jerk conflation of the lyric with the personal, interest me. I don't want to dismiss wholesale Vendler's mode of
the lyric, the particular lyricism which she advocates. (Indeed, I share
a number of her enthusiasms [though not her misgivings], especially
for Plath and Ashbery.) I am arguing for a more varied location for
lyricism, and I am arguing against the identification of the lyric
with a poignant univocalism. What, then, is the danger of Vendler's
version of the lyric? She turns the lyric into poignant sloganeering,
a refined late twentieth-century Augustan maxim of virtuous forti-
tude on the part of a diligently introspective individual (who has, of
course, achieved *a* distinctive voice).

An interesting overlap, with significant differences, from
Vendler's thoughts on the lyric comes from Theodor Adorno in his
1957 essay "On Lyric Poetry and Society." With Adorno, what is
precisely of interest is his attention to what Vendler is blind (and/or
deaf) to: the exact and paradoxical *social* nature of the lyric—of the
lyric as a manifestation and embodiment of social relations. Rather
unpromisingly, Adorno begins with a fairly standard definition of
the lyric as a poetic world apart:

> The most delicate, the most fragile thing that exists is to be
> encroached upon and brought into conjunction with bustle
> and commotion, when part of the ideal of lyric poetry, at
> least in its traditional sense, is to remain unaffected by bustle
> and commotion. A sphere of expression whose very essence

lies in either not acknowledging the power of socialization or
overcoming it through the pathos of detachment.... (37)

As an aside, I would argue that by virtue of their contrast with the
surrounding language of the poem, the lyricisms I have been citing
behave in a similar manner within the context of longer poems. Like
Vendler (who is writing on the subject forty years later), Adorno
links the lyric to processes of individuation (a definition inseparable
from European political and ideological debates of the Cold War
era?): "the lyric work hopes to attain universality through unre-
strained individuation" (38). But the key turn in Adorno's thinking
comes with his profession of the lyric's swerve away from the social
as the social gesture peculiar to the lyric:

> You experience lyric poetry as something opposed to soci-
> ety, something wholly individual. Your feelings insist that
> it remain so, that lyric expression, having escaped from the
> weight of material existence, evoke the image of a life free
> from the coercion of reigning practices, of utility, of the
> relentless pressures of self-preservation. This demand, how-
> ever, the demand that the lyric word be virginal, is itself
> social in nature. It implies a protest against a social situa-
> tion that every individual experiences as hostile, alien, cold,
> oppressive... [.] (39)

For Adorno, the lyric involves a protest against the mere utility or
instrumentality of language: "The lyric spirit's idiosyncratic opposition to the superior power of material things is a form of reaction to
the reification of the world, to the domination of human beings by
commodities that has developed since the beginning of the modern
era, since the industrial revolution became the dominant force in
life" (40). The contemporary poets I am looking at and listening
to emphasize, quite emphatically, the thing-ness of the word. Like
Adorno, Hejinian, for example, locates the lyric's social resistance
to utilitarianism in writing of the early twentieth century. In "Two
Stein Talks," Hejinian points to Stein's "discovery that language is
an order of reality itself and not a mere mediating medium—that
it is possible and even likely that one can have a confrontation with

a phrase that is as significant as a confrontation with a tree, chair, cone, dog, bishop, piano, vineyard, door, or penny" (129). Or, as Adorno concisely states the paradox, "it is precisely what is not social in the lyric poem that is now to become its social aspect" (42).

Adorno, through a reading of Stefan George's poetry, similarly affirms such a process of intensification of language. Adorno's description of George could serve equally well for Gertrude Stein, living in Paris, re-sounding American English in her composition of *Tender Buttons*: "… the ear of George, the German student of Mallarmé, hears his own language as though it were a foreign tongue. He overcomes its alienation, which is an alienation of use, by intensifying it until it becomes the alienation of a language no longer actually spoken, even an imaginary language, and in that imaginary language he perceives what would be possible, but never took place, in its composition" (52–53). (Such a description might also serve as an applicable reading of bpNichol's soundings of English and French and "nonsense" elements in the passages I've cited from *The Martyrology*.) Adorno realizes and celebrates the utopian aspect of such a language-play freed from the overwhelming demand of immediate use and reification: "in the particular does lyrical language represent language's intrinsic being as opposed to its service in the realm of ends. But it thereby represents the idea of a free humankind … [.]" (53). Similarly, Ron Silliman concludes that poetry provides a rare opportunity, especially in an advanced capitalist culture, for an unusual mode of labor: "Among the several social functions of poetry is that of posing a model of unalienated work: it stands in relation to the rest of society both as utopian possibility and constant reminder of just how bad things are" (61).

Adorno, in the passage quoted above, begins to think of the lyric as potentially distinct from spoken language. But Adorno, unlike many American poets of the latter half of the twentieth century, cannot affirm that distinction without significant qualification and backsliding. The following observation by Adorno could be lipsynched by Vendler without modification: "The 'I' whose voice is heard in the lyric is an 'I' that defines and expresses itself as something opposed to the collective, to objectivity; it is not immediately at one with the nature to which its expresssion refers. It has lost it, as it were, and attempts to restore it through animation, through im-

mersion in the 'I' itself" (41). Where Adorno's thinking moves closer
to the present is in granting greater importance to language itself
(though, oddly, Adorno expresses such a position in Vendler's [later]
vocabulary of the "soul"): "A second immediacy is promised: what is
human, language itself, seems to become creation again, while everything external dies away in the echo of the soul" (41).

But in Adorno's thinking two features begin to be united: the
lyric turn itself as social; and the lyric as existing primarily *within* the
realm of language (rather than, as for Vendler, as primarily a signature of personal identity via a personal voice):

> … the lyric work of art's withdrawal into itself, its self-ab-
> sorption, its detachment from the social surface, is socially
> motivated behind the author's back. But the medium of this
> is language. The paradox specific to the lyric work, a sub-
> jectivity that turns into objectivity, is tied to the priority of
> linguistic form in the lyric, it is that priority from which the
> primacy of language in literature in general (even in prose
> forms) is derived. For language is itself something double.
> Through its configurations it assimilates itself completely
> into subjective impulses; one would almost think it had
> produced them. But at the same time language remains the
> medium of concepts, remains that which establishes an in-
> escapable relationship to the universal and to society. Hence
> the highest lyric works are those in which the subject, with
> no remaining trace of mere matter, sounds forth in language
> until language itself acquires a voice. The unself-conscious-
> ness of the subject submitting itself to language as to some-
> thing objective, and the immediacy and spontaneity of that
> subject's expression are one and the same: thus language me-
> diates lyric poetry and society in their innermost core. This
> is why the lyric reveals itself to be most deeply grounded in
> society when it does not chime in with society, when it com-
> municates nothing, when, instead, the subject whose expres-
> sion is successful reaches an accord with language itself, with
> the inherent tendency of language. (43)

For Adorno, that particular submission and grounding constitutes the breakthrough of the lyric. Through lyricism, "the melody of the poem's language extends beyond mere signification" (53). *Exactly!* The *melopoeia* I am sounding and the heuristics I am advocating involve precisely a singing beyond mere signification. In fact, in a specific historical and cultural situation, in opposition to the tenets of theme-based reading (which we have inherited from the New Criticism and from *Understanding Poetry*) and in reaction against the univocal sloganeering and epiphanizing of the contemporary personal lyric, the lyricisms I am exploring work in a disrupted syntax and garbled (though still melodic and "beautiful") relationship to speech that make difficult customary thematic strip-minings of the poem. Such lyricisms deliberately problematize their appropriation by signification-based reading methods.

To return then to the particular gravity—the sound and drag of a specific instance of the lyrical—of a poem, we might wish to consider Clark Coolidge's "Rhymes with Monk" (in *Own Face*). A section from the middle of the poem exemplifies the particular metric of swerve that Coolidge offers as homage to Monk:

> Traps that settle and are bridges. And to the side
> it said, in time. The paper on the window
> scrape of speakage. That tugs are ever down.
> This won't change it winters. A cap that place
> it so, it stays. Wood, so untoward, metals. An egg
> to a city. The rafters, whistled by. A book's center.
> Says one, to someone, find me zero. Sun, and the flat
> keeps pace. He would laugh at the dock. Stroll by
> means the having words. Gleams mean the brittle
> instrument. And he goes, green the rest. Space
> to light lets to equal. Mishquamaquoddy. The pin to
> all weights. Not forgetting it won't and then but
> does come. All, but counter. Have to move to move it.
> Shifts by no lonesome. Music a matter of walls.

(Own Face, 18)

As Monk's expertise consists in hitting the right-wrong note, or playing a percussive piano against an absent or implied melody, Coolidge's particular poetic lyricism is an exactitude that rhymes with Monk. As with a Monk solo which advances us into unexpected options, Coolidge's sentences advance with an almost didactic (melodic?) assurance that is undermined by the direction advanced by each unexpected word. What accumulates is melodic and assured but every few words a little warped. torqued, off. As Monk's music frames the significant silences ("green the rest"?), and implies the tune it is just missing, Coolidge's poem develops an obstructive rhythm ("Music a matter of walls"). Even though we can locate persistent and familiar threads of assonance—*gleams / mean / he / green / equal; brittle / instrument; rest / lets*—Coolidge makes a familiar music quickly opaque. Whereas Oppen proposes a "room that measures years," Coolidge's room (in the concluding lines of the poem) offers a place for doing:

> Face it, room enough for the doing thing. Fly takes air,
> and has weight. Come look to the sides of which are his,
> the broughtens.
>
> As the room is quiet for the one who listens. (19)

The poem, an embodiment rather than a thematizing of jazz, gives space "for the doing thing," and is such a doing. As with Enslin, the music takes precedence (over theme or idea); but as Zukofsky notes, communicativeness too is inevitably attached to the word along with the word's musical properties. In Monk and Coolidge, there is a rapidity and joy of pointing slightly "to the sides." How else explain the way *broughtens* and *listens* interact?

———

Adorno's attention to appropriation returns us to some considerations with which I began this essay: the rapidity and importance of a shift in perception from hearing the poem as "ugly" to hearing the poem as "beautiful." Stein posited a lamentable, instantaneous shift in perception, one which doomed the most adventurous artists to equally unsatisfactory positions as outlaws and classics. Stein laments the loss of contemporaries (and the contemporaries' loss of the excitement and joy of finding a fresh, current expression of one's consciousness). Adorno's perspective is decidedly more political, and his thinking in *Aesthetic Theory* (first published in 1970) allows us to understand the dynamics of reception (including rejection/suspicion and acceptance/appropriation) as part of a process of cultural politics. He notes that

> Just as the non-specialist has trouble grasping the most recent developments in nuclear physics, so the non-expert cannot understand the complexities of modern music or painting. But there is a difference: while people resign themselves to the unintelligibility of theorems or modern physics, trusting that they are rational just the same, they tend to brand the unintelligibility of modern art as some schizoid whim. (AT, 334)

Adorno's conclusion about this state of affairs is that "the elitist segregation of the avant-garde is not art's fault but society's" (360). Where Stein seems to long for a more comprehensive acceptance, a greater community of contemporaries, Adorno savors a dialectical interdependence (and thus a necessity of opposition) between the ugly and the beautiful: "If there is any causal connection at all between the beautiful and the ugly, it is from the ugly as cause to the beautiful as effect, not the other way around.... If aesthetics were nothing but an exhaustive and systematic list of all that can be called beautiful, we would gain no understanding of the dynamic life inherent in the concept of beauty. Actually this concept is only a moment in the totality of aesthetic reflection" (75). Adorno thinks of aesthetic reflection as occasioning an "exodus." The perception of beauty, for Adorno, is not a fixed perception but is a moment within a broader exodus of reflection. Whereas Stein seems to feel genuine pain at her sense of exclusion from appreciation, though not a pain that seems in any way to have compromised the trajectory of her writing nor the radicalness of her experimentation in language, Adorno, thinking within an increasingly commodified and reified culture, offers a redeeming perception of the value of difficulty itself:

> Hermetic art works tend to be rebuked for being unintelligible. Actually, their unintelligibility is a confession that all of

art is enigmatic, and that affects traditional works with their surface intelligibility as well. When people sense that the intelligibility of traditional works begins to crumble they get angry. Many traditional works that bear the stamp of public approval are falsely considered understood. Under their veneer of intelligibility, the enigmatic rears its head again and again. Paradoxically, today the least understandable works, those that highlight the enigmatic quality rather than downplaying it, are potentially the most intelligible ones. (179)

Stein, who wrote many "difficulties that stay difficult," authored a great many seminal twentieth-century works which show us, over time (in the temporal exodus which is aesthetic reflection), the peculiar intelligibility of the enigmatic, its peculiarly apt modes of new realism. One danger of intelligibility is its related concept: appropriation. The intelligible (or, as Adorno has it, more accurately, the *seemingly* intelligible) bears with it a kind of comfort that allows for the disposal of the work of art, the completion of the exodus of aesthetic reflection. If the work of art is fundamentally desired to be a provocation to thinking, a thinking in and of itself, then a too swift intelligibility carries with it a neutralization of the art work's capacity to disturb (and thus to cause one to think). Thus, Adorno concludes,

> Reception tends to dull the critical edge of art, its determinate negation of society. Works are most critical when they first see the light of day; afterwards they become neutralized because, among other things, the social conditions have changed. Neutralization is the social price art pays for its autonomy. Once works are buried in the pantheon of cultural exhibits, their truth content deteriorates. In the administered world neutralization becomes universal. (325)

Perhaps the current lyricisms I have been sounding offer us an attractive means for entry into a relationship with larger written works which may be disturbing or disruptive (and thus provide occasions for thinking). But one might also ask, following up on Adorno's narrative of reception, when did a poetry of fragmentation, of a multiple subject, of the free play of signifiers/signs, of the thingness of the word "first see the light of day"? As the editors of *the apex of the M* hint (but do not address directly), has the mode of the new which I have been putting on display in this essay (and thus adding to "the pantheon of cultural exhibits"?) already been substantially neutralized? Perhaps the ugly beauty of Mackey's anagrammatic scat, Mullen's discourse dancing, Bernstein's clotted scientific lyricism, and Nichol's associative slippage offer some strategies for remaining trippingly on the tongue, offering an alluring and annoying tang of thinking, which, in its pronounced difficulties resists complete neutralization. As for the social efficacy of such soundings, we might wish to keep in mind Adorno's claim that "by articulating the otherwise ineffable contradictions of society, figuration takes on the features of a praxis which is the opposite of escapism, transforming art into a mode of behaviour. Art is a type of praxis and there is no need to make apologies for its failure to act directly" (AT, 330). Newly emerging versions of the lyrical speak to, sing toward, stammer about a kind of amorphous social efficacy as articulated by Adorno:

> One decisive reason why art works, at least those that refuse to surrender to propaganda, are lacking in social impact is that they have to give up the use of those communicative means that would make them palatable to a larger public. If they do not, they become pawns in the all-encompassing system of communication. If art works have any social influence at all, it is not by haranguing, but by changing consciousness in ways that are ever so difficult to pin down. (344)

At the risk of a reiteration more in the mode of *logopoeia* than *melopoeia*, it is possible to re-locate the substance of Adorno's remarks in Kit Robinson's "Lyric Strand," the opening poem in *The Champagne of Concrete*, which begins, "There it goes again, a sound/ changing the way we live" (3). Though Robinson's poem is rich in ironic and deflating complications, one essential aspect of lyricism is, as Adorno has argued, to sound out changing modes of thinking. As Robinson thinks through it in "Lyric Strand," in keeping with the examples I have cited from Nichol, Mullen, Mackey, and Bernstein, the musicality of lyricism is the mark of (or re-marks upon) a strug-

gle with the limitations and controlling implications of more transparent modes of communication:

> A caustic rush of paint slaps
> entertainment value across the side
> of the nation, faintly visible
> two centuries previous. Coughing
> stiffs. The inch repeals; its staff
> of whole notes flutters and subscribes.
> Sound is an antidote to words,
> meaning lies. It can be used
> to show that they are used and only
> exist by their use and are made of it.
> Backwater flats form the interior
> design of a signature. The image
> breaks against the rocks
> in the sound of words. It is deleted
> by normal wear and tear. What
> a relief. The only conclusion
> we can draw is that you
> heard it here first. (3–4)

One might object and point out that Robinson's pronouncements
on the potential for sound/music to erode sense/meaning is itself
presented in a mode of meaningful proposition (much the same
as MacLeish's famous dictum in "Ars Poetica," "a poem should not
mean / but be," a statement which occurs seemingly in precisely the
abstract and general manner of expression which MacLeish argues
against). But Robinson's poem, particularly in the lines "Coughing
/ stiffs. The inch repeals; its staff / of whole notes flutters and sub-
scribes," does affirm a priority of sound even as the poet offers logical propositions on the value of a sound-based playfulness. Lyricism
offers a check on meaning-making, a check on the possible excesses
of *logopoeia* and *phanopoeia*. Of the sensual affirmation which is inseparable from the lyric valuables, you may say of the news that stays
news in the lyric, "that you / heard it here first," that the lyrical is a
place where "here" and "hear" cohere.

(1996)

Works Cited

Theodor Adorno. *Aesthetic Theory*. trans. C. Lenhardt. London and New York: Routledge & Kegan Paul, 1984. (where there might be confusion, cited as AT).

Theodor Adorno. "On Lyric Poetry and Society." In *Notes to Literature*, Volume One, Ed. Rolf Tiedemann; trans. Shierry Weber Nicholsen. New York: Coumbia University Press, 1991. 37–54.

apex of the M. issues 1 & 2. "State of the Art" (in #1, Spring 1994): 5–7. "Editorial" (in #2, Fall 1994): 5–8.

Charles Bernstein. *Dark City*. Los Angeles: Sun & Moon Press, 1994.

Don Byrd. "The Shape of Zukofsky's Canon." In *Louis Zukofsky: Man and Poet*. Ed. Carroll F. Terrell. Orono, Maine: National Poetry Foundation, 1979: 163–185.

John Cage. *X: Writings '79– '82*. Middletown, Connecticut: Wesleyan University Press, 1983.

Clark Coolidge. *Odes of Roba*. Great Barrington, Massachusetts: The Figures, 1991.

Clark Coolidge. *Own Face*. Los Angeles: Sun & Moon Press, 1993. (originally published in 1978 by United Artists.)

Theodore Enslin. Interview (with Edward Foster, 25–36) and "Autumnal Rime" (37–69). *Talisman: A Journal of Contemporary Poetry and Poetics* 12 (Spring 1994: The Theodore Enslin Issue).

Lyn Hejinian. *The Cell*. Los Angeles: Sun & Moon Press, 1992.

Lyn Hejinian. *My Life*. Los Angeles: Sun & Moon Press, 1987.

Lyn Hejinian. "Two Stein Talks." *Temblor* 3 (1986): 128–139. (For a more recent publication of "Two Stein Talks," see *The Language of Inquiry*. Berkeley: University of California Press, 2000: 83–110.)

Susan Howe. *The Europe of Trusts*. Los Angeles: Sun & Moon Press, 1990.

Hank Lazer. *Opposing Poetries*. Volume 1: Issues and Institutions; Volume 2: Readings. Evanston: Northwestern University Press, 1996.

Nathaniel Mackey. "Cante Moro." In *Disembodied Poetics: Annals of the Jack Kerouac School*. Ed. Anne Waldman & Andrew Schelling. Albuquerque: University of New Mexico Press, 1994. 71–94.

Nathaniel Mackey. *Discrepant Engagement: Dissonance, Cross-Culturality, and Experimental Writing*. New York: Cambridge University Press, 1993. (Reprinted, Tuscaloosa: University of Alabama Press, 2000.)

Nathaniel Mackey. *School of Udhra*. San Francisco: City Lights Books, 1993.

Harryette Mullen. *Muse & Drudge*. Philadelphia: Singing Horse Press, 1995.

bpNichol. *gIFTS: The Martyrology Book[s] 7&*. Toronto: Coach House Press, 1990.

George Oppen. *Collected Poems*. New York: New Directions, 1975. (where there might be confusion, cited as CP) (For a more recent edition, see George Oppen. *New Collected Poems*. Ed. By Michael Davidson. New York: New Directions, 2002.)

George Oppen. *Primitive*. Santa Barbara: Black Sparrow, 1979.

Sylvia Plath. *Ariel*. New York: Harper & Row, 1966.

Kit Robinson. *The Champagne of the Concrete*. Elmwood, Connecticut: Potes & Poets Pr, 1991.

Ron Silliman. *The New Sentence*. New York: Roof Books, 1987.

Susan Schultz. "'Called Null or Called Vocative': A Fate of the Contemporary Lyric." *Talisman: A Journal of Contemporary Poetry and Poetics* #14 (1996): 70–80.

Gertrude Stein, "Composition as Explanation," In *A Stein Reader*. Ed. Ulla Dydo. Evanston: Northwestern University Press, 1993. 494–503.

John Taggart. *Loop*. Los Angeles: Sun & Moon Press, 1991.

John Taggart. *Songs of Degrees: Essays on Contemporary Poetry and Poetics*. Tuscaloosa: University of Alabama Press, 1994.

Helen Vendler. *Soul Says: On Recent Poetry*. Cambridge, MA: Harvard University Press, 1995.

Mark Wallace. "On the Lyric as Experimental Possibility." *Witz: A Journal of Contemporary Poetics*, 3, 2 (Spring 1995): 1–3, 10.

Theodore Weiss. "Reviewing the Reviewer." *The American Poetry Review* 25, 3 (May/June 1996): 37–45.

Louis Zukofsky. *"A."* Berkeley: University of California Press, 1978.

Louis Zukofsky. *All: The Collected Short Poems 1923–1964*. New York: W. W. Norton, 1971.

Louis Zukofsky. *Prepositions: The Collected Critical Essays of Louis Zukofsky* (Expanded Edition). Berkeley: University of California Press, 1981.

"Vatic Scat":
Jazz and the Poetry of
Robert Creeley and Nathaniel Mackey

In mid-February 1997, I was in San Diego. Or, I was in at
least two San Diegos. I gave a reading at UCSD, and I spoke at
San Diego State University to Harry Polkinhorn's seminar on Jack
Kerouac. Harry had suggested that I might talk to the class about
jazz and poetry. Actually, I have been doing just that in my own
classes for the past several years. More and more, to exemplify *some*
of the rhythmic/musical possibilities for poetry, I have drawn on
jazz examples, especially the work of John Coltrane and Thelonious
Monk. When I went to Harry's class, my play list included (portions
of) the following: Thelonious Monk's "(I Love You, I Love You I
Love You) Sweetheart of All My Dreams" (1964, on *Standards*), "In
Walked Bud," "Evidence," and "Criss Cross" (1947, 1948, and 1951,
from *The Best of Thelonious Monk*, Blue Note), "In Walked Bud"
(1958, *Mysterioso*), "Bright Mississippi" (*Monk's Dream*, 1963), and
John Coltrane's "The Father and the Son and the Holy Ghost" (from
Meditations, 1966). In the class, we moved back and forth from the
jazz-listenings to a reading/discussion of a number of poems from
my own sequence *Days* (several of which appeared in the Summer
1996 issue of *River City*).

Gradually, I have begun to claim that jazz as *content* may be
the least interesting way that jazz may enter into poetry. Too of-
ten, jazz-as-content becomes a heroizing of the jazz musician as a
figure of "intuition" or "imagination." Several anthologies—*The
Jazz Poetry Anthology* and *The Second Set: The Jazz Poetry Anthology,
Volume 2* (both edited by Sacha Feinstein & Yusef Komunyakaa,
Indiana University Press, 1991 & 1996) and *Moment's Notice: Jazz in
Poetry and Prose* (edited by Art Lange & Nathaniel Mackey, Coffee
House Press, 1993)—do indicate the pervasiveness of jazz's influ-
ence on contemporary poetry and some of the range of options for

a jazz-influenced poetry. But the vast majority of the poems in the anthologies re-enforce the least interesting option: jazz-as-content, or jazz-as-subject-matter. Such a use falls prey to a fairly predictable sentimentality and equally often is marked by a failure to engage the poem's (or jazz's) particular constructedness, the precision of a particular structure (even, or especially, as that structure is an irregular one). I have also gradually learned that for me the term *jazz* does not automatically lead to some loose idealization of *improvisation*. I am interested in the idiosyncrasies and the peculiarities of certain jazz compositions, and in how they might occur similarly in a poem. As John Cage said of his varied art-making: an imitation of nature *in her manner of operation*. The homage is not to a fetishized signature (written or played), not another hymn to individuality, but an homage to a collective investigation of what is possible.

The particular legacy that interests me begins with jazz of the late 1940s and early 1950s. One of the first manifestations of what I am trying to get at occurs in Robert Creeley's poetry of the early and mid-1950s, a poetry influenced both by Creeley's deep interest in jazz and by his correspondence with Charles Olson. As an antidote to the restricted resources of *Understanding Poetry* and to an era of poetic activity with a strong basis in conventional metrics, Olson advocated renewed attention to the syllable "as an act of correction, to both prose and verse as now written ... if the syllable, that fine creature, were more allowed to lead the harmony on" ("Projective Verse," 1950, in *Selected Writings*, 18). Olson's emphasis on the syllable is allied to his valorization of "the ear, which is so close to the mind that it is the mind's that it has the mind's speed" (18). It is speed of mind that Robert Creeley finds most productively in the jazz of the late 1940s and early 1950s, a jazz music which helps the poet to investigate analogous resources in his own quickly shifting poetry of that period. For example, in writing about his poem "The Whip" (from the mid-1950s), Creeley refers to the music he had been listening to:

> ... it is music, specifically jazz, that informs the poem's manner in large part. Not that it's jazzy, or about jazz—rather, it's trying to use a rhythmic base much as jazz of this time would—or what was especially characteristic of Charlie Parker's playing, or Miles Davis', Thelonious Monk's, or Milt

Jackson. That is, the beat is used to delay, detail, prompt,
define the content of the statement or, more aptly, the emotional field of the statement. It's trying to do this while moving in time to a set periodicity—durational units, call them.
It will say as much as it can, or as little, in the "time" given.
So each line is figured as taking the same time, like they say,
and each line ending works as a distinct pause. I used to
listen to Parker's endless variations on "I Got Rhythm" and
all the various times in which he'd play it, all the tempi, up,
down, you name it. What fascinated me was that he'd write
silences as actively as sounds, which of course they were. Just
so in poetry. (*Collected Essays*, 591)

As John Wilson remarks, "as early as the 1940s, while still at Harvard,
Creeley was spending hour upon hour day after day listening to
jazz" (*Robert Creeley's Life and Work*, 5). As Michael Rumaker recalls
Creeley's classes at Black Mountain College, the class "read and discussed at length William Carlos Williams's earlier poems as points
of departure towards our own possibilities in American speech, as
well as the poetry of Hart Crane and the jazz of Charlie Parker and
Bud Powell" (*Life and Work*, 54). For the listener/reader interested
in following up on Creeley's jazz interests of the late 1940s and early
1950s, there are a number of good sources, including *Charlie Parker:
Bebop & Bird, Volume 1* (Hipsville/Rhino R2 70197), which includes
five cuts from the WJZ live radio broadcasts (June 30, 1950) from
Birdland in which Parker's legendary quintet includes Fats Navarro,
Bud Powell, Curly Russell, and Art Blakey; or the many early recordings of Thelonious Monk on Blue Note (*Thelonious Monk: Genius of
Modern Music - Volume 1*, Blue Note CDP 7 81510 2, all cuts from
1947; and *The Best of Thelonious Monk*, Blue Note CDP 7 9536 2,
which includes several cuts from the 1947 sessions as well as some
important work from 1948, 1951 [with Milt Jackson], and 1952).
 Perhaps from Parker, Creeley absorbed a rapidity of motion—a
quality that Olson had also been urging Creeley to investigate. From
Parker and more especially from Monk, Creeley may have learned
about the humor and beauty of sudden shifts in direction and about
the value of silence and syncopation. In 1950, Olson was writing to
Creeley, offering suggestions on directions Creeley might explore:

… but just as his head is long, his breath is quick &
short, AND (which is, of course in a way the same thing:
any man who goes fast can't go without, *etcs*, which are
shorthand for the fastest sort of juxtapositions:
it's JUXTAPOSITIONS, that I mean by quick breath,
and that you are not yet getting in, at least in verse. (*Life
and Work*, 36)

The rapidity, urged by Olson, and informed by Charlie Parker and
Thelonious Monk, came out soon enough in Creeley's remarkable
poems of the early and mid-1950s—see, for example, "Le Fou" and
"I Know a Man."

In light of Olson's comments on the importance of the syllable, I would like to attend to some specifics of music in Nathaniel
Mackey's poetry, particularly the work represented in *School of
Udhra*. I suppose that what I am seeking is a description that would
point to the specific elements of cadence and music, the dialog of
silence and sound that is particular to Mackey's work, the signature
of what I hear as distinctive in his writing, in the same way that
one recognizes the exactness and idiosyncrasy in Thelonious Monk's
compositions. Such a description does not pretend to some objectivity; it is, obliquely, merely an attempt to articulate what captures my
attention, in the hope that such a description is of value to others
and can provide a more detailed (acoustical) access to the poetry. It is
an act of appreciation, an attempt to specify that appreciation.

Begin, for example, with this passage:
Weathered raft I saw myself
adrift on.

Battered wood I dreamt I
drummed on, driven.

Scissored rose, newly braided
light, slack hoped-for-rope
groped at, unraveled.
(*Udhra*, 9)

One might begin by asking, quite reasonably, why this passage rather than another? For me, this passage begins to point toward the hard edges between words in much of Mackey's poetry, the way our mouthing of the poem must pause decisively, must slow to say *Battered wood I dreamt I / drummed on, driven.* I think of this cadence and this anti-mellifluous quality as percussive in nature. Such a percussive quality recurs throughout *Udhra*, as in this passage:

> Arced harp. Dark
> bent-over body. Esoteric
> sun whose boat its
> back
> upheld… (26)

Often, as in these two examples, Mackey's percussiveness is re-enforced by assonance (as in *Arced / harp / dark*). Or, to cite another example, "Gruff / stutter, / scuffed horn" (34). Or, as in the deliberate word-lumps of "Blue lump love cut its / teeth on" (83). To my ear, such passages constitute a particular, distinctive lyricism in Mackey's poetry, moments of a stuttered, stammered, hard to say, beautiful music. Perhaps these passages exemplify what Mackey means by "word / let out edgewise" (38). I could distort the truth by means of my selections and claim that such percussiveness is *the* dominant feature of Mackey's writing. It is not so. And such an attempt to track *an* element of a poet's lyricism should admit as much. As a counter example to the percussiveness that I am tracking, I note, for example, the sliding mellifluousness, the easy movement from word to word, the fluid syllable boundaries between words (where the edges between words are *not* sharp) in a passage such as

> Sweet
> beast whose horns mourn lost
> amenities, mystic lament it
> appropriates,
> mad but won't say. Sings out of the
> side of its mouth. (42)

There is no point in saying, falsely, that *one* sound (or one mode of
music) is *the* sound that this poet makes. Even so, I would argue
for the importance of such distinguishing distinctivenesses and of
Mackey's stammered percussive lyricism.

   Besides providing me with an example of a jazz-based poetry
which is *not* restricted to jazz-as-content, it makes sense to ask what
is the significance of such an exploration of sound? (How might the
percussiveness that I have alleged for Mackey's poetry differ in sound
or in significance from similarly stressed poems by Ezra Pound, or
Richard Hugo, or, more similarly, by Clark Coolidge?) Is such a
study (on my part) merely a series of technical/craft observations
(and thus complicit with an ahistoricizing New Critical approach to
the poem)? If we think about the following passage, we can perhaps
begin to formulate some of the significance of Mackey's music:

> chalices lifted, consequent
> hum the what-sayer's *we*, whereof a
>   new muse might emerge, root
>   clarity,
> whimsic nearness, far-flung
>   sight …
> "Muy lejos," the chorus's refrain
>   felt beyond hearing (68)

Mackey's poem-music exists on several borders: a synaesthetic border
of sight and sound (elsewhere referred to as "anagrammatic / scat"
[44] and "vatic scat" [86]), a border between the sayable and the unsayable, the smooth statement and the stuttered stammer. Mackey's
lyricism plays at the intersection of meaning and unmeaning, of
sense and nonsense, an intersectional source for poetic composition, kin to Kristeva's *chora*, kin to Coltrane's sheets of sound, to the
honking and moaning of the saxophone leaving accustomed melodies for a more heuristic howling:

> To unmean with moaning,
> adamant,
>   guttural gist inexhaustibly
> ancestral to itself …

Bent glyph, synaesthetic,
unglimpsed ... (76)

As Mackey is quite aware, the movement into such a "guttural
gist" is decidedly *not* original. As I've been suggesting, it is a lyricism
that declares its affinity with many elements of jazz (and of blues,
and, as Mackey has pointed out, of *cante jondo*). In poetry, such
an exploration continues the work of Amiri Baraka, who in "AM/
TRAK" writes that "Trane clawed at the limits of cool / slandered
sanity / with his tryin to be born" (*The LeRoi Jones /Amiri Baraka
Reader*, 268), and whose own poem moves from thematization of
jazz's moaning into its transcription:

The cadre came together
the inimitable 4 who blew the pulse of then, exact
The flame the confusion the love of
whatever the fuck there was
   to love
Yes it says
blow, oh honk-scream (bahhhhhhh - wheeeeeeee)
                                        (*Reader*, 271)

Or most remarkably of all is the embodiment of the scream and the
moan in Baraka's extraordinary poem "Dope" (*Reader*, 263–266, a
poem which is most effectively appreciated by listening to Baraka's
reading of "Dope" on July 26, 1978 at the Naropa Institute [Tape
#36, Naropa Institute Archives]. See also the many poems on Monk
and Coltrane in Baraka's *Funk Lore: New Poems 1984–1995*, Los
Angeles: Littoral Books, 1996.). I believe that Mackey shares Baraka's
insistence that we "understand the implications of music as an autonomous *judge* of civilizations" (*Reader*, 191).

   In fact, Mackey argues that "part of the genius of black music
is the room it allows for a telling 'inarticulacy,' a feature consistent
with its critique of a predatory coherence" (*Discrepant Engagement*,
252–253). Mackey writes, "In *Sound and Symbol*,...Victor
Zuckerkandl offers 'a musical concept of the external world,' something he also calls 'a critique of our concept of reality from the point
of view of music.' He goes to great lengths to assert that music bears

witness to what is left out of that concept of reality, or, if not exactly
what, to the fact that something *is* left out" (*Discrepant*, 232). In
his critical writing, Mackey links together many art forms engaged,
through the peculiarly disruptive music of noise, in such a stammered cultural critique:

> Noise is whatever the signifying system, in a particular situ-
> ation, is not intended to transmit, be the system a poem,
> a piece of music, a novel, or an entire society. Open form
> (itself a discrepant, oxymoronic formulation, not unlike
> Williams's "variable foot") is a gesture in the direction of
> noise. Baraka's valorization of "honking" by rhythm and
> blues (R&B) saxophonists, Major's "remarkable verb of /
> things," Duncan's invocation of "disturbance," Creeley's be-
> bop-influenced deviation from expected narrative accents,
> Olson's insistence that things "keep their proper confu-
> sions," his advocacy of "shout" as a corrective to discourse,
> Brathwaite's "calibanisms," and Harris's "language as omen"
> all in their distinctive ways validate noise. (*Discrepant*, 20)

Mackey's list above, and his superb book of criticism, *Discrepant
Engagement: Dissonance, Cross-Culturality, and Experimental Writing*,
argue forcefully for the cultural and ideological implications of an
innovative "noise-making." Equally exciting, his arguments point
toward the profoundly enriching possibilities of a multi-arts cross-
fertilization that we see and hear at work in his own poetry and in
the poetry of writers such as Robert Creeley, John Taggart, Yusef
Komunyakaa, Amiri Baraka, and others.

Mackey points to the ways that "Brathwaite helps impeded
speech find its voice, the way Thelonious Monk makes hesitation
eloquent or the way a scat singer makes inarticulacy speak. This
places his [Brathwaite's] work in the New World African tradition of
troubled eloquence, othered eloquence" (*Discrepant*, 274). Perhaps as
an innovative extension of a tradition of call-and-response, Mackey
describes this emerging tradition of "troubled eloquence" as "the tor-
menting lure of anomalous beauty and the answering dance of defor-
mation" (*Discrepant*, 241). In "Slipped Quadrant," the concluding
poem to Mackey's *School of Udhra*, he proclaims

Ominous music made a mumblers
                                    academy
    vatic scat,   to be alive
was to be warned it said (86)

It is, however, an ominousness not without promise, for Mackey's
"mumblers academy" is also "seed / within a seed sown elsewhere"
and "In oblique / league with majesty" (86). Though a historically
informed cultural critique and a noise critical of dominant (en-
forced) harmonies, Mackey's stammered eloquence, as in the concluding passage to *School of Udhra*, retains utopian desires as well:

            Dream of a just world.
    Saw the in we sought ran deep, sat us
        down with chills, polyrhythmic
                                    shivers…
    Pinched earth, outrun by longing.
        Whimsical inlet.   Renegade
                                    wish   (87)

    For me, that renegade wish factors in the rhythmic and ideo-
logical implications of Monk, Mackey, Baraka, Creeley, Taggart,
Coltrane, and an expanding list of eloquent stammerers.

Works Cited

Amiri Baraka. *The LeRoi Jones / Amiri Baraka Reader*. Edited by William J. Harris. New York: Thunder's Mouth Press, 1991.

Robert Creeley. *The Collected Essays of Robert Creeley*. Berkeley: University of California Press, 1989.

Nathaniel Mackey. *Discrepant Engagement: Dissonance, Cross-Culturality, and Experimental Writing*. New York: Cambridge University Press, 1993. (Reprinted, Tuscaloosa. University of Alabama, 2000)

Nathaniel Mackey. *School of Udhra*. San Francisco: City Lights Books, 1993.

Charles Olson. *Selected Writings*. Edited by Robert Creeley. New York: New Directions, 1966.

John Wilson, editor. *Robert Creeley's Life and Work: A Sense of Increment*. Ann Arbor: University of Michigan Press, 1987.

Lyricism of the Swerve:
The Poetry of Rae Armantrout

> but clarity need not be equivalent to
> readability. How readable is the world?
> —Rae Armantrout

Rae Armantrout begins "Cheshire Poetics"[1] by giving us a simple narrative which she then calls into question:

> I spent my twenties (during the 1970's) in the Bay Area—at one of the origin points for what came to be known as "language poetry" and I am, of course, one of the people associated with that group. Most of you know that—but when you know that, what do you know? (24)

Such doubleness—in this case, assertion and critique—done with brevity and humor, characterizes Armantrout's poetry. Her poetry is of special importance because of the particular nature of her commitment to precision and to new possibilities within lyricism. These commitments mark Armantrout's poetry as unusual within the writings known as language poetry; they also mark her work as a noteworthy extension of an innovative lyric tradition from Dickinson to the present. My attempt in this essay is to pay particular attention to the movement in Armantrout's poetry. It is an idiosyncratic movement—what I think of as a peculiar mode of swerving—that, for me, characterizes a kind of lyric poetry that Armantrout has been pursuing for quite some time. In reading her poetry with some care, yes, it is possible to differentiate her writing from various other modes of swerving such as we find, for example, in the poetry of Robert Creeley, bpNichol, and Emily Dickinson. Attuning our hearing/reading constitutes a beginning.

---

1 *American Women Poets in the 21st Century*, ed. Claudia Rankine and Juliana Spahr, Middletown, CT: Wesleyan University Press, 2002: 24–26.

———

Is there a describable lyricism of swerving? For those poems
for which the swerve, the turn, the sudden change in direction are
integral, can we begin to articulate a precise appreciation? Is there a
describable and *individualistic* lyricism of swerving?

I have heard Rae Armantrout spoken of as the most lyrical of
all Language poets. And, I have heard her work described as an important instance of contemporary innovative lyricism. As a poet, my
own work (particularly *Days* and "Well Yes Then") explores such
current possibilities. As a critic, I have written about new lyricisms[2].
But the terms themselves—lyric, lyrical, lyricism—at present, mean
so many different things. Of my particular current favorites in such
modes—Larry Eigner, Robert Creeley, bpNichol, Theodore Enslin,
John Taggart, Harryette Mullen, John Ashbery, Nathaniel Mackey,
Lyn Hejinian, Susan Howe—none is a (precise or identical) twin
to Armantrout. Initially, I offer descriptions and readings of several
different kinds of contemporary lyricisms as a means of situating
Armantrout's particular contribution.

Perhaps one task of critical writing (and of intensive reading) is
to attend to, in George Oppen's words, "the thing and its distinction."[3] A most important recent "thing" by Armantrout is her Chax
book, *writing / the plot / about / sets* (1998). Oppen's complete observation is of "the thing and its distinction / (which of course reveals
actually the human / subjectivity: human meanings)," and it is with
an eye toward those particularities of subjectivity that I wish to attend to Armantrout's poetry.

---

2 See "The Lyric Valuables: Soundings, Questions, and Examples,"
Modern Language Studies Volume 27, Number 2 (Spring 1997): 25–50; and
" 'Vatic Scat': Jazz and the Poetry of Robert Creeley and Nathaniel Mackey,"
River City: A Journal of Contemporary Culture, Volume 17, Number 2
(Summer 1997): 100–108. (Chapters 1 and 2 in *Lyric & Spirit*.)

3 Included in unpublished Oppen manuscripts, included in the
George Oppen Archive, housed in The Archive for New Poetry at
Mandeville Special Collections at the University of California at San Diego
library, edited by Stephen Cope. This passage Cope locates as 16:19:1:2;
his marking system refers to the Archive, Box, Folder, and Leaf numbers of
the given page.

I am tempted to think toward a brief taxonomy of swerving. I begin with what for me is a touchstone for a particular kind of musical/sound swerving in an energetic passage of perpetual modulation and transformation from bpNichol's *Martyrology*:

> an infinite statement. a finite statement. a statement of infancy. a fine line state line. a finger of stalemate. a feeling a saint meant ointment.

> tremble.

> a region religion
> reigns in. a returning. turning return the lover. the retrospect of relationships always returning. the burning of the urge. the surge forward in animal being inside us. the catatosis van del reeba rebus suburbs of our imagination. last church of the lurching word worked weird in our heads.

Such a category of swerving could and would be found elsewhere, for example, in many passages of Louis Zukofsky's work, most notably in "Songs of Degrees," which begins "Hear, her / Clear / Mirror, / Care / His error. / In her / Care / Is clear."[4] Another category would highlight instances where the swerving occurred much more gradually, and my examples would come from extended quotation from the poetry of John Taggart or Theodore Enslin.[5] For example, Enslin's "Autumnal Rime" begins

---

4 See Louis Zukofsky, *ALL: The Collected Short Poems, 1923–1964* (New York: Norton, 1971), particularly "Songs of Degrees" (pp. 151–159) and "The Translation" (235–240); see also *"A"* (Berkeley: University of California Press, 1978), particularly *"A"-19* (pp. 408–434).

5 The specific examples cited come from Theodore Enslin, "Autumnal Rime," *Talisman: A Journal of Contemporary Poetry and Poetics*, Number 12 (Spring 1994, The Theodore Enslin Issue), p. 37; and John Taggart, "The Rothko Chapel Poem," in *Loop* (Los Angeles: Sun & Moon Press, 1991), p. 150. While Enslin's earlier work is also highly musical in nature, the particular mode of gradual change that I'm highlighting is more readily visible/audible in later work such as "Scripturals" (December 4, 1993–February 7, 1994) published in *First Intensity*, issues 5, 6, 7, and 8; "Autumnal Rime," *Talisman* #12 (Spring 1994), pp. 37–69; "Propositions for John Taggart," *tel-let* #57 (1996); and "Mad Songs," Backwoods Broadsides.

Mindful   mindful only of quality
the quality of moritura   of need
of the need to die . that all dying
dying out of the need   the need
to die the quality   the moritura
of quality   moritura in dying
need to   of need in the mores
that all is mortal   is mortally
wounded   the mind is a wound mindful

In Taggart's poetry, the swerving transformations take shape a bit
more gradually. Perhaps if we were to imagine a topology of swerving,
we would locate Enslin's musical turns somewhere between the quick,
precise syllabic turns of Zukofsky's "Songs of Degrees" and Taggart's
more extended modulations in "The Rothko Chapel Poem," Taggart's
musical turns taking place not so much at the level of the syllable- or
word-transformed but at the level of the phrase slowly modified:

Really only one has been moving us
only one within itself moving us
one scream within itself moving us
screams within the one move us away
away from the weddings wedding rooms
from those to this this black room
to our wandering in this black room
moving in this room means wandering
wandering's moving without meaning
no end to moving in this black room
it is like moving in a writhing sea

Chaplet Series, Number 6 (1995). Additional examples in Taggart's *Loop*
include "See What Love" (17–21), "In True Night" (57–59), "Were
You" (99–102), "Repetition" (113–123), "The Rothko Chapel Poem"
(137–171), and "Marvin Gaye Suite" (216–224). There are many other
examples in Taggart's *Crosses: Poems 1992–1998* (Stop Press, 2005), especially "What She Heard" and Taggart's extended discussion in "Jesus'
Blood: Notes & Overlays" (a meditation on Gavin Bryars' "Jesus' Blood
Never Failed Me Yet"). See also John Taggart's *Dehiscence* (Milwaukee:
Membrane Press, 1983).

we are wandering in a writhing sea
seething and writhing in this room.

Perhaps one might make analogies to minimalist music, or one
might call this swerving a kind of gradual modulation (and link it
to the studies of gradual changes in time in Stein's *The Making of
Americans* [completed in 1911, and first published in 1925] and in
her *Lectures in America* [first presented in 1934, and first published
in 1935]). The particular sound-swervings of Zukofsky, Taggart, and
Enslin seem to me to be fundamentally musical in nature.

Then, there are the more tentative, tenuous, miraculous, mystical
turns in a Larry Eigner poem. In many of Eigner's poems, as in the
beginning of "Letter to Duncan," those shifts occur not at the musical
level of the syllable or word but at the level of the phrase, re-enforced
by the shifting but precise location of the phrase on the page:

> just because I forget
> to perch different ways
>   the fish
>   go monotonous
>
>
>   the
>   sudden hulks of the trees
>   in a glorious summer
> you don't realize
>   how mature you get
>   at 21
>
>
>   but you look back
>
>
>   wherever a summer
>   continue 70 seasons
>
>
>   this one
>   has been so various
>
>
>   was the spring hot?[6]

_____

6 Larry Eigner, "Letter for Duncan," in *Selected Poems* (Berkeley:

As in much of Creeley's poetry, the exact tension between the phrase—its seeming autonomy—and the sentence (which may attempt to subordinate and coordinate the various phrases) constitutes a drama of the poem's lineation and spatial arrangement. Thus, such poems enact an important ambivalence—one which is central as well to Armantrout's poetry: the tension, humor, play, and desire of what-goes-with-what.

Or, one might examine a quite different swerve-category called the wacky juxtaposition, perhaps best exemplified in John Ashbery's poetry, when there is a sudden shift in tone, or register, or discourse, or subject matter. In "Grand Galop," for example, Ashbery's address to Surrey turns sharply (in tone and subject matter) in another direction:

> Surrey, your lute is getting an attack of nervous paralysis
> But there are, again, things to be sung of
> And this is one of them, only I would not dream of intruding on
> The frantic completeness, the all-purpose benevolence
> Of that still-moist garden where the tooting originates:
> Between intervals of clenched teeth, your venomous rondelay.
>
> Ask a hog what is happening. Go on. Ask him.[7]

Or, one might look to another example twenty years later in the opening lines of "A Day at the Gate": "A loose and dispiriting / wind took over from the grinding of traffic. / Clouds from the distillery / blotted out the sky. Ocarina sales plummeted."[8] Armantrout, in my opinion, does have some similarities to Ashbery's sense of humor; but her poems really are not much like his. That category of the wacky juxtaposition—particularly when it is based on a quick change of subject—moves me in the direction of John Cage's realization "that two notations on the saMe / pIece of paper / automatically briNg / About relationship."[9] (Cage, interestingly, completes this re-

---

Oyez, 1972), p. 60.

7 John Ashbery, "Grand Galop," in *Self-Portrait in a Convex Mirror* (New York: Penguin, 1976), p. 20.

8 John Ashbery, *Can You Hear, Bird* (New York: Farrar, Straus & Giroux, 1995), p. 3.

9 John Cage, *Composition in Retrospect* (Cambridge, MA: Exact

alization by adding the conclusion that "my Composing / is actuallY unnecessary.")

Armantrout's particular and distinctive skill lies in the peculiarly teasing, humorous, thoughtful (and thought-provoking) engagement at those junctures, joints, and sites of adjacency.

~~~~~~

Just as with the title to her Chax book—*writing / the plot / about / sets* (1998)—in which there are various possible combinations and multiplicities (or a simple list as a table of contents), so Armantrout's poems turn and tease, combine and resist combination, as in the opening lines of "about"[10]:

What's the worst that could happen?

"Schools of fish are trapped
In these pools,"
Say the anchors

Who hang
On nursing home walls.

Reference is inimical,
We find out now;

Its Moebius strip
Search called

Vital
To security.

Change, 1993), p. 22.

10 Armantrout's Chax book is unpaginated. With twelve pages of actual text, the passages are easily located. The poems included in Armantrout's Chax chapbook are also included in *The Pretext* (Green Integer, 2001) and *Veil: New and Selected Poems* (Wesleyan, 2001). In subsequent citations to Armantrout's various poetry, *E=Extremities*; *I= The Invention of Hunger*; *P=Precedence*; *N=Necromance*; *M=Made to Seem.*

Her poems are, as her line break helps us to realize, how "we find out now." And her poems constitute specific embodiments of "now." Increasingly, I have come to think of poems as particular intervals of consciousness, as thinking singing instances of now.

As we decipher what goes with what, Armantrout works the lyricism of that simultaneous gap-and-connection. From the outset of "about," there is an element of discomfort, combined with a resistance to a simple tendency for the poem to be "about" anything static—an edginess marked by one of the last lines of the poem: "*We're* the target audience." It is that quality of targeting and being targeted that "about" circles about. Does the first line of the poem refer to the confinement implicit in a poetry that must somehow be "about" something in a sustained, controlled manner? If such a critique is begun, the critique of "about-ness," of a subject or theme-based poetry/poetics, then we'd expect the schools and the schooled to be "trapped / In these pools," though *which* pools remains indefinite.

For me, the characteristic Armantrout swerve—with a mixture of play and investigativeness—occurs with the word "anchors." At first, we swim along from fish to pools to anchors, and it is a quiet aftershock as we must redecipher these anchors in light of their position of hanging "On nursing home walls," thus being transformed into TV anchors, hanging in and on the hypnotizing and consoling TV sets of the nursing home. These anchors do indeed anchor us—we are the target audience, and that CNN factoid "we" is part of the smart-bomb targeting of inclusivity and normalization. The hook is an authoritative voice which inevitably and clearly tells us (and informs us) "about" something, relaying a digested narrative "about" current events (to the trapped, mesmerized viewer).

If, as Oppen suggests, "a poem may be devoted to giving clear meaning to one word,"[11] then for me Armantrout's poem clarifies, by focusing attention on, "inimical." "Reference is inimical" and extends its dominion as modes of organization that bombard us, and as modes of organization that we impose and superimpose. "Inimical," from *inimicus*: enemy; hostile; viewing with disfavor; having the disposition or temper of an enemy; harmful; adverse; prejudicial in tendency, influence, or effects. Not that there is a place utterly *out-*

11　Unpublished manuscript, University of California, San Diego, edited by Stephen Cope, 16:19:3:29.

side reference or outside about-ness either. The strip we read and ride on twists Moebius-style; it is a continuous one-sided surface upon which we circulate and re-circulate. That surface continues smoothly unless there is a sudden interruption; thus Armantrout breaks the continuity with a poet's principal resource, the line break, so that the continuous strip becomes a "strip / search," though that momentary glitch is taken into account as part of a greater habit of security and as part of a process that makes sure we "just keep moving." If we are the target audience, the target of what? Targeted to do or be or become what? In the imperial gathering of "we" in the factoid world,[12] as good Americans, as consumers of the news, soon, as in Armantrout's next poem, we'll learn that " "We're" bombing Iraq again." As with about-ness and reference, two inimicals, there is not a space outside of the collectively imposed and imposing "we."

A danger of the lyric: preciousness; (calculated) scarcity; a romantic exaltation of intensification. The lyric may not be enough. As a friend says of the reception of Susan Howe's poetry: so much fuss over so few words?!

In "sets," the final poem in *writing / the plot / about / sets*, Armantrout concludes:

> Time's tic:
> to pitch forward
> then catch "itself"
> again.
>
> "We're" bombing Iraq again.

---

12 Much of Bob Perelman's poetry is pertinent to such in inquiry into the political uses of pronouns. See particularly "Seduced by Analogy" in *To the Reader* (Berkeley: Tuumba Press, 1984) and "We" in *The First World* (Great Barrington, Massachusetts: The Figures, 1986).

If I turn on the news,
someone will say, "We
mean business."

*

Eyes open wide
to form

an apology?
Disguised as what
might be surprise
over the raised
spoon.

That quotation-marked "we" means a certain kind of business. In our time, the rhetoric of that pronoun is no longer the kingly "we" but the "we" of fact, data, and of persuasion of our collective deeds (and, implicitly, of our collective strength).

Is Armantrout's ending fully complicit in innocent "wonder"? Is this ending a typical or formulaic instance of lyrical closure? Or/and its mockery? That last stanza has a delicacy of sound/music—it is typically "lyrical." It is still evasive, pleasant, not overbearing in its crafted charms. I register the echoes of the long I-vowels in the sequence *eyes, wide, disguised, might, surprise,* modulating slightly into *raised,* playing off of the sequence of raspy s-z sounds in *eyeS, disguiSed, aS, surpriSe,* and *raiSed.* I hear, as well, a dialog of high and low vowel sounds (as in Plath's "Morning Song"), the high treble I and A vowels beside the low bass O-sounds of *Open, apolOgy, Over,* and *spOOn.* These pretty echoing sounds incarnate the lyrical moment.

Are eyes open wide over the raised spoon an effective gesture of skepticism (by means of a feigned surprise)? Do these gestures offer a fit defense against and a reply to the inimical? Or, as the first poem, "writing," warns, "But here's the joke: syntactic space predates and dominates these words." "We" are the target audience. The smart bombs find us. We launch them all the time. "We hunker down / with short pencils / in front of the ticket booth."

A ticket to what? A ticket to the next poem called "the plot,"
which begins:

> The secret is
> you can't get to sleep
> with a quiet mind;
> you need to follow a sentence,
> inward or downward,
> as it becomes circuitous,
> path-like, with tenuously credible
> foliage on either side of it—
> but you're still not sleeping.

Or, as Charles Bernstein has written, a pronouncement inseparable from its humor, "Poetry is like a swoon, with this difference: /
it brings you to your senses."[13] For Rae's analytic lyrics *do* attempt to
bring us to our senses. As Lyn Hejinian asks, "isn't the avant garde
always pedagogical?"[14]

———

Let us backtrack, then. In Armantrout's first book, *Extremities*
(The Figures, 1978), some pitfalls of lyricism are all too apparent, as
in "Paradise" (23):

> Paradise
> *is* golden.
>
>   Sun
> on wicker chair.
>
> It is as one knew!
>
> The joyful song
> ascends

13 Charles Bernstein in "The Klupzy Girl" in *Islets/Irritations* (New York: Jordan Davies, 1983), p. 47.

14 Lyn Hejinian, *My Life* (Los Angeles: Sun & Moon, 1987), p. 92.

The poet risks clarity and simplicity; the poem is restricted to momentary phenomena. As in a later poem in the same volume, the poem stakes its value on the possible depth of singularity: "A single truth now occupies the mind: // the smallest // distance // inexhaustible" (34). But once we know that—the Blakean infinite in a grain of sand, the depth and value of each particular—then what? We are left to assess and access the poet's moments of such integrity and realization. It may be a state about which we might say later, "Disguised as what / might be surprise / over the raised / spoon." Or, we might encounter the self-promoting medium of such proclamations, as in one of the final poems in *Extremities* (41), "Show":

> Big Red Tomatoes - Dangling
>   from Plain Sticks
>
>   To Show
>
>   Miracle
>   Creation of Flesh

But a mysticism of the particular is inextricable from its presentational rhetoric, and the need to capitalize already brings on a countering skepticism.

     I would argue that a flat mysticism of the particular is a problem. What's needed is a twist or turn, a kind of swerve in another direction—as Louis Zukofsky suggests, "thoughts' torsion."[15] From her earliest writing on, Armantrout brings in qualities of skepticism, self-criticism, and self-opposition to provide the kind of torsion that Zukofsky advocates. There is an element of critique (of a naïve poetry of mystical affirmation) in the capitalized display of "Show," and if we re-examine "Paradise" that poem too contains an important twist. The potential for the poem to be a flat declaration and a simple "joyful song" of a discovered paradise gets critiqued by the exclamation "It is as one knew!" As Armantrout explains,

---

15   "Mantis," in *ALL: The collected Short Poems, 1923–1964* (New York: Norton, 1971), p. 73.

I intended an irony in the line "It is as one knew!" If paradise is as one knew then is it paradise or is it merely a stereotype? The exclamation makes it sound like discovery—but one can't discover what one already knew. So I think that line takes that poem out of the realm of "momentary phenomena."[16]

Exclamation marks, italics, capitalization, and quotation marks become essential print-based markers as Rae develops a subtly polyphonic lyricism. From early on in her writing, Armantrout gives us a typically lyrical moment, but that moment inevitably is tied to some counterbalancing skepticism, so that the moment becomes ironized or self-conflicted. Rae deploys a lyricism of the moment that highlights its own rhetoric of presentation. The result is a swerving within the moment itself—a two-faced or two faceted lyrical moment, which, at its best, leaves us both engaged and on edge.

The lyric, to sustain our interest, to have complexity and beauty, and to remain compelling, requires "torsion"—that is, motion, tension, torque, and a twist. Such torsion is evident in Armantrout's "Travels" (*E*, 33):

> Among the zinnias I once thought
> I had recovered silence
>
> The power to be
> irretrievably lost
>
> Is death
> what's wrong?

It is the vertiginous swerve from the commonplace tone and diction of the first four lines in this passage (with its conventional lyrical intensifiers—*among, once, recovered, silence, power, irretrievably lost*) to the disruption and deepening of the concluding two lines that begins to characterize Armantrout's idiosyncratic lyricism. In this first book,

---

16 E-mail, Rae Armantrout to Hank Lazer, September 20, 1998. I'm grateful to Rae Armantrout for her helpful critique of my initial reading of "Paradise."

Rae's poetry begins to become a poetics of edges and verges, as in the concluding six lines of the title poem, "Extremities" (7):

> the glitter of edges
> again catches the eye
>
> to approach these swords!
>
> Lines across which
> beings vanish / flare
>
> the charmed verges of presence

Armantrout's attention to edges reminds me of an earlier poetics of the edge in Williams' *Spring and All* (1923), particularly the seventh poem which begins

> The rose is obsolete
> but each petal ends in
> an edge, the double facet
> cementing the grooved
> columns of air—The edge
> cuts without cutting

and which includes this wonderfully odd embodiment of the edge:

> What
>
> The place between the petal's
> edge and the
>
> From the petal's edge a line starts[17]

But Armantrout's is not a poetics of the edge enacted on the page (which is Williams' exuberance, his investigation [in the dawning age

17 William Carlos Williams, *The Collected Poems of William Carlos Williams, Volume 1: 1909 – 1939*, edited by A. Walton Litz & Christopher MacGowan, (New York: New Directions, 1986), pp. 195 – 196.

of the typewriter] of the line and the line break as a sculptural and visual means). Armantrout's edge-world is more one of sudden transitions and transits, sudden charges and charms. It is less effable than Williams' sense of edge, less a celebration of hard edges, more a sense of quiet pleasure, as when we see and hear "approach these swords!" as kin to "approach these words." Armantrout begins to spell out her own erotics of the edge (*E*, 26–27):

> Precision.   Clitoris.
> The searing crystals.
>
> Wicked.   Stylish.   True
>
>   stars
>   of sensation
>
> flicker all night between
> meanings.

Or, Armantrout's swerve (as in "Dusk," the concluding poem in *The Invention of Hunger*, Tuumba, 1979) can be away from the implicit and often habitual correspondence of self to nature:

> spider on the cold expanse
> of glass, three stories high
> rests intently
> and so purely alone.
>
> I'm not like that!

In *Precedence* (Burning Deck, 1985), Armantrout becomes increasingly involved in a critical relationship to the premises of the lyric, critiquing instances "When the particular / becomes romantic (19)," the lines which follow her parody of William Stafford's "Traveling through the Dark." The lyric, perhaps at all times, but certainly in our time, has a history of abuse, danger, and habit—

perhaps typified by the bloated self-dramatization in Stafford's poem (and his ponderous and manipulative evocation of the scene of wonder). Armantrout, increasingly, draws tension, attention, and depth from her critique of the lyric (while, interestingly, remaining within a lyrical praxis). For example, "Round" begins by asking, "Do the children want a face drawn on everything?" (41). The lyric too often does become a neat vehicle for an act of comparison, an act of anthropomorphizing that, post-Emerson, has a habitual and reductive quality to it, adhering all too readily to the tenets established by Emerson in the Language section of "Nature": "Nature is the symbol of spirit....The use of natural history is to give us aid in supernatural history; the use of the outer creation, to give us language for the beings and changes of the inward creation."[18] One danger of the lyric formulaic is to rob the external world of its radical otherness by turning it into an Emersonian code book of the spirit world or into a mere vehicle for revealing the speaker's (professed) epiphanic state.

As Armantrout observes in "Another Tongue" (*P*, 34), "Coercion lets us understand what a thing means." *We* coerce those meanings into being—by our steady capitulation to given (and inadequately questioned) modes and protocols of meaning-making. And, "Early learning brackets / the notorious product" (*P*, 37). Or, as we learn in the very first page of *writing the plot about sets*: "But here's the joke: syntactic space predates and dominates these words."

Obliquity. That kind of swerving? As mathematical, at an angle. A reticence, an ethical reticence, perhaps as with Oppen, in the pursuit of a kind of integrity, a clarity, a clarifying which bears a relationship to truthfulness, though Rae, unlike George, does not proclaim it so. Though by now, even in Rae's mode of lyrical reticence, we can begin to notice how many of her sentences are, in fact, declarations. Armantrout, in a discussion of Bob Perelman's "China," suggests about simple declarations, "There is a pathos in

18 *"Nature,"* in *Selections from Ralph Waldo Emerson*, edited by Stephen E. Whicher, (Boston: Houghton Mifflin Company, 1960), p. 31.

the contrast between these minimalist statements and the missing totality of the world."[19]

Rae's poetry is often characterized as less overtly "political" than the writings of her Bay Area language poet peers. But such a characterization fails to grasp the inherently political nature of her calculated subversion of comfortable and comforting assumptions. In "Irony and Postmodern Poetry," Armantrout responds to the critique of irony as politically paralyzing—the claim (by Fredric Jameson and others) being that an ironic perspective delights in "pointing to problems instead of imagining solutions." Armantrout's view "is that it's probably elitist as well as unrealistic to think art can point out solutions. Art is the play of resonance and dissonance. To the extent that it can foreground social dissonances, it can serve a political end by increasing people's discomfort."[20]

〰

"Until I see a beauty / in disinterest, in digression!" (*P*, 40). But in the role of poet-juggler, be sure to de-center the juggler, for it is what is juggled not the juggler that is of import. Find that disinterest which is of interest to us.

〰

Rae's lyricism may, at times, become a mobile of critiqued observations, as in "Postcards" (*P*, 12):

> Man in
> the eye clinic
> rubbing his
> eye—
>
> too convincing. Like
> memory.

---

19 "Irony and Postmodern Poetry." In *Moving Borders*, edited by Mary Margaret Sloan, (Jersey City: Talisman, 1998), p. 677.

20 "Irony and Postmodern Poetry," p. 675.

My parents' neighbors' house,
backlit,
at the end of their street.

It is this teasing relationship to consecutiveness, to relatedness, that
constitutes the humor and the ethics of such lyricism. Like the man
in the eye/I clinic, Rae's poems ask us to join her in rubbing our
eyes/I's so that we might disentangle our seeing and our self-con-
struction from merely habitual and unselfconscious activity.

Or, Armantrout may offer us attention to being on edge, as in
the beginning of "Single Most" (*P*, 13):

Leaves fritter.

Teased edges.

It's vacillation that pleases.

Who answers for
the 'whole being?'

This is
only the firing

Only the firing of what? What follows (after a section division,
an asterisk, or a division sign): "Daffy runs across / the synapses,
hooting / in mock terror." The poem's drama—of the sub-genre
analytic lyric—centers on the synaptic crossing, in the teased relationship at the intersection of sense-making, connectedness, relationship, and difference.

For such a poetics, the poem "Admission" (*P*, 20) tells the primal
story of the analytic lyric as the story of the eye/I thinking:

The eye roves
back and forth, as
indictment catches up?

If shadows tattoo
the bare shelf,
they enter by comparison?

A child's turntable fastened
to the wall with a white cord
will not?

Unless on its
metal core
an unspeakable radiance ...

Think in order
to recall
what the striking thing

resembles.
(So impotently
loved the world

Yes, think. But think *in order*? And *in order to recall*? And think only toward resemblance? Such sense-making and ordering may be an impotent love in light of that core of unspeakable radiance....

〜〜〜

   In "Feminist Poetics and the Meaning of Clarity," Armantrout contrasts the poetry of Lyn Hejinian and Lorine Niedecker to Sharon Olds' poetry. Armantrout critiques Olds for keeping "her imagistic ducks in a row" and writing poems which employ "a totalizing metaphor" (290).[21] Armantrout has little patience with Olds' tendency to create "an impression of order and clarity by repressing any consciousness of dissent" (290). What's at issue here

---

   21 "Feminist Poetics and the Meaning of Clarity," in *Artifice and Indetermin-acy: An Anthology of New Poetics*, edited by Christopher Beach (Tuscaloosa: The University of Alabama Press, 1998), 287–296. (Armantrout's essay was originally published in *Sagetrieb* 11.3 [1992]). All subsequent references are to page numbers in Beach.

is what we mean (and desire) by clarity. In Rae's reading of Olds' poetry, "only information tailored to the controlling code is admissible; no second thoughts or outside voices are allowed" (290). The issue here is not simply an evaluation of Olds' poetry. Armantrout writes toward a fundamental redefinition of clarity and readability: "Whether such a poem [as Olds'] is clear depends upon what one means by clarity" (290).

Armantrout prefers a different mode of order: in the poetry of Hejinian and Niedecker, she locates "a polyphonic inner experience and an unbounded outer world" (290). Her readings allow Rae to identify an important alternative version of clarity:

> but clarity need not be equivalent to readability. How readable is the world? There is another kind of clarity that doesn't have to do with control but with attention, one in which the sensorium of the world can enter as it presents itself. Am I valorizing a long-enforced feminine passivity here? I think not. Writing is never passive. Hejinian's and Niedecker's poetry is subversive. Their poems are dynamic, contrapuntal systems in which conflicting forces and voices (inner and outer) are allowed to work. (290)

The particular mode of clarity that Armantrout's poetry embodies (as she notes in "Cheshire Poetics") depends upon "an equal counter-weight of assertion and doubt."[22] If such clarity is called "ironic," then we should keep in mind Armantrout's version of that concept: "Irony, in its broadest sense, marks the consciousness of dissonance." While Rae's poetry is insistently precise, it is a precision, as we have seen, determined to swerve. As Armantrout explains

---

22 Throughout this essay, I confine my attention to examples of swerving in Armantrout's poetry. I would point out that there are many similar instances—particularly of assertion and doubt—to be found in her wonderful autobiographical prose book, *True* (Berkeley: Atelos, 1998). In particular, I refer the reader to the story of Rae's mother's mother (page 14); the story of Rae being "saved" from landing on a "harrow" (page 18); and her account of interactions with Denise Levertov during the People's Park demonstrations (page 61)—all excellent examples of the questioning and self-questioning essential to Rae's swerving.

in "Cheshire Poetics," "I wanted my Imagism and my slither too. My precision and my doubleness." This insistence on at least doubleness (if not on multiplicity or polyphony) lies at the heart of Armantrout's version of clarity. Her intensification—an inseparable quality of a brief, lyric poetry—leads to an idiosyncratic clarity and precision that refuse and avoid singularity.

Rae has assiduously avoided what George Oppen (in "Of Being Numerous") refers to as "the shipwreck / Of the singular."[23] Or, in her own succinct and deflatingly declarative mode, she evades what she refers to in "Necromance" as the "[m]orbid / glamour of the singular" (*N*, 7). In "Necromance," one sees an analogy to the sequestered clarity of the singular as "Couples lounge / in slim fenced yards / beside the roar / of a freeway" (*N*, 8). Armantrout's poetry shows us that any "true"—or truly "clear"—picture must honor the juxtaposition of the fenced yard and the freeway.

In "Feminist Poetics and the Meaning of Clarity," Armantrout directs our attention to Hejinian's essay "Strangeness," particularly Hejinian's consideration of metonymy. Hejinian's analysis of metonymy (and how it differs from metaphor) offers an especially valuable perspective on a juxtapositional poetics which provides a foundation for Armantrout's own poetry as well. Hejinian explains,

> Metonymy moves attention from thing to thing; its principle is combination rather than selection. Compared to metaphor, which depends on code, metonym preserves context, foregrounds interrelationship. And again in comparison to metaphor, which is based on similarity and in which meanings are conserved and transferred from one thing to something like it, the metonymic world is unstable. … Metonymic thinking moves more rapidly and less predictably than metaphors permit—but the metonym is not metaphor's opposite. Metonymy moves restlessly, through an

---

23 "Of Being Numerous," in George Oppen, *Collected Poems* (New York: New Directions, 1975), p. 151.

associative network in which the associations are compressed rather than elaborated. (147)[24]

In Armantrout's poetry, metonymic thinking points toward the simultaneously readable and unreadable nature of the world. Rae's unexpected swerves and juxtapositions—what Hejinian refers to as metonymy's moving attention from thing to thing—place us within a perceptual environment where connections and disconnections become the object of our attention. Hejinian cites Jakobson's observation that "a connection once created becomes an object in its own right" (147). Hejinian claims that "a metonym is a condensation of its context" (147). The specific context of an Armantrout poem remains irreducibly multiple (or polyphonic) and stands, implicitly, as a rebuke of a more prevalent poetics (practiced by Olds and many others) which organizes perception around a monological metaphor or theme.

⁓

If, then, Rae's ways of swerving often mark disconcerting shifts in direction "about," a significant but not self-glorifying turn, not exactly one perception leading directly to another but one perception placing one somewhat askew in relation to the next, so that one becomes aware of being both engaged (perhaps "alerted") and a bit decentered.... Then, as in *Necromance* (Sun & Moon, 1991), one might, as in "The Garden," move through a garden or gallery of shifting (and humorous, though also culturally contrived) perceptions:

Oleander: coral
from lipstick ads in the 50's.

Fruit of the tree of *such* knowledge.

---

24 "Strangeness," in *Artifice and Indeterminacy: An Anthology of New Poetics*, edited by Christopher Beach (Tuscaloosa: University of Alabama Press, 1998), pp. 140–154. (Hejinian's essay originally appeared in *Poetics Journal* 8 [1989]). Subsequent page numbers refer to Beach.

To "smack"
(thin air)
meaning kiss or hit.

It appears
in the guise of outworn usages
because we are bad?

Big masculine threat,
insinuating and slangy. (11)

Within such a mobile of perceptions—at once phenomenological
and cultural—Rae runs the hazards of either a cool ironizing (as
"we" are the ones able to note the crude cultural manipulations that
surround us) or a flat detachment. Within such a process of swerving
notation, Armantrout's distinctive humor leavens both the irony and
the disinterest:

> Buoyant continuum: a lapping made of chatter about
> who controls the ranch. Possession flickers back
> and forth, filling the room like breathing. Simile
> and alibi. If human limbs *entwine*, the morning
> glory *embraces* the fence. (Can we still drain the
> energy in sex repression off landscape?) (*N*, 13)

So that the swerve becomes Armantrout's tweaking of the cli-
ched (and often italicized) phrase, the re-imagining of the italicized
phrase that has become a mere cultural counter: "In a dream language, the *troubled region* has returned as a showgirl with masses of
fruit on her head" (*N*, 16). Thus the humor comes from noticing
precisely how (often subliminally, though sometimes quite frontally)
"we" have been targeted: "Photos of lighthouses / line the walls / of
banks" (*N*, 28). How carefully did someone plan, at a bank, to reas-
sure us with such photos steeped in nostalgia but also of beacons
that light up to warn us and save us? One might say (to oneself, or
to a few others in a poem), with a barely detectable smile, "Traffic /
in surplus meaning / quite heavy of late" (*N*, 27). In fact, the media
and mediated culture we live in are increasingly about this process of

aggregate self-monitoring: "Now the news is of polls which measure our reactions to duplicity" (*N*, 21). Thus, as she notes in "Cheshire Poetics," where she cites "A Story" (in *Made to Seem*) as a particular example, Armantrout's poems "often parody and undermine some voice of social control."

Odd, then, is it, to have a lyricism—of focus, of scope, for what else can we call a poetry of intensifying brevities?—paired so insistently with a flatness of affect and a flatness of statement? Perhaps Rae's reticence occurs as it does so as *not* to interfere with our attention to something other than her *craft*. So many lyricisms run the opposite risk: they turn the poem into an occasion (merely?) for our attention and attunement with the poet's craft-on-display. In Rae's deliberate reticence, I detect (at a remove) an *ethics* of writing (perhaps akin to Oppen's quest for clarity). And yet that reticence and flatness are hardly unselfconscious productions: "Empty likeness / as the perfect tease: / her "mysterious smile" / which he must recognize / quickly" (*N*, 23).

Such reticence, such a finely tuned swerving away from the too easy automatic mode of comparison, serves Rae best in her carefully drawn attention to the natural world:

> Twigs stiffen
> the fingers.
>
> Love of nature
> is a translation.
>
> Secret nodding
> in the figurative:
>
> a corroboration
> which is taken for
> "companion."

A saw warbles,
somewhere,
and the yards too
are terraced. (*N*, 24)

"Nature," then, becomes one site to trace the entry into language
of figuration and comparison. But we are far away from some
Emersonian faith in correspondence. The two worlds, human and
natural, both bleed into one another and resist any sort of mutual
incorporation. Thus, the saw *warbles*, and the yards are *terraced*.
Especially when the "natural" too readily suggests some human quality, Armantrout quickly reasserts the autonomy, the distance, and the
strangeness of that other world:

Beauty appeals
                              like a cry

for help
                              that's distant

or inhuman
                              so foreclosed. (*N*, 26)

This insistence on the primacy of distance and autonomy remains
throughout Armantrout's poetry, beginning with such early poems
as "View" with its concluding exclamation, "The Moon // none of
our doing!" (*E*, 25).

     Armantrout, though, unlike Robinson Jeffers or W. S. Merwin,
does not fetishize that autonomy, nor does she turn that distance
from human modes of meaning-making into some fortune cookie
formulaic for wisdom. Instead of Jeffers' masculinist heroics of
tough, existential inhumanism, Armantrout's declared affinity, with a
quiet humor of recognition, may be with a linguistically impersonal
oddity: "The "you" / in the heart of / molecule and ridicule" (*N*, 39).
Her ethic, then, is one of clarifying notation, of proper perspective:

Perspective is a can of worms
but nausea defends us
against distraction

as a bird noise seethes
from everywhere at once
unlike the human

fugue where each note
is compensatory,
ringing "true." (*N*, 31)

For most of what "we" call "true" proves to be, upon further scrutiny, as Armantrout notes, "compensatory" and self-serving. With Armantrout, we may take pleasure in a world of perspective where nothing is required or expected to ring "true."

~

One particularly productive tension at work (and play) in Armantrout's poetry is between an infinite variability of relationship and an utterly finite act of willful placement (which establishes or declares or notices a certain relatedness). On the one hand: "On conditions / so numerous / nothing can begin" (*N*, 48). On the other hand: "Place things / in relation / when I want them / permanent" (*N*, 27).

~

In *Made to Seem* (Sun & Moon, 1995), Rae's humor is a bit more pronounced. Why not explore how what we see /know is *made* to seem? If we are within the circle of shared analysis, then we share in the humor of unraveling the codes and constructions of order-making:

The sky darkened
then. It seemed
like the wrong end
of a weak simile.
That was what shocked us.
None of our cries
had been heard,

but his was.
When something has happened
once, you might say
it's happened, "once and
for all". That's what
symbols mean
and why they're used
to cover up envy. (*M*, 36)

Such an analytic lyric involves more than merely unmasking the plots of others. One may, midway in the deed, critique the lyrical pathway one is in the process of making:

Leaf still
fibrillating on the vine;

watch it closely
for a minute

as if listening
to a liar. (*M*, 38)

The lie may stem from the habitual associations with the too readily symbolic, organic leaf. The swerve is a humorous one, ethical as well, as one withdraws from the heart-felt verbiage of "fibrillating," that *fib*-word itself marking the space of a (possibly inadvertent) liar. In part, then, an ethics of self-correction, an analytic lyric marking out what is possible or plausible once the suspected contaminants are identified:

It's strange to see traffic backed up at this checkpoint— people scattering—heading for the hills or darting across the freeway toward the beach. There are words connected with this scene. "Aliens" is one. If I can avoid these words, what remains should be my experience. (*M*, 45)

Perhaps the space of attention becomes lyricized by means of an activating desire for clarity. At times, I have referred to such desire in Armantrout's poetry as involving reticence and a muted ethical imperative, so that we might see with something approaching accuracy:

> Evenly spaced
> on the heavenly floor,
>
> those hairy stalks
> do not object
>
> to duplicating
> one another's work.
>
> This is creation's
> diligence
>
> in which we
> stand apart. (*M*, 50)

If Armantrout's poetry explores "our" "place," it is a placement that stands apart from hieratic poetic impulses of self-aggrandizement. Where we are is in a world of highly particularized making:

> Cellophane grass and
> foil eggs.
>   The modesty
>
> of standard presentation
> does remind me of home
> sickness.   (*M*, 57)

It is a world in which the line break between "home" and "sickness" is all to the point. It is a world, too, of placements and turns, the swerves of the line breaks, that revivify our attention to the colloquial:

With waves
shine slides over
shine like skin's
what sections
same from same. (*M*, 58)

As in the best of Creeley's poetry, the tension between the order
of the sentence and the line break puts us in an anti-Evelyn-Wood
mode of reading, a slowed lyrical reading that invokes an awareness
of our decision-making as we place what-with-what, fashioning and
re-fashioning the modes of order available to us in these particular
word-arrays. To Armantrout's credit, that perspectival pedagogy occurs with considerable (if muted) humor and tenderness:

"Well, look who missed
the fleeting moment,"

Green Giant gloats
over dazed children.

If to transpose
is to know,

we can cover our losses.

But only
If talking,

Formerly food,

Now meant
Not now

So recovery
Ran rings.

If to traverse
is to envelop,

> I am held
> and sung to sleep. (*M*, 12)

Sung to and held in a word-world of precise declarations, "if to
transpose / is to know," it is time to take inventory of the particular
traversings and envelopings in Rae Armantrout's poetry. To invent
along such lines would be to tell anew how such is made to seem.

———

Armantrout's poetry—in part through the idiosyncratic swerves
that I have been examining—achieves an arresting mixture of clarity, audacity, surprise, and enigma. In "The Plan," each section of
the poem has its own quick form of double-faceted self-engagement.
From its audacious beginning—" 'Who told you / you were visible?'
// God said, // meaning naked / or powerless" (V, 140)—the nature
of the visible, the summoning into visibility, and the self-awareness
of being visible appear in a Genesis story set in motion by a question
rather than a command. In the poem's second section, our planned
meeting with the divine gets couched in the language of an assigna-
tion. Our considerations—"how we'd address each other, // how
we'd stand / or kneel"—become at once reverential and comical.
Appropriately, "our intentions / are different // from our bodies, /
something extra, // though transparent / like a negligee" (V, 140). In
a poem which begins with the shock of visibility, we soon enter the
realm of transparency, where our intentions—like a filmy negligee—
are, perhaps enticingly, seen through.

That is the complex site of many of Armantrout's best poems:
intensified vision that takes us along a moebius strip of, if not its
undoing, then its endless circulation. As Bob Perelman aptly general-
izes, "Rae Armantrout's poems rely tenaciously on the intelligibility
of language, though the world is finally no more lucid for all that."[25]
While Rae's language is often simple and intelligible, her vision is
not susceptible to simplification. It is a poetry that is aptly and precisely enigmatic.

---

25 *The Marginalization of Poetry: Language Writing and Literary
History* (Princeton: Princeton University Press, 1996), p. 136.

In "Cheshire Poetics," Armantrout asks how we define what we
mean by radical poetries. She suggests, "Perhaps by how much is put
at risk in the text, how far the arc of implication can reach and still
seem apt." In "The Plan," that arc of implication—which has already
involved a complex tracking of human visibility being questioned by
the divine—ends in a remarkable simile:

> Like a lariat made of scalloped bricks
>
> circling a patch
> of grass   (V, 141)

It is an arresting image—perhaps as clear a picture as is possible
for the quasi-closure (deliberately without any ending punctua-
tion) of a lyric poem—an enigmatic closure that, in keeping with
Rae's sensibility, registers equally resonances and dissonances. The
lariat—literally, *la reata* (Spanish, for the rope)—is, oddly, made of
scalloped bricks. Perhaps most lyric poems are a thrown lasso—or, as
most dictionaries tell it, a rope used for tethering grazing horses. Is
the human story of the divine—that negligee-like filmy tale of self-
dignifying encounter—not also a lasso? Or, is the divine question
hurled from an invisible realm back upon the exposed, visible mortal
not also a circumscribing gesture? And the poem of its telling plays
out just enough rope to seem apt, and to remain taut. Armantrout's
poems give us that encircled patch of grass (as she concludes in
"Cheshire Poetics") "held together in the ghost embrace of assonance
and consonance, in the echoed and echoing body of language."

Works Cited

Poetry by Rae Armantrout

E=*Extremities*. Berkeley: The Figures, 1978.

I= *The Invention of Hunger*. Berkeley: Tuumba, 1979.

P= *Precedence*. Providence: Burning Deck, 1985.

N= *Necromance*. Los Angeles: Sun & Moon, 1991.

M= *Made To Seem*. Los Angeles: Sun & Moon, 1995.

writing the plot about sets. Tucson: Chax, 1998.

The Pretext. Los Angeles: Green Integer, 2001.

V=*Veil: New and Selected Poems,* Middletown: Wesleyan University Press, 2001.

The Early 1950s and the Laboratory of the Short Line

I aim to attend to the exploration and discovery of the resources of the short line in poetry as manifest mainly in the early 1950s. The particular poets I have in mind are Charles Olson, Louis Zukofsky, Lorine Niedecker, Robert Creeley, and Larry Eigner.[1] We can begin by keeping in mind three different starting points from 1950: the influential third edition of *Understanding Poetry*; Charles Olson's essay "Projective Verse" (first published in *Poetry New York*, No. 3, 1950); Louis Zukofsky's formula (in "*A*"-12, also 1950) of a poetics based on the integral with speech as the lower limit and music as the upper limit.

In the 1950 third edition of *Understanding Poetry*, we find virtually no attention at all paid to the resources of the short line. By my reckoning, in the 727 pages of the 1950 edition, even though the editors claim that the new edition "does give a fairly full showing of contemporary practice" (xxvi), only nine poems are categorized as free verse; there are a few examples of dimeter and trimeter; there is one poem by e. e. cummings that indicates some of the possibilities for deploying words on the page [other than the customary left-justified poem]; there are a couple of short-line poems by H. D. and by that bold experimentalist Robert Frost. In the most influential and

---

1 This essay, in a much-abridged version, was initially presented at the June 1996 National Poetry Foundation conference "American Poetry in the 1950s" at the University of Maine. I have made only minor revisions to the full text of the essay I wrote in 1996. Since that time, there have been some important new editions for all four poets under consideration. The most important new resource is the superb Lorine Niedecker, *Collected Works*, University of California Press, 2002, edited by Jenny Penberthy. At the time I presented the paper in 1996, I had the privilege of reading the manuscript for Mark Scroggins' *Louis Zukofsky and the Poetry of Knowledge* (now in print from the University of Alabama Press, 1998). As is anyone who reads and studies Zukofsky with care, I am indebted to Mark Scroggins' insights.

widely-used poetry primer of mid-century, there is little or no sense of newly emerging possibilities in poetry. Williams merits one poem, while Pound is granted three poems. Needless to say, the work of Olson and Zukofsky has no representation. And the development of an invigorating short-lined poetry, about to be published over the next decade by poets such as Creeley, Zukofsky, Niedecker, and Eigner, is simply not foreseen as a possibility by Brooks and Warren, the editors of *Understanding Poetry*. It is against this limited background—a mainstream and increasingly entrenched and institutionalized authority—for the line that the developments and directions presented by Olson and Zukofsky might be understood.[2]

One of the many generative paths from Olson's "Projective Verse," with its considerable emphasis on the authority of voice, speech, and breath, will be the long-lined poetry of Allen Ginsberg and others. But a careful re-reading of "Projective Verse" shows Olson to have a recurrent interest in the function, nature, and possibilities of the line, a mode of attention that might lead equally to the extraordinary accomplishments with the short-line that will be launched in the 1950s.

Early on in "Projective Verse," Olson cites a crisis of resources in 1950: "Verse now, 1950, if it is to go ahead, if it is to be of *essential* use, must, I take it, catch up and put into itself certain laws and possibilities of the breath, of the breathing of the man who writes as well as of his listenings" (15, *Selected Writings*)[3]. As we will hear/see shortly, for Olson's friend Robert Creeley those listenings involved an education of the ear, in part, by means of jazz. At any rate, for Olson, 1950 marks a time when new resources are called for, principally resources of breath and ear. Olson begins with the syllable: "It is the king and pin of versification, what rules and hold together the lines, the larger forms, of a poem" (17). For Olson, renewed attention to the syllable is allied to newly emergent possibilities of beauty: "It is by their syllables that words juxtapose in beauty, by these

2 For a more detailed consideration of *Understanding Poetry*, see Alan Golding, *From Outlaw to Classic: Canons in American Poetry* (Madison: University of Wisconsin Press, 1995), especially pages 102–113.

3 References to "Projective Verse" cite Charles Olson, *Selected Writings of Charles Olson*, edited by Robert Creeley (New York: New Directions, 1966).

particles of sound as clearly as by the sense of the words which they
compose. In any given instance, because there is a choice of words,
the choice, if a man is in there, will be, spontaneously, the obedience
of his ear to the syllables" (17 – 18).

———

> Old man who seined
> to educate his daughter
> sees red Mars rise:
>   What lies
> behind it?
>
> Cold water business
> now starred in Fishes
> of dipnet shape
>   to ached
> thru his arms.
>   (Lorine Niedecker, 1950s?, p. 14, *The Granite*
>   *Pail: The Selected Poems of Lorine Niedecker*)[4]

> Lights, lifts
> parts nicely opposed
> this white
>   lice lithe
> _____ pink bird   (Niedecker, 1950s?, p. 32)[5]

4   Jenny Penberthy, in *Collected Works*, places this poem as part of the
series "For Paul and Other Poems," typescript dated December 1956.
5   Penberthy notes this poem as from the mid-1960s. With the
beautifully researched sense of chronology that Penberthy's work allows,
I would add two particular Niedecker poems from the early 1950s to
this list of examples: "So this was I" (manuscript dated November 1951),
opening stanza:

> So this was I
> in my framed
> young aloofness
> unsuspecting
>   what I filled

In the narcotic and act
of omniscience

a gain, of the formal,
is possible   (Robert Creeley, from *The Charm*,
                                          early 1950s?, p. 56, *Collected Poems*)[6]

A song.

Which one sings, if he sings it,
with care.   (Creeley, from *For Love*, 1950–1955,
                                          p. 112, *Collected Poems*)

⸻

As an antidote to the resources of *Understanding Poetry* and to an era of poetic activity with a strong interest in conventional metrics, Olson sees renewed attention to the syllable "as an act of correction, to both prose and verse as now written … if the syllable, that fine creature, were more allowed to lead the harmony on" (18). Olson's emphasis on the syllable is allied to his valorization of the ear, "the ear, which is so close to the mind that it is the mind's that it has the mind's speed…" (18). It is a speed of mind that Robert Creeley finds most productively in the jazz of the late 1940s and early 1950s, a jazz music which helps the poet to investigate analogous resources in his own quickly shifting poetry of that period. For example, in-writing about his poem "The Whip" (from the mid-1950s), Creeley refers to the music he had been listening to:

⸻

and "Some have chimes" (manuscript dated August 21, 1950, published first in *New Direction* 12 [1950]).

    6 It remains difficult to determine a precise date for this poem. It is part of the collection called *The Charm*. Creeley, in his notes introducing the poems from *The Charm* in the *Collected Poems* observes that the poems begin with one written in 1945. The publication history is *The Charm: Early and Uncollected Poems* (Mt. Horeb, Wisc.: Perishable Press, 1967; enlarged as *The Charm: Early and Uncollected Poems* (San Francisco: Four Seasons Foundation, 1969; London: Calder and Boyars, 1971).

... it is music, specifically jazz, that informs the poem's manner in large part. Not that it's jazzy, or about jazz— rather, it's trying to use a rhythmic base much as jazz of this time would—or what was especially characteristic of Charlie Parker's playing, or Miles Davis', Thelonious Monk's, or Milt Jackson. That is, the beat is used to delay, detail, prompt, define the content of the statement or, more aptly, the emotional field of the statement. It's trying to do this while moving in time to a set periodicity—durational units, call them. It will say as much as it can, or as little, in the "time" given. So each line is figured as taking the same time, like they say, and each line ending works as a distinct pause. I used to listen to Parker's endless variations on "I Got Rhythm" and all the various times in which he'd play it, all the tempi, up, down, you name it. What fascinated me was that he'd write silences as actively as sounds, which of course they were. Just so in poetry. (*Collected Essays*, 591)

As John Wilson remarks, "as early as the 1940s, while still at Harvard, Creeley was spending hour upon hour day after day listening to jazz" (*Robert Creeley's Life and Work*, 5). As Michael Rumaker recalls Creeley's classes at Black Mountain College, the class "read and discussed at length William Carlos Williams's earlier poems as points of departure towards our own possibilities in American speech, as well as the poetry of Hart Crane and the jazz of Charlie Parker and Bud Powell" (*Life and Work*, 54). For the listener/reader interested in following up on Creeley's jazz interests of the late 1940s and early 1950s, there are a number of good sources, including *Charlie Parker: Bebop & Bird, Volume 1* (Hipsville/Rhino R2 70197), which includes five cuts from the WJZ live radio broadcasts (June 30, 1950) from Birdland in which Parker's legendary quintet includes Fats Navarro, Bud Powell, Curly Russell, and Art Blakey; or the many early recordings of Thelonious Monk on Blue Note (*Thelonious Monk: Genius of Modern Music - Volume 1*, Blue Note CDP 7 81510 2, all cuts from 1947; and *The Best of Thelonious Monk*, Blue Note CDP 7 9536 2, which includes several cuts from the 1947 sessions as well as some important work from 1948, 1951 [with Milt Jackson], and 1952). Perhaps from Parker, Creeley absorbed a rapidity of motion—a quality that Olson had also been urging Creeley to investigate. And from Parker and more especially from Monk, Creeley may have learned about the humor and beauty of sudden shifts in direction and about the value of silence and syncopation. In 1950, Olson was writing to Creeley, offering suggestions on directions Creeley might explore:

> … but just as his head is long, his breath is quick & short, AND (which is, of course in a way the same thing: any man who goes fast can't go without, *etcs*, which are shorthand for the fastest sort of juxtapositions:
>   it's JUXTAPOSITIONS, that I mean by quick breath, and that you are not yet getting in, at least in the verse (*Robert Creeley's Life and Work*, 36)

That rapidity, urged by Olson, and informed by Charlie Parker and Thelonious Monk, came out soon enough in Creeley's remarkable poems of the early 1950s such as "Le Fou" and "I Know a Man":

> Le Fou
>   *for Charles*
>
> who plots, then, the lines
> talking, taking, always the beat from
> the breath
>   (moving slowly at first
> the breath
>   which is slow —
>
> I mean, graces come slowly,
> it is that way.

So slowly (they are waving
we are moving
                              away from   (the trees
                                    the usual   (go by
which is slower than this, is
                                    (we are moving!
goodbye

                                    (from *For Love*, 1950 – 1955,
                                    Collected Poems, 111)

I Know a Man

As I sd to my
friend, because I am
always talking,—John, I

sd, which was not his
name, the darkness sur-
rounds us, what

can we do against
it, or else, shall we &
why not, buy a goddamn big car,

drive, he sd, for
christ's sake, look
out where yr going   (from *For Love*, 1950 – 1955;
                                    Collected Poems, 132)

———

    To return, then, to Olson's thinking in 1950 in "Projective
Verse," we find that in that essay Olson develops a mythology for
the birth of the syllable: "it is from the union of the mind and the
ear that the syllable is born" (18). But Olson's mythology is doubled;
the syllable has a twin: the *line*: "And together, these two, the syllable *and* the line, they make a poem" (18 – 19). In pinpointing the

problems of verse in 1950, Olson singles out inadequate attention to the line: "The trouble with most work ... is: contemporary workers go lazy RIGHT HERE WHERE THE LINE IS BORN" (19). The line, for Olson, is crucial because it is the site for a possible mode of immediacy in poetry: "And the line comes (I swear it) from the breath, from the breathing of the man who writes, at the moment that he writes" (19). (Olson's description reminds me of Zukofsky's earlier phrase, in "Mantis" of the mid-1930s, 'thoughts' torsion.")

For Olson, it is in the making of the line "that the shaping takes place, each moment of the going" (19). As the examples from Creeley point out, the line itself, particularly the sudden breaks and shifts that are a principal resource of the short line, are a means to embody that sense of movement. Intellect for Olson, "the dance of the intellect," is manifest in the syllable. Olson's thinking about the line and about the syllable mark an important shift away from a theme-based obsession with the content of poetry, particularly content as (in the mode of *Understanding Poetry*) restateable or para-phrasable summaries. Though Brooks and Warren argue that there is no substitute for the poem itself, they also show the reader/student in example after example that the highest integration of a reading experience is a well-wrought argument for the poem as a complex but unified expression of a theme or key idea. Brooks and Warren see analysis of the poem as the highest integration of a study of various elements of the poem. They teach the reader, by studying poems in an ascending scale of difficulty, to discuss "the relations of the vari-ous aspects of a poem to each other and to the total communication intended" (xvi). Olson, on the other hand, by way of the syllable and the line, asks, "is it not the PLAY of a mind we are after, is not that that shows whether a mind is there at all?" (19). For Olson, when a poet fails to pay adequate attention to the line, the result is a dead-ness, a poetry which then relies on "slow things, similes, say, adjec-tives, or such, that we are bored by" (19).

Olson's essay, however, manifests an oddly ambivalent or con-tradictory understanding of the basis of poetry in the twin resources of the line and syllable. Olson is prone to overly literalize the reli-ance of poetry on speech: "Because breath allows *all* the speech-force of language back in (speech is the "solid" of verse, is the secret of a poem's energy)...." (20). Interestingly, in a passage that might lead just as easily to some of the anti-speech based writings of Robert Grenier, Susan Howe, Charles Bernstein, Bruce Andrews, and others, Olson equally appreciates the thing-like possibilities granted to the word and the syllable: "because, now, a poem has, by speech, solidity, everything in it can now be treated as solids, objects, things; ... yet each of these elements of a poem can be allowed, once the poem is well composed, to keep, as those other objects do, their proper confusions" (20–21). Olson, while leaning on speech as a normative resource, can also begin to argue for a thing-like quality of poetry, for an anti-absorptive quality in poetry. He extends this portion of his argument by critiquing the constraints of normative grammar and syntax:

> Which brings us up, immediately, bang, against tenses, in fact against syntax, in fact against grammar generally, that is, as we have inherited it. Do not tenses, must they not also be kicked around anew, in order that time, that other governing absolute, may be kept, as must the space-tensions of a poem immediate, contemporary to the acting-on-you of the poem? I would argue that here, too, the LAW OF THE LINE, which projective verse creates, must be hewn to, obeyed, and that the conventions which logic has forced on syntax must be broken open as quietly as must the too set feet of the old line. (21)

Olson realizes—as we will see in the writings of Creeley, Eigner, Zukofsky, and Niedecker (and more recently in the poetry of, among others, Nathaniel Mackey, Jake Berry, Harryette Mullen, bpNichol, and Charles Bernstein)—that his particular emphasis on the syllable allows, as in Thelonious Monk's compositions for the piano, a percussive quality to emerge: "It is my impression that *all* parts of speech suddenly, in composition by field, are fresh for both sound and percussive use ..." (21).

Overall, though, Olson's concept of the resources for a new poetry boils down to voice. In his assessment of the importance of the typewriter, Olson's emphasis falls not on a kind of sculptural or spatial possibility for the poem—the poem as a kind of mobile made of words—but upon the machine's capacity to transcribe with greater accuracy the poet's reading voice: "It is the advantage of the typewriter that, due to its rigidity and its space precisions, it can, for a poet, indicate exactly the breath, the pauses, the suspensions even of syllables, the juxtapositions even of parts of phrases, which he intends. For the first time the poet has the stave and the bar a musician has had" (22). Here, Olson is off base; he fails to foresee the spatial possibilities (which, ironically, his own poems would explore) as seen in the work of Susan Howe, or Ronald Johnson, or Larry Eigner. For Olson, the typewriter would allow the poem to become a more accurate script for its vocalization. What interests me is that two slightly divergent possibilities are being enunciated and conflated in Olson's famous essay: possibilities of renewal via the breath; and possibilities of renewal via the line. My own concern is with the latter. Olson too recognizes how crucial a building block the line is: "The dimension of his line itself changes, not to speak of the change in his conceiving, of the matter he will turn to, of the scale in which he imagines that matter's use" (24). In his essay of 1950, Olson puts forward the dual importance of the breath and the line, but in his most flamboyant moments in the essay, his allegiance is with the possibilities of breath:

> It is in this sense that projective act, which is the artist's act in the larger field of objects, leads to dimensions larger than the man. For a man's problem, the moment he takes speech up in all its fullness, is to give his work his seriousness, a seriousness sufficient to cause the thing he makes to try to take its place alongside the things of nature. This is not easy. Nature works from reverence, even in her destructions (species go down with a crash). But breath is man's special qualification as an animal. Sound is a dimension he has extended. Language is one of his proudest acts. (25)

But for many poets of the latter half of the twentieth century, that thing-like status of the poem (first enunciated clearly by Williams in the 1920s) is achieved in part through an exploration of the spatial possibilities of the poem on the page.

Olson's thinking drifted in the direction of the large-scale project, even as his essay of 1950 (as a kind of side-bar) indicated possibilities for a poetry of a much smaller scale. Olson hoped that projective verse would allow poets and verse to "carry much larger material than it has carried in our language since the Elizabethans" (26). Oddly enough, Louis Zukofsky would achieve a poetry of epic proportions founded on the words "A" and "An." Zukofsky's wife, Celia, would claim that much of Olson's thinking in "Projective Verse" was a rehash of many of Zukofsky's own ideas.

Before I turn to an examination of Zukofsky's writing of the early 1950s, let us take a quick look at some of Larry Eigner's early poems, particularly as an instance of some of the spatial possibilities for the line which Olson, in his attention to the typewriter, does not emphasize. Eigner's first book-length collection, *From the Sustaining Air* (1953), contains several examples of a new deployment of phrases on the page:

> *From the sustaining air*
>
> from the sustaining air
>
> fresh air
>
> There is the clarity of a shore
> And shadow,   mostly,   brilliance
>
> summer
>   the billows of August
>
> When, wandering, I look from my page
>
> I say nothing
>
>   when asked
>
> I am, finally, an incompetent, after all   (*Selected Poems*, 5)

so the words go up

so the words go up
into thin air

      parlor   the speaking
   room

      birds pass the window
         a plane lengthens through fog
            or cloud bends away
        the curves together

     the phone the hallway
       all my life   (*Selected Poems*, 11)

William Carlos Williams, upon receiving a copy of Eigner's first book, wrote to Robert Creeley:

> Eigner's book is charming. I haven't got such a relaxed feeling from anything in years. There is no tension whatever, but a feeling of eternity. It is hard to say how he achieved this in the world today. As far is I can see it comes from a perfect ear.... Let me see anything he writes, it is contagious. (*Eigner: A Bibliography*, 2)[7]

While Eigner's early poems show some of the rapidity of motion that Creeley was seeking, particularly within a line like "the phone the hallway," there is also a quality of settled exactness in the lines' placement on the page, a quality linked more to elements of perception than to Olson's notion of a scoring of the speaking voice. Eigner's phrases take on the quality of things; the phrases themselves become

---

7 *A Bibliography of Works by Larry Eigner, 1937–1969*, compiled by Andrea Wyatt (Berkeley: Oyez, 1970). I am grateful to Jack Foley for providing me with a copy of the Bibliography and of *Sustaining Air*, and for introducing me to Larry and for giving me the opportunity to spend time with Larry and to get to know his work.

objects to encounter (as well as words for vocalization). Their placement on the page constitutes a kind of off-rhyme or homeomorph with other similar objects in the world. Eigner's work, important to Williams and Creeley, had a crucial impact too on Robert Duncan, who coined the term "stanzaic phrasings" (in writing retrospectively in 1967 about the range of Eigner's accomplishment) to describe Eigner's deployment of words on the page:

> We wanted not fragments of consciousness or utterance but immediacies set into motion, comparable to the localities of color in which Cezanne built up his visual world, to the instances of impulse in which American action painters workt, to the immediacies of the music in which Webern composed; and here, Larry Eigner, 'against the abyss' which he knows as a spastic, has over the last fifteen years raised the very body of a world whose reality we sought in poetry. … Eigner has suggested a new development of Williams's line: his phrasings are not broken off in an abrupt juncture but hover, having a margin of their own—stanzaic phrasings—suspended in their own time within the time of the poem, the immediate occasion of Eigner's life consciousness, has a time of its own in the continuity of poems. (*Eigner Bibliography*, 10 – 11)

⁓

To my mind—to my ears and eyes—the major masters of the short line are two: Robert Creeley and Louis Zukofsky. Each had achieved major understandings by the early 1950s. They were good friends, and each appreciated the virtues, especially of sound and the line, in the work of the other. Creeley, as editor of the *Black Mountain Review*, published Zukofsky's *"A"*-12 (in issue #5) and "Songs of Degrees" (in issue #6). Creeley, with his Divers Press in Majorca, also published the first collection of Larry Eigner's poems, *From the Sustaining Air*, in 1953. Creeley, in writing about Zukofsky's work (at the time of the publication of Zukofsky's *All: The Collected Short Poems, 1923 – 1958*), proclaimed that "it is a peculiar virtue of Zukofsky's work that it offers an extraordinary handbook for the writing of poems" (*Collected Prose*, 56—Creeley is writing about Zukofsky in a review published in *Agenda* in 1966). He ends his review, which attends to a range of work but especially Zukofsky's *A Test of Poetry* (1948) and "*A*"-12, with a note from Zukofsky:

> ... How much what is sounded by words has to do with what is seen by them, and how much what is at once sounded and seen by them crosscuts an interplay among themselves—will naturally sustain the scientific definition of poetry we are looking for. To endure it would be compelled to integrate these functions: time, and what is seen in time (as held by a song), and an action whose words are actors, or, if you will, mimes composing steps as of a dance that at proper instants calls in the vocal cords to transform it into plain speech.... (57)

In the years 1950–1955 (by the reckoning of dates in Celia Zukofsky's "Year by Year Bibliography" in LZMP[8]), Zukofsky completed "*A*"-12 and "Songs of Degrees." In my limited attempt to historicize the development of short-line resources in the early 1950s, I would like to juxtapose (beside Olson's breath/voice statements of "Projective Verse") Zukofsky's famous definition of poetics found in "*A*"-12: "An integral / Lower limit speech / Upper limit music" ("*A*," 138). For me, the short-line poetry from the early 1950s to the present constitutes a kind of laboratory or crucible for studying the interplay of sight and sound: the sight *of* words, and the *site* of words (some significant instances of which can be found in Eigner's spacing and in Olson's later Maximus poems). In Zukofsky's remarks to Creeley, we might do well to dwell on the parenthetical notation of words as a location for what is seen "*as held by a song*." The words might be thought of, as Zukofsky suggests, as actors (on the stage of the page?). What Zukofsky imagines (in his note to Creeley) is

---

8 Celia Zukofsky's "Year by Year Bibliography" appears in *Louis Zukofsky: Man and Poet*, edited by Carroll F. Terrell (Orono: National Poetry Foundation, 1979), pp. 385–392. All references to "A" are to the University of California Press 1978 edition. Readers may also wish to consult the more recent 1993 edition, The Johns Hopkins University Press.

an instant of transformation, but, interestingly, particularly when set side by side with his famous integral, it is a transformation "*into plain speech.*" I think that it is very important, when re-considering Zukofsky's integral, to note that his upper limit, "music," is *not* a contrary of speech. Plain speech, as Zukofsky shows from "Poem beginning 'The'" (1926) to the end of his career, and as Creeley has demonstrated for fifty highly productive finely nuanced years, is, and can be, quite musical.

We might, then, re-integrate Zukofsky's foundational statement of poetics—re-integrate it back into its self-clarifying (and self-complicating) context in "*A*"-12:

> You remember
> The houses where we were born
> The first horse pulsed
> Until the evening and the morning
> Were the first day?
>
> I'll tell you.
> About my *poetics*—
>
> $$\int_{\text{speech}}^{\text{music}}$$
>
> An integral
> Lower limit speech
> Upper limit music
>
> No?
>
> To excel in humility
> Is not to be humble.
> Humility does not glaze
> Other bodies,
> With fellow creatures
> Sees agony,
> Is the stronger body,

With the eye of sky
Eats food that
Guano dressed
Not a swallow made that summer.

Time qualifies the fire and spark of
I can't improve *that*.
That closed and open sounds saw
    Things,
See somehow everlastingly
Out of the eye of sky.

Poetics. With constancy.

My father died in the spring. (137 – 138)

When extracted and presented as if it were a fixed pronouncement, Zukofsky's calculus of poetics might sound, as do most equations or statements of first principles, so definite and inflexible, as if *logopoeia* might, as in the dreamy reaches of the law and of mathematics, do away with the more playful and subversive fuzzy logics of *melopoeia*. But read in context, Zukofsky's statement of poetics is found to be embedded in an ongoing enactment of the resources of speech and of the complex associative capacities of assonance and resemblance (or off-rhyme). The equation itself follows one of the many compressed Genesis stories of "*A*"-12 (where, as in Jewish reckonings of time, each day begins with sundown, this first day too begins with evening). Even this seemingly casual, almost chatty, version of Genesis, with its off-handed "You remember," invokes echoic resemblances that constitute a music simultaneously audible with the flatly stated question. We hear the sound-path of *houses* / *horse* and *born* / *horse*. The immediate lead-in to Zukofsky's famous equation is also deceptively casual: "I'll tell you./ About my *poetics* —". The period at the end of the first line points to the importance of slight alteration in Zukofsky's micro-poetics. He does not write "I'll tell you about my poetics." The equation itself thus is embedded between a tiny, carefully calculated end stop and a Yiddish-sounding rhetorical question, "No?" (which I hear as said by my grandparents, exact contemporaries of Zukofsky's, said as "no" or "nuh," sometimes affectionately, "nuh, bubulah?"—a rhetorical asking, with a decidedly affectionate warm tone to it, of "isn't it so?"). But the specific music, of speech, surrounding the equation enacts the equation, and *is* its simultaneous manifestation. The equation is not, as it is often misread, a statement of a hierarchy, speech at the bottom and music at the top. The integral in calculus is simply a (value neutral) means for measuring (by tiny increments, as "Songs of Degrees" is a similar measuring of syllabic resources) the area under a curve in a graph. The integral accumulates all of the bits beneath a particular curve, adds them together, comes up with a result even when the line of the graph may extend infinitely, the limits being approached asymptotically. What follows Zukofsky's rhetorical "No?" is a further exemplification of the complex resources, and equally complex intertwining, of speech and music, full of puns and resemblances. The passage, at the level of sense or meaning, offers a musically pleasant passage that is difficult to paraphrase. Perhaps speech offers the illusion of transparent communication, the illusion of a certain assuredness and communicability, as one might say, seemingly directly, "To excel in humility / Is not to be humble," a kind of simple equation. But as the equation is extended, as the word "humility" is deployed in the very next sentence, musical play and syntactical complexity/indeterminacy reassert the more variable resources of music (which lie *within* the capacities of speech). In "sees agony" we hear "seize agony." One acoustic pathway comes from the conjunction of *glaze* / *sees* / *eats*. Another from *eye* / *sky*, still another from *glaze* / *agony* / *Guano*. The talk of food is punned upon by the word "swallow." And perhaps all thinking about "humility" and its consequences boils down to a consideration of what food arises from shit. And if we navigate that passage of integrated speech and music, Zukofsky then places us in the synaesthetic awareness of sounds as sights (which, as I've been arguing, is a particular resource of the spatially focused poetry of the short line):

> That closed and open sounds saw
>   Things,
> See somehow everlastingly
> Out of the sky.

The placement of "Things" in the middle of the passage enacts as
well the thingness under discussion, the word placed in the sky of
the page, that sky though too (as Olson might remind us) the site
of breath and drawing of air, the place where *spiritus* circulates. As if
all that had preceded were obvious, "nuh?," Zukofsky adds, "Poetics.
With constancy." And then, to close (partially) a passage that began
with a first day beginning with evening, we have his father's death
"in the spring." Zukofsky's equation is thus situated in a genesis-
passage where beginnings and endings are integrated, as are the
resources of speech and music. If there is a certain playful and el-
liptical quality to this reasoning, we should be prepared to read carefully. His equation is not equal to his poetics; it is his telling *About*
his poetics, in and around his poetics, *OF* his poetics, in a precisely
thought through circular musing, a *BOUT* of his poetics, in which
we see, somehow, a sound, a sounding. As in Zukofsky's note cited
by Creeley, it is "what is seen in time (as held by a song)."

Zukofsky's famous integral of 1950 is also not a unique nor definitive statement, particularly when read in the broader context of
"*A*"-12 read in its entirety. Zukofsky, in the midst of a meditation on
being and non-being, offers a doubled use of the integral:

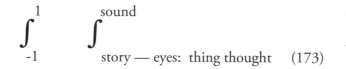

$$\int_{-1}^{1} \int^{sound}_{story} - \; eyes: \; thing \; thought \quad (173)$$

In this instance, sound sits atop the second integral, seemingly opposed to (or at the other end of) the schematic of the story which
Zukofsky perhaps characterizes as a visual manifestation of thinking.
Or, later still in "*A*"-12, again he attempts a definition or description
of his poetics:

> My poetics has old ochre in it
> On walls of a civilized cave,
> Eyes trapped in time, hears foam over horses,
> All of a style, surge
> Over six thousand years
> Not one of their mouths worrying a bit. (238–239)

Again, Zukofsky's emphasis is on the surge or pulse as the sustaining quality of the work, re-enforced by the pun on bit, the bit held
lightly in the poet's mouth, unworried. Similarly, in his letter to
L.N., Zukofsky writes,

> . . .   — — — Each writer writes
> one long work whose beat he cannot
> entirely be aware of. Recurrences
> follow him, crib and drink from a
> well that's his cadence — after
> he's gone. (214)

This single long work is the opposite of the 1950 *Understanding
Poetry* model which ultimately emphasizes a thematic coherence
and the subordination of the work to a conceptual whole. For
Zukofsky, the nature of the long work has as its core a particular
pulse, a beat, a cadence whose precise nature the poet does not
know either. He must sound it out and seek to be attuned to it (as
others will afterwards).

For Zukofsky, a poetics is tied to the idiosyncrasy and recurrence
of cadence, pulse, surge, and beat:

> Like the sea fishing
> Constantly fishing
>   Its own waters.
>
> The continuity —
> Its pulse. (215)

It is in "*A*"-12 that Zukofsky lays some crucial groundwork
for the succeeding sustained study of the resources of the short
line—a study engaged in by many poets over the last forty-five years.
According to Celia's Year by Year Bibliography, Louis Zukofsky began "*A*"-12 in 1950, completed it in 1951, wrote "Songs of Degrees"
sections 1, 2, 3 (original version) in 1953, "Songs" 4 and 5 in 1954,
and in 1955 wrote "Songs 3 (revised), 6, and 7. Though Zukofsky

did some work in the short line earlier in "*A*" (especially in "*A*"-3
and "*A*"-10), and though one can argue that it is later in "*A*" (such
as in "*A*"-13 part iv, "*A*"-14, and most especially in the incredibly
masterful "*A*"-19) and in other poems that Zukofsky achieves and
displays a greater and more sustained mastery of the possibilities of a
short line poetry, a reading of "*A*"-12 clarifies the key terms. issues,
and poetics of Zukofsky's short line writings. While I do not wish
to argue for either the uniqueness or the originality of "*A*"-12 (for
indeed, in a strict sense, one could point to Williams' short line work
in *Spring and All* twenty-seven years earlier), Zukofsky's thinking
in "*A*"-12 can be considered as a kind of arbitrary starting point or
threshold for many subsequent short line writings.

  For Zukofsky, one might contend that an investigation into music is also a study of a particular kind of truth-making:

> The order that rules music, the same
>   controls the placing of the stars and the feathers
>   in a bird's wing.
> In the middle of harmony
> Most heavenly music
> For the universe is true enough. (128)

Interestingly, Zukofsky, as he himself will do (in this passage and
many others throughout "*A*"), fuses sound and sight by thinking of
music as a precise and true placement. To make use of a phrase developed much earlier by Zukofsky—"thoughts' torsion" (in "Mantis"
of the mid-1930s)—music, particularly as deployed in a short line
(with its extremely important disjunctive line breaks), by sound and
placement offers a kind of truth-making. When Zukofsky remem-
bers his father, Pinchas, that extended memory begins to fuse with a
complex colloquial Yiddish syntax and inflection:

> Measure, tacit is.
> Listen to the birds —
> And what do the birds sing.
> He never saw a movie.
> A rich sitter, a broad wake.
> Not a sign that he is not here,

Yet a sign, to what side of the window
He sat by, creaks outside.
A speech, tapped off music. (156)

Zukofsky gives us an idiosyncratic music, rich in puns, *tacit is* =
Tacitus?, broad wake = *Broadway?* (also a "broad," she a rich sit-
ter?), the double sense of sign, the flow of memory in a sound that
creaks/creeks. As in the earlier integral, the concluding terms are those
lower and upper limits, speech and music. Here, "speech" is apposed
to "tapped off music," being both a shut off music and a sounding tapped from music. For Zukofsky, a truth of music is precisely
the reckoning by subtle degrees (as he himself demonstrates, in a
kind of well-tempered song-book for poets, "Songs of Degrees"). As
Gertrude Stein had argued in her lectures of 1934–35 that there
was no such thing as repetition, Zukofsky too, principally by way of
music, argues too for a kind of spiritual dimension to the principle
of uniqueness. Zukofsky presents the principle as a kind of Hasidic
parable (with his father as the sage/rabbi),

> Rabbi Pinhas: It teaches a man.
> There is no one who is not
>   every minute
> Taught by his soul.
> A disciple: If that is so
> Why does it not rule?
> Rabbi Pinhas: The soul teaches,
> It never repeats. (159–160)

Zukofsky himself will enunciate a more poetic version of such teaching: "that cannot be praiseless / Which considers each word" (163).

   Zukofsky's increasing attention to a kind of micro-music involves both the enigmatic, unique, indeterminant (or multiple) quality of musicality, as well as the precise placement of the words on the
page. Zukofsky is thus, in *"A"*-12, increasingly interested in ways of
shaping information:

Shall I graph a course,
Say *look at* but le this not take you:

MAN ———▶ EARTH ———▶ WORLDS

His more or   Waters   Radiance
less body   curst   heat
                   and   dispersion
| what's within
                                  |
Speaking |
cutting | Beneath
   his   Look at   and beyond
   story   animated   color
                     things
| |
                   |
At his |
crafts,   Their place
a-this's —   and places
inanimate
   or   I AM THAT I AM
   heady   and – or –
   and   Euhius Euan
   souled

For tenure
   of
"history"
(*his* story)
   and   1
characters   being
   and
character
   and   0
commerce   non-being

                 Texts: Thinks
                 Axiom: He composed – or
                          hunted, sowed and
                          made things –
                          with hand or bent –
                          is matter and thinks   (163-164)

Zukofsky's studies of music and the shape/deployment of words on the page inevitably involve his thinking about the complex relationship between eye and ear. Acknowledging that some forms of knowing are inaccessible to our dominant sense, sight, "nor do eyes / Know *the nature of things*" (166), Zukofsky does not choose to re-inscribe a new primary sense. No one sense (and its sense of knowing) supplants another:

> Can ears judge eyes,
> Or touch debate ears,
> Or mouth refute touch
> Or smell disprove it
> Or eyes show it false.
> One sense cannot prove
> Another false. (167)

Even so, his immediate claim is "There are places out of sight / Filled with voices" (167). And my suggestion is that "*A*"-12, in part through an exploration of the resources of the short line, marks a turn toward the peculiar modes of knowing to be found in those enigmatic differential musics. Perhaps the most attractive feature of Zukofsky's sensual knowing is its basis in love:

> All men by nature desire
> (It is put — but, in effect, *love*) to know
> We delight in our senses
> Aside from their usefulness
> They are loved for themselves —
> And most of all the sense of sight
> Brings to light differences
>   between things. (169)

That attention to differences, which can be apprised especially through sight but also through sound, will form the basis for Zukofsky's masterful series "Songs of Degrees" (written just after "*A*"-12). For Zukofsky, learning and knowing involve degrees, involve an understanding of minute particulars and the significant specifics of slight difference: "So the instrument of knowledge / Plays only when the beloved's head / Turns from Passing to Being / So learns by degrees —" (177). What we arrive at is Reb Pinhas' lesson of infinite difference, of infinite particularity (or, as Oppen has it in "Of Being Numerous," "Surely infiniteness is the most evident thing in the world" [*Collected Poems*, 174]) as a principle for poetic composition and as a mark of knowing:

> From a body's nature
> From nature
> Under whatever
> Attribute
> Follow
> Infinite things:
>
> Thought
> Not image
> Or word,
>
> Tongues
> That fail quiet,
> Desires
> That may order,
>
> And what
> Men desire
> With such love
> Nothing can
> Remove
> From their minds. (232–233)

To parse, or present, or exemplify, while stating clearly, that ethic of infinite particularity, it is not accidental that Zukofsky resorts to the clarifying display of the short line. Increasingly, as "*A*"-12 proceeds, Zukofsky attends to the peculiar quality of song's truthfulness, and he does so consistently in a torsioned short line poetry. For Zukofsky, song itself, especially the finely tuned song of the short lined work, marks an emergence into being, an unambiguous *yes*:

The form of a song,
                equity,
Reflect no *yes*
That means *no*
If it sang then
It still sings. (199)

The song is, as Zukofsky thinks in and through it, a mode of undivided being:

The song does not think
To say therefore I am,
Has not wit so forked. (200)

Though still clearly a thinking, Zukofsky's song involves an especially valued mode of non-ironic knowing. (If it is forked, it is attuned to a tuning fork, not to a fork in the road....) Even William Carlos Williams, a long-time reader and admirer of Zukofsky's poetry, had not fully understood the centrality of this mode of musical knowing to Zukofsky's work. In his end-note to *"A"* 1–12 (Origin Press, 1958), Williams acknowledges his own errors in reading Zukofsky: "Intent on the portrayal of a visual image in a poem my perception has been thrown frequently out of gear. I was looking for the wrong things. The poems whatever else they are are grammatical units intent on making a meaning *unrelated* to a mere pictorial image" (LZMP, 406).

By way of his praise for the being made manifest in and by song, Zukofsky moves to his most celebratory expression of that infinitely nuanced being (which he chooses to embody in the shifting, nuanced capacities of the short line):

Between the simple
And *therefore*
Is a chasm.
Only our thought
Says, our cave
Was not simple
Dark once — a false leap,

That our clear art
Moved to diversity
Understands and
Depicts our lives better.
Hope says this
With cave in us sometimes
And art in others
With art in us sometimes
And cave in others —
As thought, extended,
As body, minded
With countless effects of
The same infinite
Not infinite
As affected by
One of us
Actual as he is
But only in so far
As it is affected
By another
As actual
And still another
And so on
To infinity —
This is history
— You say
You speak and sing
And that you dread
The abstraction?
— The song in the head?
Why should I dread
What outlasts
Snarled hope,
Is more than
Where no one is,
There where anyone is. (200–201)

Perhaps for Zukofsky, a short lined poetry marks a minimal declaration of being, a singing that demarcates a position just within the realm of the existent. Yet, any conclusion to be drawn from such a "simple" song crosses a great chasm before a legitimate "therefore" may emerge. As in his earlier integral poetics, here, too, Zukofsky writes in terms of speech and music ("You speak and sing"). What Zukofsky displays is that infinitely nuanced differential existence upon which he thinks, a quality of being marked by the exchange of "art" and "cave," of "body" and "mind" (with body "minded"). It is this doubled doubling, literally a "di-versity," that becomes the premise for our new art, which "Moved to diversity / Understands and / Depicts our lives better." The procession of infinite difference, when told as the story of infinitely different particular bodies, constitutes "history," the tale of an infinite sequence of "another" and "still another." As Reb Pinhas had suggested, and as Zukofsky suggests throughout "A"-12 and in "Songs of Degrees" (in the nearly infinite discriminations of the short line), each being counts (though, paradoxically, or *di-versely*, part of the "countless effects of / The same infinite") and amounts to "more than / Where no one is." And though I cannot fully specify the correctness of the form, Zukofsky's serpentine short lines (perhaps an efficient poetic equivalent to Thomas Jefferson's structurally sound one brick thick serpentine walls for the gardens surrounding the lawn at the University of Virginia) enact that procession of similarity and difference, a simple if di-verse fact, from which no precise *therefore* can result, except the ethical/spiritual imperative of appreciation of being in its infinite difference. It is an ethic already stated in "A"-12:

> Reject no one
>   and
> Debase nothing.
> This is all-around
> Intellect. (135–136)

In spite of his daunting reputation for intellectuality and allusive complexity, Zukofsky, particularly in "A"-12, is a poet of love. (As in the work of his friend George Oppen, that love involves a love of consciousness and insight, in Oppen's words, "The virtue of the

mind // Is that emotion // Which causes / To see" [*Collected Poems,*
87].) Near the end of "*A*"-12, Zukofsky proclaims "Thinking's the
lowest rung / No one'll believe I feel this" (260). But earlier in "*A*"-
12, he had proclaimed (in yet another of his poetics equations): "As
I love: / My poetics" (151). And one of the governing commands of
"*A*"-12 has been: "Voice: first, body — / Speak, of all loves!" (132).
On the last page of "*A*"-12, Zukofsky recapitulates:

> Living, you love
> So I love
> With the dead
> In me
> Thru wet and dry
> For the living (261)

As the *i* and *o* exchange places in *living* and *loving*, Zukofsky's
quiet differential music proceeds. In his simultaneous celebration of
BACH and of his own domestic loving relationship, Zukofsky closes
the first half of his twenty-four part "small" epic with a carefully
placed enigmatic music:

> Blest
> Ardent
> Celia
>   unhurt and
> Happy. (261)

And such an ending constitutes a rewriting—both a re-vision
and reassertion, a partial enclosure, a re-configuring, as well as a dis-
tilling—of one of the opening statements of "*A*"-12:

> Blest
> Ardent   good,
> Celia,   speak simply, rarely   scarce, seldom —
> Happy, immeasureable love
>   heart or head's greater part unhurt and happy,
>   things that bear harmony
>   certain in concord with reason.   (127)

Thus all of "*A*"-12 is, lovingly, a bearing out of "the order that rules music" (128), or "time, and what is seen in time (as held by a song)," marked in the end by a simplifying return, a fugal recurrence with a difference, yet another marker of the reverently musical speech possible in a discriminating short-lined poetry, of Zukofsky's prayerful domestic blessing. By simple, I mean literally a statement in fewer words, a kind of simplification that is spiritual, ethical, and mathematical in nature. Zukofsky's laboratory of the short line fuses the lessons of his father and of Einstein. Of the former, Zukofsky says, "Had he asked me to say Kadish / I believe I would have said it for him. / How fathom his will / Who had taught himself to be simple" (143). And the lines that immediately follow make the link to Einstein: "Everything should be as simple as it *can* be, / Says Einstein, / But not simpler." And that is the virtue of Zukofsky's accomplishment in "*A*"-12, a virtue active in the short-lined work of Creeley, Eigner, Niedecker, and a number of other practitioners whose own lab work began in the early 1950s.

Nice Work If You Can Get It: John Taggart's *Pastorelles*

John Taggart's *Pastorelles* (2004) is yet another beautifully designed book from Flood Editions. Miraculously, the book was reviewed in the *New York Times*—unusual both for an independent press such as Flood Editions, and equally long odds for an idiosyncratic, independent poet such as Taggart. Furthermore, the back cover of the book provides two sensible sets of approaches to the book: one, a decent summary—"Taggart draws on the culture of rural Pennsylvania to consider the permutations of the human mark"; the other, an on-target blurb from Robert Creeley which begins, "John Taggart has long been master of accumulating, complexly layered patterns of sound and sense, and here he uses his formal powers with a perfect, unobtrusive authority. In these modest 'songs' of quiet reflection Taggart echoes the world in which he's lived, making particular the mind and heart's persistent need."

John Taggart's *Pastorelles* is a beautiful, serene, musical work. Set in a time of drought, Taggart's book proceeds with dry humor, as in "Pastorelle 14," a poem that begins with some history of Jacob Ramp for whom Ramp's Bridge (in Taggart's rural Pennsylvania—Taggart's home was originally occupied by Jacob Ramp's son) is named: "proof you can leave your mark / if you leave / and if you're remembered" (93), a poem destined to end: "1804 Theodore Burr patented the truss principle + arch / like Mozart / buried in an unmarked grave" (97). The structures, the forms, the pastorelles, the modulating phrasing of this book exist for a single reason: "that music may enter as through a welcoming portal may enter this" (104).

A work of labor and grace, *Pastorelles* requires us to slow down, to attend to a gradual modulation of phrase, to dwell in the sights we are given, to take in the sounds. Though there are some poems that we might call highly personal—most especially "Car Museum," one of Taggart's quintessential Midwestern poems—or that are situated in the circumstances of Taggart's home and garden

in Newburg, Pennsylvania, the overall effect of *Pastorelles* confirms
George Oppen's observation at the end of "World, World —":
"'Thought leaps on us' because we are here. That is the fact of the
matter. /…The self is no mystery, the mystery is / That there is
something for us to stand on. // We want to be here. // The act of
being, the act of being / More than onself." Such an orientation
is crucial to Taggart's conclusion to a reflection upon shadows on
water in "Pastorelle 11," "wonderful still for having nothing to do
with your selves or mine" (79). Taggart's new book is precisely that
slow interrogation (with moments of grace) of how and what we are
here, and how we come to know what it is to *be* here. We know by
work. As the popular song has it, and as Taggart has it in "Work,"
it is "nice" work, if you can get it, "And you can get it / if you try"
(76), a getting and a trying (and a being tried) that begins "try = in
the woodshed in the young years of your life" (76). Begin, then, the
labor by practicing, the sax, the pen, the guitar/ax/saw, the voice,
the cuts, the cross-cuts in the shed (or, as in Henry David Thoreau /
Sonny Rollins, alone in the woods or alone on the bridge). Working
it out out there is perilous,

> it = your work with the beat crazified and
> more than crazified
> your work a saw
> cross-cut saw that cuts across/against the grain of the beat
> leaves a body gruesome/real gruesome all over (77)

Why enter such perilous, crazifying work?: "to get a new father and
to be a new father who is the law of the saw / and the prophets yet
to come" (77). To make a new cut, a cross-cut, a chord bent a new
way. Or, as Oppen/Kierkegaard/Genesis would have it, labor that
precedes Taggart's labor (and is recorded in "Of Being Numerous"),
"'and only he who unsheathes his knife shall be given Isaac again.
He who will not work shall not eat… / but he who will work shall
give birth to his own father.'" Or, a labor that, on occasion, as at the
end of "Not Egypt," may become ecstatic: "from the creek through
another woods under another road / through another woods to the
creek again / millrace / made by a number of men with their tools /

by their labor / which is my labor also // a labor of ecstasy / considerable labor of ecstasy" (17).

Pastorelles is a book of severe beauty, of hard labor which, on occasion, yields to moments of rest and pleasure. Ultimately, Taggart's gradually developed music and carefully sited observations point toward mortality, as in "Pastorelle 1," where the precise description, "Glance to the right all that's possible / driving south / on 641 what was the old stage coach route / curve on 641 curve and descent / hard on the horses / weight bearing down on them" ends "this is where my ashes are to be scattered / driving south and west" (2). Such a statement is quintessentially Taggart's style (and also characteristically Midwestern, in the mode of Grant Wood)—flat, and made with a thoughtful, labored integrity of consideration. I'm not sure how I know this, but I do; I'm not sure that the flat words themselves are the basis for my belief in the truthfulness of Taggart's statement. Perhaps it is the gradually accumulating earnestness of the entire book that creates such a compact with this reader.

There are many noteworthy poems in this book—poems that one can read and re-read, dwell with, listen to, sound out, consider. They repay the investment of attention; they are not used up by one or two readings. Among the best in the book (and for different reasons): "In the Kitchen" (Taggart's blues-fugue, a variation on the Robert Johnson blues standard "Come on in My Kitchen," a song recorded quite beautifully by Cassandra Wilson among others); "Rhythm & Blues Singer" (a history of James Carr); "Work"; "Shadyside School"; "Magdalene Poem"; and the various Pastorelles that run throughout the book. Though for my money, the finest poem in the book is "Henry David Thoreau / Sonny Rollins."

A hazard of Taggart's slowly modulating musicality—I think of it as a kind of extended or maximal lyricism—is its deliberate flatness. Rather than the savored sound within the individual word (highlighted, for example, in the echoing, assonant vowels of linked individual words), Taggart orients us toward a more extended phrase as the pertinent unit of composition and thus of our attention. As Taggart makes clear at the outset of "The Compulsion to Repeat," underlying this particular music is an ethic or an epistemology of attention and its ends:

Gradually how gradually
one comes to understand the poets
as gradually as
the compulsion of one's own compulsion the compulsion
    to repeat

the expense of
spirit (62)

It is not a music that most readers will already be attuned to. Just as novice readers are often puzzled by, deaf to, and thus irritated by the minute modulations of Stein's prose in *The Making of Americans*, or, as some listeners hear music by Phillip Glass and Steve Reich as simply and thus annoyingly repetitious, the solemnity, seriousness, and unspectacular nature of Taggart's gradual musicality requires learning a different pace of reading. It is a taste and a sound well worth learning. As such, it is one of the most important, distinctive, and pleasurable lyricisms of our time.

Taggart's book schools us in such slow, deliberate learning. In "Shadyside School," in addition to the literal and factual attention to the site of an old one-room school, we see how the students learned to bring back water: "reward and honor and a matter of care / pail / pail on a stick / notched in the middle not to let the pail slip / how slow how very careful they must have been all the way back" (19). In Taggart's care, we see and learn with him how to be schooled, slowly, by the world, by the precise labor of gardening, by a study of place, by a gradually attuned listening to music, by reading, and by considering and weighing carefully the words of other thinkers.

Taggart's gradualist music accompanies what thinking becomes. His finest articulation of the premises of this gradualism occurs in the opening section of "Parmenides / Fragments 3 and 15A":

To think = to be

statement needing to become
image

you will come to know what you think although not when
  you see
what you say
when you see what it is that you are doing

most gradual of images. (80)

The form of Taggart's writing—by virtue of its own gradations—engages us in what Zukofsky called "thoughts' torsion," the turning and twisting of thinking in its immediacy. Taggart's particular music allows us to enter into thinking-singing, thinking made manifest in its process of becoming image (not merely visual image, but acoustical image as well), as we see and hear and thus bear witness to what we are doing. Perhaps one could conclude that such a gradual music is necessary precisely because the nature of human being is exactly and elusively that "most gradual of images"?

Taggart's new poems, precise in their placement and his observation of place, keep to Zukofsky's observation (in *Bottom: On Shakespeare*): "Insight moves sight to the site, or the site moves sight to insight. Each makes *natural* sense: i.e., a purposeful thought; a thought felt as purposeful. But the term *site* must always be there with the other two—sight and insight—or they will not be there." Taggart's is a precisely differential sense of place, description measured with care (and by degrees of difference) against others texts, poets, and perceptions, as in "Pastorelle 4" and the study of the view, "The road from Jacob Ramp's / window" (26). The view that Taggart establishes sets out toward a similarity, somewhat like Trakl's wanderer, then pulls back and differentiates itself from that wanderer, becomes its own wandering, and finally notes and swerves away from implicit echoes of Frost's horse/travelers (from "Stopping by Woods on a Snowy Evening" and "Come In"):

looking directly down on the road

Trakl's wanderer

and his blue steps in the blue snow notwithstanding not
Trakl's wanderer I watch my wandering self

a plodding sort of wanderer / a slow horse he does not stop

nor comes in. (26)

The poets and makers that Taggart tunes into (and has tuned into for
many years) tend to be isolated, neglected, and troubled, but mak-
ers of art that reeks of commitment, necessity, and integrity. Over
the years, Taggart's studies have focused on Mark Rothko, Edward
Hopper, Brad Graves, Herman Melville, John Coltrane, George
Oppen, Louis Zukofsky, Emily Dickinson, and Marvin Gaye. In
Pastorelles, there are compelling studies of William Bronk and Lorine
Niedecker. Taggart explores a lineage similar to the one examined by
Edward Foster in his book of essays, *Answerable to None: Berrigan,
Bronk, and the American Real*. It is a tenuous community of isola-
toes, in the Emersonian tradition of individualism—a community
of representative individuals connected to one another. Taggart is
famous for his extensive, candid, thoughtful (hand-written) correspondence—part of his own substantial investment in establishing
and sustaining this scattered community of makers.

   In *Pastorelles*, Taggart attends (as he has throughout his writing
life) to key carriers of the tune, from Charles Wesley to James Carr.
A word or two on these particular figures might be illuminating.
Even a cursory google-search (via the Wholesome Words / Christian
Bookshop website) yields interesting information regarding Wesley,
brother of John Wesley, known as the "sweet singer of Methodism"
and one of the greatest hymn-writers ever, author of over 5,500
hymns (including *Hark! The Herald Angels Sing*). One quick sketch
of him suggests, "If ever there was a human being who disliked
power, avoided prominence, and shrank from praise, it was Charles
Wesley." His conversion was a slow one. While his brother John
moved more steadily into a position of authority and prominence as
a scholar and a minister, Charles defended his own slower path, resisting his brother by asking, "Would you have me to become a saint
all at once?"

   Greg Johnson's blues obit for James Carr (*Blues Note*, February
2001) gives us a quick sketch of a blues artist born in rural
Mississippi, known for a string of hits in the mid-1960s including "The Dark End of the Street" (referenced in Taggart's poem),

known as the equal of soul-singers such as Otis Redding and Aretha
Franklin. A victim of drug and alcohol abuse, subject to bouts of
manic depression, Carr disappeared from the music scene, spending
much of his life in mental hospitals while later battling lung cancer.
After a few concert appearances in the 1990s, Carr settled into a
nursing home and died at age 58 in 2001.

Robert Gordon's portrait of James Carr, though, offers a portrait that suggests (on every count) the reasons for Taggart's affinity
with him:

> James Carr has been accorded the title "World's Greatest
> Soul Singer," though certainly other great soul singers are
> more renowned. From the mid to late 60s, he established
> himself with sad songs and songs of desperation, singing
> them not like his life depended on them, but like what his
> life depended on was gone and these songs were what was
> left. His voice is deep and full, operatic even, and though
> heavy with conviction, he can soar like a preacher giving
> warning.
>
> Like many of his peers, Carr has been influenced by the gos-
> pel tradition. Unlike Otis Redding, however, he is not a roll-
> er and shaker whose energy reflects the hand-clapping and
> swaying of the choir. Nor, like Sam and Dave, does he work
> into a frenzy through call and response. Carr has always been
> a quiet person, and his best work is with slower material,
> ballads. His father was a Baptist preacher, and one imagines
> Carr as a youth in church, eyes trained on his father, observ-
> ing the hysteria but absorbing the solemnity. ("James Carr:
> Way Out on a Voyage," from Britain's *Q* magazine and the
> *L.A. Weekly*, 1992).

Taggart, in the four-part "Rhythm and Blues Singer," presents Carr
as a "rhythm and blues singer / who never learned to read or write /
superior / so superior to Bartleby who failed to unlearn reading and
writing" (48). Though he tells a story which he knows to be impli-
cated in "the invention of romance" (51), Taggart's Carr takes us to
a language (a music) that is "before writing" (as well as *other* than

writing): "acoustic / river / a river of sound / river / a river of action / charm and more than charm / conferred by sound / action / for survival / what to do / how to / do / what to do" (49). It is that river of charm and more than charm that runs through *Pastorelles*, a channel, a millrace, labored on and sounded precisely below the written river, beneath the "silent signs in silent lines" (50).

By my accounting, the finest poem in *Pastorelles* (and one of the finest of Taggart's ever) is "Henry David Thoreau / Sonny Rollins," a poem that stands as summary and conflation of Taggart's inquiry into the pained, idiosyncratic isolated (and isolating) labor that may lead to a lasting breakthrough. The paired figures—Thoreau and his two year and two month stay at Walden Pond; saxophonist Sonny Rollins and his two year retreat from public playing so that he could practice alone on a bridge at night—are at once Taggart's guides and figures of his own practice. Thoreau, "alone in the woods / where he had vast range and circuit // his nights black kernels / never profaned by any human neighborhood" (21), "having spent youthful days / costly hours / learning words of an ancient language / an ancient language of perpetual suggestion and provocation" (22), chooses to live in a site "singing if it can be called singing / to sing along with the sound of owls" (22). Rollins "fled the clubs /… for two years / alone with the alone // alone with the alone saxophone / in the air / alone in the night air and high above the East River / heimarmene and black water of the river" (24). Of course such stories risk and are inevitably complicit with a kind of heroic, romanticized American individualism. Rather than being a merely correct and cautiously "good" experimentalist, Taggart enters that domain willingly, finding that there really is no better way to be located, as Rollins was (and Thoreau too) in the quiet night air where the "planets in material orbits / so huge and moving at so great a speed must produce sound // harmonia of heimarmene // ringing and roaring sound the sound of a grinding down / "heavenly harmony" in waves and particles" (25). That music, though, heard in quiet and isolation, away from cities and neighborhoods of human commerce, away from the clubs, becomes an internal music as well, or, better yet, a correspondence, "in the air in the ear in the heart / since birth / in the heart there is a melody of heaven's harmony / ringing and roaring // alone with that / without a song with that" (25). Alone, heart, heaven, harmony—these are the notes from which Taggart builds the ringing and roaring music to remind us of our little-listened to birthright. The five-part poem pivots around a third section—a kind of schematic or intersection for the two figures and for the stepping out or the cutting out that each made—"Cut of the slash / which cuts / which cuts and which connects" (23). This cut can be read as "the cut of / time itself" (think of Thoreau's "nick" of time) or "as a kind of bridge." What Thoreau and Rollins, and by extension, Taggart, show us is that some developments in our art, in writing and in playing, in knowing what we are, can only come about by breaking ties ("Rhythm and Blues Singer": "to sing is to be untied" [48]) and by finding alone a new music, though the "new" music will, of course, involve a listening to something that was already there.

"Magdalene Poem," the poem that precedes "Henry David Thoreau / Sonny Rollins," offers a delicate music—an etude or prelude, Taggart's own small song of degrees—that sings of transformation:

> Love enters the body
>
> enters
> almost
> almost completely breaks and enters into the body
>
> already beaten and broken
>
> peaceful if breaking if breaking
> and entering the already broken is peaceful
>
> untouchable fortunately
> untouchable. (20)

Is it the body that is already broken? Is love itself already broken? In the violent moment of breaking and entering, the moment of grace is oddly peaceful. What enters is untouchable, and, I would add, perhaps unknowable as well. In contrast to somewhat similar love-songs by Zukofsky, Taggart's poem is more impassioned, almost shameful, and perhaps more Christian (as a moment of grace), and retains an eroticism in its gradually made statement. *Pastorelles* is principally a book of painful labor, of isolation, of drought, of unrecognized accomplishments. To Taggart's credit, poems such as "Magdalene Poem" attempt an equal clarity and directness in providing a phenomenology of moments of extraordinary grace.

Though the music and structure of *Pastorelles* and of its predecessor, *When the Saints* (1999), may be a bit more modest in scope than the more symphonic works in *Loops* (1991, with the thirty-five page "Rothko Chapel Poem" being the exemplar of the symphonic Taggart) and the forthcoming large collection *Crosses* (long delayed by the failure of the book's originally intended publisher), I believe that these two most recent books (particularly as *books* of poetry) are Taggart's finest. *Pastorelles* in particular offers a music of considerable integrity and solemn beauty. It is a fit and exacting bridge to walk out on, a fine place to fine tune one's listening and seeing.

Q & A Poetics

Q. You've recently completed a rather provocative essay for the *Boston Review*. In that essay, "American Poetry in the 1990s and First Years of the 21st Century,"[1] you offer some assessments of the state of American poetry. What's the most important element missing from that essay?

A. The non-community or non-public element of writing and living with poetry. Such an essay—a sort of history of the present moment—inevitably, like a moth drawn to an intense light, tells a story of movements, careers, reputations, group principles, points of contention. Perhaps such a history only describes the side of the moon that faces us. It is, as perhaps nearly all literary histories are, a kind of externally derived narrative. Thus, in a literal sense, it is superficial.

The description of the shadow-side, or an internally derived narrative, though, would not be a story of *pure* isolation, even if of a series of detached heroic figures like Emily Dickinson, Henry David Thoreau, William Bronk—of the lineage of the American isolato, of Emerson's representative men (humans). But there is also a necessary idiosyncrasy, a resistance to belonging, an evasion of "success," that matters tremendously, particularly if a poet will ever manage to disentangle professionalism or careerism from the more enduring and fundamental nature of the activity. It is my good friend Glenn Mott[2], himself a poet in this individualized tradition, and as I am, who got me thinking about this topic. In his own way, Glenn insisted that I think about that other history as I completed the externally derived account for the *Boston Review*.

It seems to me that in fact the most interesting work of the time does come out of the portion of a writer's life that does *not* fit into a social belonging. Of course, it's not a binary situation by any

1 See "The People's Poetry." (American Poetry in the 1990s and in the First Years of the 21st Century) *Boston Review* Vol. 29, No. 2 (April/May 2004): 47–51. (and online:http://www.bostonreview.net/BR29.2/lazer.html)

2 See Glenn Mott's *Analects* (Chax Press, 2006).

means—member-of-a-community vs. one-of-a-kind. I certainly have substantial conversation and dialog with a range of language and post-language poets—what might in a hazy way be described as an experimental writing community—but it really is my *differences* from that community and my points of tension and discomfort as well as my geographical location or isolation (in Tuscaloosa, Alabama) that I think are crucial to what I'm doing, or, that are at least somewhat distinctive.

Q. Over the years, I've heard you use the term "serial heuristics." What do you mean by the term, and why do you do it? That is, why have you, for approximately twenty years, made such a commitment to the practice of serial heuristics? What are, so to speak, the losses and gains of such a practice?

A. Serial heuristics, to me, means the developing of a particular procedure or form or set of rules for a series of poems which become, either for a pre-determined number of poems or a pre-determined span of time, where and how I will live in poetry for that period. Once the habitation is over with, I develop another way of proceeding in poetry, and occupy that new methodology until its time is up.

I hit upon such a method of writing—really, an extended way of living in and with poetry—from thinking about the way some other writers have structured their writing lives: Ron Silliman and the various forms of his long-term project *The Alphabet* (as well as earlier work such as *Tjanting* and *Ketjak*); the procedural work of John Cage; and the notion of radical difference (from poem to poem) in many of Charles Bernstein's books, particularly his earlier books of poetry. I became drawn to the number 10 as a central part of my practice, thus works such as *INTER(IR)RUPTIONS* (Generator Press, 1992), a series of ten collage poems; *3 of 10: H's Journal, Negation, and Displayspace* (Chax Press, 1996), three ten-poem series; the ten-line format for *Days* (Lavender Ink, 2002); and the ten-poem cycle *The New Spirit* (Singing Horse Press, 2005).

One might reasonably ask, why learn a form, live with it, only to abandon it? To avoid mastery and to avoid self-imitation. I have been struck by how many poets, perhaps taking their cue from market forces in the world of the visual arts, develop a style or voice and stick with it for a boringly elaborated career. Sure, their poems have a certain recognizable identity, but I cannot understand why one might continue to read lots of their poems (much less continue to write them, poem after poem, book after book). My commitment is to the poem—as well as the *series* of poems—as a site of discovery. Through a different form, which I also think of as a different lens, I gradually learn what I might think, feel, experience, and know in that place, from such a perspective, and within such a methodology of writing.

It seems that the marketplace—gallery world—in the visual arts encourages a painter to develop a recognizable style. A "signature" which becomes a fixed product to be valued by its recognizable distinctiveness, so that one can "own" a representative product. The art work as commodity. So, too, in poetry, the parallel notion is "finding your voice"—which, of course, misses the rich fact that poems don't at all have to be constructed of "voice." Perhaps the most egregious examples of achieving a voice, and repeating and repeating that voice's limited range of utterances, would be the poetry of Philip Levine and Gerald Stern. But there are plenty of others. True, this repetition does lead to a certain refinement, perhaps even something that approaches a form of mastery (or a display of a certain practiced craft). Many readers, no doubt, find the predictability of such poetry comforting—perhaps even the source of a nuanced reading pleasure (as one notes the minute variations of the voice). The downside is the frontal lobotomy—for reader and writer—required to pursue such a version of poetry.

Yes, I do, on occasion, begin to experience a certain sense of regret when I reach my bargained time or number to leave behind a certain form of poetry. That most definitely was the case as I reached the (forestalled) end of writing *Days*. And sometimes, it is necessary to practice a rather severe form of revision or decision-making: saying that an extended experiment did not work out (and gets consigned to the desk drawer, or file, or disk). But there is also a compelling ethical drive that convinces me of the value of sticking to this serial heuristics. It is a way to avoid some aspects of self-imitation—of a narrowing, habitual form of writing. Of course, the idea that one changes, by will, by design, after a set number of poems is an overstatement too, since of course over time traces of a style or a set of concerns do emerge in spite of outward appearances of change.

Q. "This One" is the most recent poem included in your new collection *Elegies & Vacations* (Salt Publishing, 2004). What's the history of that poem's composition (in relation to serial heuristics), and what have you been working on since the work collected in *Elegies & Vacations*?

A. When I completed the series of ten poems called *The New Spirit*, I remained at a loss for quite some time as to what and how to write next. During the year and a half that I spent investigating what to do, I wrote only one new poem, "This One." I had originally intended for *Elegies & Vacations* to be yet another of my assemblages based on the number ten—in this case, ten poems that were different from one another (a principle of the collection thus being self-difference). But when it finally came time for an actual publisher, Salt turns out to have a tendency to print large collections (i.e., more than the more customary 48–64 pages format—in fact, more on the order of 120 pages), so I began to think about how "This One" might function in that larger context. I decided to include it in *Elegies & Vacations*.

So, in relation to serial heuristics, "This One" is an oddity—a singularity of sorts. It does have elements (of the lyricism) of the prior work *Days*; and it most definitely has some of the composition by phrase and the loose narrative of *The New Spirit*. And it really has the self-differing quality of the overall work *Elegies & Vacations* (as each section of "This One" is often quite different from what precedes and follows it).

The New Spirit (Singing Horse Press, 2005) is the work that follows *Elegies & Vacations*. *The New Spirit* is another series of ten poems, with poems 1, 4, 7, and 10 being somewhat open-ended, and poems 2, 3, 5, 6, 8, and 9 having a more terse form and lyrical quality to them. The original form for the shorter poems remains most visible in section one of poems 5 and 8. Initially, these poems were all composed in three word units; each line consists of three three-word clumps; thus, nine words per line, six lines per section (or 54 words per section), and three sections per poem. Eventually,

and with the help of a friend who read an early version of the manuscript, I realized that this form had been enabling but did not (with
the two exceptions noted) match up well with the way the poems
were spoken. So, in their final form, these poems retain the trace
(and precise line and word count) of the initial compositional form,
but the layout of the words on the page—their spacing, the use of
blank space—honors the speaking voice. Eventually, the work with
that 54 word structure re-surfaced when I began work on *Portions*.
The overall form of *The New Spirit*—the extended poems for 1, 4, 7,
and 10, and a briefer form for 2, 3, 5, 6, 8, and 9—is an approach
I'd taken previously in *Displayspace* (in *3 of 10*).

Early on, about ten or twelve years ago, I had imagined an over-
arching work—a book of books—called *10 X 10*, which, ultimately,
would collect 10 sets of 10-poem projects. *INTER(IR)RUPTIONS*
would be one set of 10, as would the three ten-poem cycles of *3 of
10*, and *Days* began as another 10-poem series (though it took a
different direction, retaining the ten-line form, but eventually occupying a year-and-a-day of writing). Eventually, I realized that this
imagined large structure existed to create the allure for new writing.
It gave me a space to write toward and into. But if I stuck to the rigidity of the imagined super-structure, I began to feel a greater sense
of loss—through a compulsiveness that ran contrary to the *heuristic*
aspect of serial heuristics—than gain. Thus, without much anxiety
or fanfare, I abandoned (perhaps temporarily, perhaps permanently)
the overall structure imagined as *10 X 10*. In some sense, that change
of plans may also represent my departure from the kind of determined large structure that Ron Silliman will fulfill in *The Alphabet*.
The abandoning of *10 X 10* has also gotten me to focus more intensely on the composition and form of the individual book.

After *The New Spirit* is *Portions*, a form that I've inhabited for
nearly three years and which, I'm beginning to realize, is coming
to an end.[3] In *Portions*, I was drawn again to the compression and
lyricism that I had experienced in *Days*, but I wanted to explore a
somewhat more twisted, under pressure version of the short poem.
The form for *Portions* is three words per line, three lines per stanza,

---

3 The guess hazarded in this interview (regarding the end of *Portions*)
turned out to be a bit premature. I wrote exclusively in the fifty-four word
form of *Portions* for five years, 2001–2006.

six stanzas, for a total of 54 words (or 3 X 18, the number 18 being
in jewish mystical lore a magical number meaning life). The term
Portions is a translation of the Hebrew *parashiot*, which refers to the
54 Torah portions read at Sabbath services throughout the calendar year (plus two additional portions for the High Holy Days?),
each portion of the Torah being known by a key phrase or word.
Thus, each poem in *Portions* bears a one word title. I had also been
doing considerable reading of Paul Celan's poetry, prose, and biography—examining translations by Michael Hamburger, Rosmarie
Waldrop, John Felstiner, and Pierre Joris—and, while not imitating
any particular Celan poem, trying to achieve in American English a
similar torsion, or twist, or turn within the poem, using the resources of the line break and the brief form. *Portions* continues the exploration of finding new ways of writing "spirit" that began in *The New
Spirit*, as well as the interval of consciousness experiments of *Days*.

Q. By page count and by location in the overall book,
"Deathwatch for My Father" is the central poem for *Elegies
& Vacations*. Yet I've heard you say that you won't read from
"Deathwatch" when you give readings from *Elegies & Vacations*, and
that you've only read "Deathwatch" aloud once. Why is that?

A. I'm not sure I fully understand it either. In some sense, I'm
going with a fairly deep instinct about what is "right" to do with that
poem. I could simply say that it is a very long poem and that for the
purpose of a reading it is not a poem that works well through being
abridged. But that's not really the reason. I feel that the poem, to be
read aloud, requires an occasion appropriate to the poem itself. Thus
far, the only time I've read the poem aloud was on February 16,
2003, the seventh anniversary of my father's death. I read the poem
to a group of around twelve people at my house. The group included
several close friends (some poets), several new friends (some poets),
and my wife and son (who had not read or heard the poem before).
That occasion felt right. I suppose that if another occasion felt right,
I would consider reading the poem aloud.

Q. What is the story behind the cover picture for *Elegies &
Vacations*? Did you pick the cover photograph?

A. Yes. For all of my book publications, I've had the luxury, opportunity, or necessity of picking out the cover. Truly, this situation
resulted from my first book, *Doublespace*, taking so long to appear.
By the time that book found a publisher, I had already laid out a
cover design and produced several mockups. The same has been
true for every book since that first one. For *Elegies & Vacations*, I
had a tough time finding a suitable cover—because, as the title
suggests, the poems seem to sort themselves into two seemingly
contradictory or irreconcilable directions. I was looking through
my friend Wayne Sides' photographic work, and this particular
photograph caught my attention. The more I studied the image,
the more it seemed to suggest the kind of relationship I had in
mind between the worlds of elegy and vacation. The photograph is
from Wayne's first book, *Sideshow*, and the image is from 1977 in
a park (Linn Park?) in Birmingham, Alabama. Perhaps the boys are
on vacation; perhaps the "preacher" (or, as Wayne titles the photo,
the "prophet") is in an elegiac space. That the two worlds exist in
the same frame is very important to me. That the photo continues
to reverberate and reveal its enigmatic details—is there someone
else behind one of the boys? why is the black man wearing a suit?
why is the scene roped off?—help me to realize that it is the right
image for this book.

As is often the case, it took someone else to articulate the relationship suggested both by the photo and the book's title. Susan
Schultz wrote me: "And it makes sense to me now why elegies and
vacations should go together. To each of them is reserved "time"
to think, to reshape relation, to write." Or, as I've thought of it
in light of Susan's off-handed perceptive remarks, each involves a
stepping aside (or beside)—a perspective that asks for a recalibrat-
ing, an assessing, an accounting, though the ostensible pleasures
of these two worlds are supposedly quite different. Perhaps those
worlds do share the habit of intensification and clarification, as
each asks for reflection.

Q. I thought that in an earlier version of *Elegies & Vacations*
that you had a couple of epigraphs to lead off the book. What happened to the epigraphs? And just as *E&V* is structured around the
colliding and colluding worlds of elegy and vacation, wouldn't it be

fair to say that the figures of John Ashbery and George Oppen also form two distinct polestars for the overall book—two figures that act as radically different models, both for purposes of emulation and argumentation?

A. You're right. There were supposed to be two epigraphs, one by Ashbery, and one by Oppen:

> Floating heart, why
> Wander on senselessly? The tall guardians
> Of yesterday are steep as cliff shadows;
> Whatever path you take abounds in their sense.
> All presently lead downward, to the harbor view.
> (Ashbery, from "Business Personals")

> Like theirs
>
> My abilities
> Are ridiculous:
>
> To go perhaps unarmed
> And unarmored, to return
>
> Now to the old questions—
>
> (George Oppen, from "Guest Room")

And you're suggestion, I think, is correct, that Ashbery and Oppen form conflicting or radically different polestars for the book: Ashbery's lush extended languorous sentences constituting a pleasurable (almost sinful or hedonistic or self-indulgent) "vacation" within language, and Oppen's more astringent, ethical and metaphysical questioning being more in keeping with the intensity and seriousness of "elegy." The Oppen quotation actually appears in the book (as one of the passages cited in "Diamond Head"); Ashbery is most explicitly spoken to, spoken through, and critiqued in "Portrait" and "The Abacos," though the specific passage does not appear.

Actually, it's through a fortuitous error that the epigraphs were
dropped. Somehow, when Chris Hamilton-Emery (editor of Salt
Publishing) and I were sending page proofs back and forth electroni-
cally, we missed the fact that the epigraphs had been dropped. After
I received the first few copies of the book, I was showing the book
to a friend, Josh Edwards, and I was explaining to him the presence
of Ashbery and Oppen as organizing perspectives in the book, and
when I went to show him the epigraphs, that was the first time I realized they had disappeared. At first, this was very upsetting. I
e-mailed Chris at once, and he said that it would not be a problem
to restore the epigraphs (since Salt is using a print-on-demand system for publication). But after giving it more thought, I realized
that the book ended up cleaner and better without the epigraphs. I
ended up deciding that the epigraphs were a case of bad didacticism:
pushing the reader in particular directions and framing the book too
narrowly. If the Ashbery and Oppen presences matter in the book,
they are already there for the reader to find and experience through
a reading of the book. If not, the heavy-handed approach of the "get
it" epigraphs wouldn't really help in a fundamental way. So, in a moment of Cagean instruction, I learned and accepted that the error
was better than my intention.

Q. I'm struck by an intensely lyrical moment in the book—the
section of "Every Now & Then" that is dedicated to Theodore
Enslin. What led to that particular section, and what accounts for its
distinctive lyricism?

A. "Every Now & Then" is probably the most hybrid composition in *Elegies & Vacations*, including at the less lyrical end of the
spectrum a book order, marginalia, and a reminder note, and at the
more lyrical end of the spectrum a Father's Day composition and the
section (6/22/96) dedicated to Ted Enslin. I was participating in the
1950s poetry symposium at Orono (Maine), and, at John Taggart's
urging, I had been reading Enslin's work avidly and extensively for
about a year. John urged me to meet Ted at Orono, and to spend
some time getting to know him. The symposium at Orono was a
like a marathon poetry camp—breakfast at 7 a.m., talks beginning
around 8 a. m., the final events of the day often winding up as late

as midnight. Enslin's poetry reading was one of those taking place at
the end of the day. Everyone was very tired, myself included. I found
his reading to be phenomenal—a gorgeous wake up call, a hypnotic
and energizing experience, one of the most memorable readings
I've ever attended. I suspect that for me the timing was right. I had
recently (approximately a year earlier) completed my lyric laboratory *Days*, and had begun my Enslin studies after that project. I had
also been reading lots of Zukofsky, and my particular approach to
Zukofsky was one quite congenial to Enslin. In the 6/22/96 entry,
I try to imitate (as well as vary from) the rhythmic insistence, variation, and beauty that I heard in Ted's reading. At readings, it is a real
pleasure to read this one aloud. In fact, at a recent reading here on
campus, afterwards someone referred to this as the poem that I sang
at the reading. It is the rhythm, repetition, musicality, and slight
variation that would leave the impression of the piece having been
sung. Enslin, of course, has an infinitely more precise sense of musical composition, having studied composition many years ago with
Nadia Boulanger.

For me, two of the most important (and significantly contrasting) lyrical models available for poetry today can be found in the
work of Enslin and John Taggart, with the latter working in larger
lyrical units of assembly. Perhaps their two lyricisms span a micro-
lyricism and a macro-lyricism.

Q. If I recall correctly, I thought I heard you say that *Days*,
Elegies & Vacations, and *The New Spirit* constituted a trilogy. Care
to explain?

A. There's a particular narrative thread that I have in mind when
I refer to these three books as constituting a trilogy. That thread has
to do with my father's life and death. *Days* begins the process of
coming to grips with his being diagnosed with leukemia. There are,
for example, poems in *Days* such as #101 (5/13/95) which track his
blood counts, his health becoming one of the particular aspects of
dailiness recorded sporadically in the poem-journal of 1994–95.
In *Elegies & Vacations*, the central poem is "Deathwatch for My
Father," which records the last six months of his life. *The New Spirit*

continues my conversation and relationship with him after the time of his death.

Q. You seem to me to be immensely productive as a poet and a critic. By one count, *Elegies & Vacations* is your eleventh book in twelve years. I know you have a full-time job as an academic administrator.[4] How have you found the time to write and publish at this pace?

A. I think I have been reasonably active and perhaps productive. But, as you know, the relationship between writing and publishing is murky at best. I published a limited edition chapbook of poems in 1976—*Mouth to Mouth* (Alderman Press). My next book publication wasn't until 1992 when Generator Press brought out *INTER(IR)RUPTIONS* (a chapbook consisting of a ten-poem collage series) and Segue brought out *Doublespace: Poems 1971–1989* (a book that opens in two directions—a nearly 200 page collection of early work and three series of more innovative work). Though I found it difficult (or nearly impossible) to get my books of poetry into print, I did not stop writing and did not stop assembling book-length projects. So, I've always worked from a backlog. When *Elegies & Vacations* was published (March 2004), I had two other book-length collections completed or nearly completed. As for the critical writing, I tend to write several essays and reviews each year. Eventually, I stop to see what lines of thinking have begun to emerge, and I attempt to collect these into some sort of coherent book format. Thus, in 1996 Northwestern University Press published a two volume collection of essays (Volume 1 = Issues and Institutions; Volume 2 = Readings), *Opposing Poetries*. If there is an area that suffers from the time demands of my job, it is my critical writing. I simply have not had the time to collect and revise work (including talks and lectures) over the past few years. I know that I have two lines of thinking in my critical writing of the past seven to ten years: writing on new modes of lyric/lyricism; and writing on "spirit." Eventually, I'll find the time to work on these essays and

---

4 At the University of Alabama: Assistant Dean (1991–1997); Assistant Vice President (1997–2006); currently, Associate Provost.

talks, and I should have enough material for two new collections of critical writing.

Q. You've suggested that the poem "This One" in *Elegies & Vacations* bears some kinship to the writing in *The New Spirit*, but it also seems to me to suggest elements that appeared in your very first published poetry. Let's conclude this conversation with some additional observations pertinent to that poem. How about unpacking a few of the possibly more obscure references, names, and phrases?

A. As I mentioned earlier, "This One" continues the phrasal composition process and concerns of *The New Spirit*, though fused perhaps more explicitly with family history that gets presented in my first poems in *Doublespace*, poems written mainly in the 1970s. Thus, the memories of my Russian Jewish relatives—grandparents, great aunts (Sonia) and great uncles, the kitchen in my mother's parents' house, the story of their move to New York and then to California, the scene of family gatherings. As in "to what are we ancestral," the first poem in *Elegies & Vacations*, a poem incidentally that begins with a line from Oppen, "This One" too asks and wonders about what elements of the dead remain with us and of surprising pertinence. The more disruptive and seemingly less continuous moments in the poem arise from an insistent and intervening musicality—an eruption from within the language itself (starting, possibly, with the section that begins "serendipitous   encryption"). There are, for me as the writer or medium of "This One," certain phrases that erupt, are overheard, or are transmitted, that insist upon their entry into the poem, such as "*breaker   breaker / cable to the ace*" or "hello   m'night / illuminate."

I am interested in poetry as a disruptive force—within one's personal life as well as within one's endeavors to write poetry. (Of course, poetry is also an enriching, deepening, intensifying force too.) In this poem, at the level of the phrase or syllable, there are elements that arise that radically change the poem's direction. I also think of the sound of the individual word as having a highly specific location. Thus the middle aged man's single drawn out word, "*dog*"—a Southern idiomatic expression—near the end of the poem, a word of wonder, but also a word that has an almost genetic specificity to it, a word that is at once "his" and radically "other" at the same time.

The concluding line comes from a science unit that I was study-ing with my son. It seems to me to enunciate a simple and profound compositional secret.

(March–April, 2004
Tuscaloosa, Alabama)

Thinking / Singing and the Metaphysics of Sound

> Poetry is a first relation to the sounds of a
> day and only subsequently the relating of
> itself in sentences and lines.
> —Donald Revell, "Joyful Noise:
>   The Gospel Sound of Henry D. Thoreau"

> Acoustics were my field of study. The path
> of sound was my liberation. By the time I
> had located it, I was part of it.
> —Fanny Howe, "The Sparkling Stone"

This essay has been through several distinct stages of composition and represents a culmination of many years of consideration. The impetus for this particular iteration was an interview with Jeffrey Side for his website *The Argotist Online*.[1] In the course of our interview, Jeffrey asked, "However, what you say is interesting especially with regard to your investigation of meaning through the musicality of language. Can you tell us something about this investigation and what you have concluded so far?" I knew that a full response to his question would take me into what has become a very lengthy, ongoing process of investigation. I decided to suspend the interview and pursue the full implications of his question. And once I had begun to develop a full answer to Jeffrey's question, I had also written the material for my part in a panel presentation at the AWP Conference in Austin in 2006.[2]

---

1 My deep thanks to Jeffrey Side, both for the fine interview, and for the specific question that triggered this essay. To see the complete interview: http://www.argotistonline.co.uk/Lazer%20interview.htm

2 AWP Conference, Austin, Texas, March 9, 2006. "Thinking in 'Song': New Lyric Modes of Thought and Music," Brenda Hillman, Afaa Michael Weaver, Annie Finch, Hank Lazer, John Gery, Cynthia Hogue, with Elisabeth Frost as chair of the panel. It's intriguing to ponder what

This investigation (which, for me, takes place concurrently in poetry and in critical prose) has been going on with some focus and continuity for a little over ten years. Recently, in 2005, I engaged in an interview with Scott Inguito for *1913: a journal of forms*.[3] The interview focused mainly on my most recently published book of poetry, *The New Spirit*, but early in our dialog, I offer a description of my most recent three books of poetry that may be of pertinence in setting a context for my current elaboration of "thinking / singing":

> Increasingly, I've come to trust the music of the poetry as an initiating force. *Days* (Lavender Ink, 2002) is a kind of lyric laboratory for the possibilities of the short-line (within a ten line format). In *Elegies & Vacations* (Salt Publishing, 2004), the long poem "This One" is closest in spirit to the musicality of *The New Spirit*. If *Days* consists of preludes and etudes—brief exercises—perhaps then *The New Spirit* moves toward a symphonic exploration of sound possibilities over an extended composition.[4] (25)

Later in the interview, I speak a bit more directly about what it means to consider "the music of the poetry as an initiating force":

> By following the lead of the sounds of words, the poems take me to unexpected places. Thus the poem does not set out to be about something, but is the emergence and actualizing of something—with its own specific music—an experience in sound.

made this panel so controversial or undesirable that we had to propose it for three consecutive years before it was accepted for presentation.

3 Scott Inguito: Interview with Hank Lazer, *1913: a journal of forms*, Issue #2 (2005): 25–29.

4 On *Days* and musicality, see Cynthia Hogue, *Rain Taxi* (Summer 2002, Online Edition: http://www.raintaxi.com/online/2002summer/lazer.shtml; on *Elegies & Vacations*, see Bill Lavender, *Big Bridge* #10: Vol 3, No 2 (2004), http://bigbridge.org/issue10/fictblavender2.htm; on *The New Spirit*, see Rachel Back, "On Prayer, Poetry and Song: A Review of Hank Lazer's *The New Spirit* and selections from *Portions*." *Golden Handcuffs Review* 1.5 (Summer–Fall 2005): 128–134, http://goldenhandcuffsreview.com/past/on_prayer.html

I recently ran across something that Joan Retallack had written about Gertrude Stein: "…to compose contemporary time into language. (An essentially musical ambition, since music is time made sensually present.)" That gets at some of what I'm after—an actualization of a feel for time, for our being in time, the infinitely variable pace and sound of such experience. (26)

My most extended critical consideration of this topic—of new modes of musicality in poetry—was published nearly ten years ago: "The Lyric Valuables: Soundings, Questions, and Examples," in *Modern Language Studies*.[5] In "The Lyric Valuables," I listen to, read, and discuss a range of specific new modes of musicality and lyricism, including work by Clark Coolidge, Theodore Enslin, Louis Zukofsky, Charles Bernstein, Nathaniel Mackey, Susan Howe, Lyn Hejinian, Robert Creeley, John Taggart, George Oppen, bpNichol, Harryette Mullen, and Kit Robinson.

Here are two key passages from "The Lyric Valuables" that will have a bearing on my current exploration of innovative modes of the lyrical:

> The lyricisms I am listening to are resistant; they depend, in part, on sounding out uncustomary thought. They postulate immersion in various musical priorities: a kind of integral, lower limit quickly shifting musics (as in Clark Coolidge's poetry) or an upper limit of imperceptibly slowly changing music (as in Theodore Enslin's work). (27)

> To my ear and eye, Robert Creeley's poetry (particularly in its cadence, in its brilliant use of hesitation and shift in direction) and Larry Eigner's poetry (particularly in its deployment on the page) constitute two of the more noteworthy adventurings into music that respect and partner silence. To

5 "The Lyric Valuables: Soundings, Questions, and Examples," *Modern Language Studies* Vol. 27, No. 2 (spring 1997): 25–50. (And Chapter One of *Lyric & Spirit*.)

take the term *music* more literally, it would be difficult to
consider the resources of silence without careful attention to
the music of Thelonious Monk (an important influence on
Creeley, who tells us repeatedly that his attention to jazz, not
to poetic models, gave him his fundamental sense of rhythmic and aural possibilities for poetry). (41)

More recently, I've come to refer to that new lyricism and the
sounding out of uncustomary thought as "thinking / singing." Here
are two examples from *Days* (cited below). My first suggestion with
respect to this pair of poems is that "meaning" and "musicality" are
inseparable, coincidental, and simultaneous. It's not that a poet "has
something in mind" and "tries to express it." The poem *is* the thinking, is an embodiment, a highly specific incarnation and manifestation of an interval of consciousness. While I don't mean to suggest
that poems do not have meaning, I do think that viewing a poem as
an object to be re-stated in terms of a theme or an underlying idea
amounts to a kind of linguistic strip-mining—a process that extracts
an element at the expense of the overall verbal terrain. Instead, I'd
ask a reader/listener to hear and see the poem (as clearly and atten-
tively as possible, perhaps in the state of mind that Shunryu Suzuki
calls "beginner's mind,"[6] or in a state that Keats called "negative
capability"[7]). That is, read for appreciation and read without preconception—as much as possible.

With these considerations in mind, here is poem #3 from *Days*:

3

and then again back

in it witness

6 See Shunryu Suzuki, *Zen Mind, Beginner's Mind: Informal Talks
on Zen Meditation and Practice* (New York: Weatherhill, 1970), especially
pages 21–28.
7 Letter to George and Thomas Keats, 21 December 1817.

serendipitous atoms drip

& cripple the im

perceptible ache of it

jack she *took* her

life a parent's love

called a darkening

of the heart emily to

susan avalanche or avenue

If musicality matters to the degree that I have been suggesting, how then to proceed with this poem? First, by noting and hearing similar sounds—the riffs on the short *i* sounds in the opening lines—*i*n, *i*t, w*i*tness, serend*i*p*i*tous, dr*i*p, cr*i*pple, *i*m-, *i*t. The poem then moves into a different musicality—the more percussive play of the hard *k* sound: the first line ba*ck*, leads to *c*ripple, to a*ch*e, and then becomes a more insistent music with greater proximity and rapidity of ja*ck* and too*k*, extending to *c*alled and dar*k*ening. In my experience of the poem, the key echo though is in the concluding line, with "avalanche or avenue." My ear had been drawn to those paired words before I understand their meaning.

If we do begin to unpack the meaning of this particular poem, I think that the interdependence and simultaneity of sound and sense become apparent. The Emily and Susan of the concluding lines are Emily Dickinson and her sister-in-law Susan, Emily's sister-in-law lived a few hundred feet away; Emily and Susan carried on a steady (written) correspondence, exchanging letters with considerable frequency. Emily said that aside from Shakespeare that Susan had the greatest influence on her life and writing. This phrase, "avalanche or avenue," concludes a letter of condolence that Emily wrote to Susan on the death from typhoid fever of Gilbert (Susan's son, Emily's favorite nephew) at age eight.[8]

The sound-paths through the poem begin to take on a particular coherence restrospectively. The opening lines riff on (and quote from) Sylvia Plath's "Nick and the Candlestick," a poem I had read twenty-five years earlier, but a poem and, more importantly, a musicality that, though I had not re-read the poem in many years, had stayed with me. Plath's life and death, and the musicality that I had imported into *Days #3*, lead into a consideration that centers on the phrase "she *took* her life," and become linked to my correspondence with a poet-friend, Jack Foley. At the time of the composition of *Days #3* (10/1/94—all of the poems in *Days* are dated), Jack had been in residence at the Djerassi Foundation. This artists' retreat (along the central coast of California, in Half Moon Bay) gives artists an opportunity to work in seclusion. The site is dedicated to the memory of Carl Djerassi's daughter, a promising poet who committed suicide in her twenties. Most artists visit and see the daughter's poetry and think of it as quaint or sentimental. Jack, instead, began to read her work with compassion and empathy—with a beginner's mind—and ended up writing a beautiful long poem meditating on her death.[9] (An added irony, Carl Djerassi, now also a novelist, accumulated his fortune through a particular invention: the birth control pill, itself perceived by some as a cancellation or a taking.)

Finally, when I was traveling in China in the early 1990s, shortly after the birth of my son, Alan, I was told about a particular word for parental love, a word that (via the constituent Chinese radicals) had embedded within it the sense of a darkening of the heart.

The entire poem itself took a matter of a few minutes to write. I would suggest that it only could have been written through a giving over of my immediate attention to the pathway of sounds, to the music of the quickly shifting phrases and directions of the poem—not through a preconception having to do with meaning or message.

---

8 See Richard B. Sewall, *The Life of Emily Dickinson* (New York: Farrar, Straus and Giroux, 1970), pages 204–206.

9 See Jack Foley, "Stanzas from Djerassi," pp. 65–91, in *Exiles* (Berkeley: Pantograph Press, 1996).

A different kind of musicality presents itself in poem #5 of *Days*:

5

quick zig zag attack

blue black ink jet

on stock white bond

thelonious all alone

hit hard the off beat

white space dark rec

tangular pitch arm or

tar which chuck called it

a clip joint chili davis

legged out the grounder

I guess that part of what I'm after in re-emphasizing the musicality of poetry is a shift in how we read, particularly how we read poetry that is somewhat innovative, poetry that defies well-established habits of theme-based (and thus meaning-based) reading. As my suggestions for poem #3 illustrate, I'm not seeking to establish a binary: musicality OR meaning. Instead, a careful listening to the music of the poetry (as a kind of first intensity, an initial lyricism of reading) allows for different concepts of meaning to emerge.

In poem #5, I'm most interested in considering the movement of the poem. When I've suggested that Thelonious Monk's piano solos are a crucial model for the poems in *Days*, I also hasten to point out that I'm not trying to write poems "about" Thelonious Monk. Instead, I'm hoping to embody in the words of the poem qualities of movement, shifts in direction, humor, the hitting of the right-

wrong note that are essential ingredients and constituent elements of
Monk's playing. In #5, the tempo of the poem is much more rapid
than #3—i.e., the poem should be read much more rapidly (in keeping with the percussive quality of "quick zig zag attack").

In my hearing of it, the poem pivots (and changes direction) at
two key junctures: in line 8 with the word "chuck"; and in line 9
with "chili." (In case you're curious, Chuck was my father's name;
Chili Davis the name of a baseball player.) Poems don't have to be
about something; *the poem itself is a primary thing in the world*. I
think of poems—as in the best of Creeley—as intervals of consciousness. And the musicality of the poem—including shifts in
direction, shifts in tempo, playing off of similar sounds—is intrinsic
to the embodiment of a particular interval of consciousness. Think,
then, of #5 as a kind of brief performance—a mind in motion, a
thinking-in-process, a move that has some kinship with a flock of
birds shifting direction mid-flight or a school of fish in clear water
suddenly turning in another direction. It is the grace and humor and
uniqueness of these intervals of verbal engagement that intrigue me,
and the unpredictable directions that arise when poems begin with
the musicality of an initiating phrase that takes on a life of its own.

Let me conclude my thoughts on the lyricism[10] of *Days* by citing
one other poem from that work, this one with minimal commentary:

84

slow to slogan

voracious to

veracity amen

to mendacity

----

10 For an excellent discussion on what's at stake in the terms "lyric"
and "lyricism," see Rachel Blau DuPlessis, *Blue Studios: Poetry and Its
Cultural Work* (Tuscaloosa: University of Alabama Press, 2006), especially
pages 222–223, which make specific reference to my conception of "the
lyric valuables."

flesh to pleasure

legs to legendary

costly to apostle

mesh to measure

& i wake up

next to you

If the reader/listener has (by this point in the book) become attuned to the musicality (and attuned to it as a primary fact and major location of attention), then this poem perhaps becomes self-evident, a kind of love poem that depends upon the reader/listener experiencing a kind of loving adjacency.

The New Spirit initiates a more symphonic exploration of the possibilities of musicality and of thinking/singing. As such, *The New Spirit* provides the room for writing that is both a thinking about musicality and a thinking within musicality (or an embodiment of it). From the very beginning of the book ("Prayer"):

> any one   could be the one   the sudden
> stun   you'd waited for
> > > > arrest again
> a rest   against the elements

The book-length poem focuses on how we hear and considers spiritual experience as something that occurs in large part through a summoning to hear (as in the central Hebrew prayer, the Shema—"Hear O Israel..."). *The New Spirit* waits for, attends to, and seeks after that moment and that instance that might be the sudden stun you'd waited for. That attending, as the opening lines propose, will require discerning, sifting, and determining—the ability to hear and enjoy the kinship (and difference) of "arrest again" and "a rest   against". As noted in a three word phrase that occurs more than once in *The New Spirit*, the poem moves along "the echoing way".

The (empty) hub for the wheel of sound is breath itself, an inspiration and an expiration:

	spell chant	the god name
a simple exhalation	*yah weh*	*yah weh*
a gust of wind	a single breath	a sacred expiration

That breath, that barely enunciated gust, a whisper or a breath on the border of becoming a word, may be as close to the forbidden name of the divine as is permitted.

As in *Days*, the play of sound in *The New Spirit* affirms play itself, sides with the Hebrew word *leeshma*, which means for its own sake. In fact, *The New Spirit* makes explicit this identification: "*leeshma*   the lyric" (14). At issue in such play is something quite serious: the function of language itself. We are, from our earliest language and reading lessons to courses in composition, journalism, and advertising, educated into a utilitarian sense of language, as if the "proper use" of language had to be to "carry" information or to present a certain mode of argument or to persuade or manipulate a listener/viewer to think favorably of a product (or politician or a politician's position on an issue).

In *The New Spirit*, this utilitarian or merely functional sense of language is referred to as "loading up the wheelbarrow" (51), a sense of language that reduces it to bearing an assigned load rather than considers language as having a life of its own and undiscovered capacities allied more with pleasure than utility. In Johan Huizinga's ground-breaking work *Homo ludens: A Study of the Play Element in Culture*,[11] which identifies play as an essential and defining characteristic of the human animal, the non-utilitarian nature of play is highlighted: "As regards its formal characteristics, all students lay stress

---

11 Written in the late 1930s and first published in an English translation in 1950; subsequently (Boston: Beacon Press paperback), 1955, the edition referred to here.

on the *disinterestedness* of play. Not being 'ordinary' life it stands outside the immediate satisfaction of wants and appetites, indeed it interrupts the appetitive process. It interpolates itself as a temporary activity satisfying in itself and ending there" (9).

But as we saw (and heard) in the several examples from *Days*, play does not necessarily exist apart from meaning. In fact, as Huizinga points out, play itself as an activity is meaningful: "In play there is something 'at play' which transcends the immediate needs of life and imparts meaning to the action. All play means something" (1). Huizinga finds play to be "just as important as reasoning and making" (ix), *Homo sapiens* and *Homo faber* being key defining features of human activity, and so Huizinga adds the term *Homo ludens* to accord play its essential role in defining human being. In *The New Spirit*, play (often in the form of musicality) stands over and against a merely utilitarian language (51):

art   a

rhythmic charm   magical rant   against loading up the
    wheelbarrow

instead a load

      unloaded

           enigmatic   as anything   irreducibly real

But the significance or import (or meaning) of that oppositionality does not end in mere contrast. Instead, the "serious" suggestion is that charm and play and an unforeseen language exploration constitutes a form of realism, a mode of representation that includes the enigmatic and the irreducible quality of the real (as opposed to a more tidy thematized reduction of the real), that recognizes the playful as a constitutive (and perhaps less predictable) element of the real.

The New Spirit, both didactically and by means of its musicality, offers a celebration of language functions that move away from mere enumeration of possessions (55):

said he went   said i went   set to go

they know &   walk across these   silences   they walk

know how   to go over   all the way across

            over frozen archipelagoes   axe heads   yes   &
                    their pictographs

                                        when began then
            not mere enumerating   not only toting up who
            has what

                        began then singing

                                        play of thinking

The "play of thinking," inextricably linked in poetry to the musicality (or capacity of words to be apprehended primarily as sound and
as song), supports a profession of poetry's role as a kind of heuristic
activity—a risked and adventuring process of discovery which does
not depend upon naming pre-existing objects or possessions but
makes new things in a kind of composition and improvisation in real
time. Such heuristic poetry may be seen as a branch of what John
Cage explored in music, what he frequently referred to as "sound
come into its own." My own work, particularly *The New Spirit*,
provides a dialectical space within which "sound come into its own"
and a more conceptual or logopoeic declaration are in dialog and in
an ever-shifting partnership. [12] Certainly, more extreme or radical

---

12 As a sidebar, and one that if included in the body of the essay
might totally derail the essay, I remain fascinated by a rather extended
exploration by Emmanuel Levinas of the relationship of doing and
hearing. In *Nine Talmudic Readings* (translated by Annette Aronowicz;
Bloomington: Indiana University Press, 1990), Levinas ponders a passage
where the "Israelites committed themselves to doing before hearing" (30).
Levinas refers to this odd reversal of standard processes as "a secret of angels," concluding that "'We will do and we will hear,' which seemed to us
contrary to logic, is the order of angelic existence" (45). Levinas elaborates:

explorations of pure musicality are possible as in the sound-poetry of poet-performance artists as varied as Tracie Morris and Richard Curtis, though that asymptote or extreme possibility does not lie at the heart of this particular essay.

I realize that a hazard of my enthusiasm for "thinking / singing" is that the term "thinking" remains extremely hazy, remains elusive and undefined. In my current reading, in Franz Rosenzweig's *The Star of Redemption*,[13] I come across a tantalizing phrase: "Poetry is not a kind of art of thought, but thinking is its element..." (263). In spite of my wholehearted agreement with Rosenzweig's remark, I am not especially tempted to delineate the nature of that thinking. Such an endeavor is of metaphysical and spiritual import, and has been done quite capably by Heidegger, particularly in *What Is Called Thinking?*.[14] In other contexts, I am interested in the questions that Heidegger poses: "what is called thinking—what does call for thinking?" (44) and "what is it that calls us, as it were, commands us to

---

The yes of "we will do" cannot be an engagement of a doing for doing's sake, of an I know not what wonderful *praxis*, prior to thought, whose blindness, even it if be that of trust, would lead to catastrophe. Rather, the yes is a lucidity as forewarned as skepticism but engaged as *doing* is engaged. It is an angel's knowledge, of which subsequent knowledge will be the commentary; it is a lucidity without tentativeness, not preceded by a hypothesis-knowledge, or by an idea, or by a trial-knowledge. But such knowledge is one in which its messenger is simultaneously the very message. (48)

I have spent considerable time thinking about Levinas's explanation. I have come to conclude that the composition of the poem, as in the instances cited from *Days* and *The New Spirit*, constitutes such a "doing before hearing." Though the musicality of the "message" (if a poem can be termed a "message") is central, the initial doing, the faith in an action, occurs in the writing of the poem and in the receiving of the words which compel the poem. It is only later—often much later in time (as this essay being an exploration five and ten years after the initial composition)—that a carefully delineated hearing becomes possible and a commentary that re-enters a more customary and less immediately volatile world of statement.

13 Translated by Barbara Galli, Madison: U. of Wisconsin Press, 2005.

14 Translated by Fred D. Wieck and J. Glenn Gray, New York: Harper & Row, 1968.

think? What is it that calls us into thinking?" (114). As Heidegger understood, "Our own manner of thinking still feeds on the traditional nature of thinking, the forming of representational ideas" (45), and thus "we moderns can learn only if we always unlearn at the same time. Applied to the matter before us: we can learn thinking only if we radically unlearn what thinking has been traditionally" (8).

If it does not sound too dismissive and evasive, I am really not too concerned (at least in *this* essay) with what thinking is nor with what calls for thinking—in Heidegger's case, a profound meditation on the nature of being. By means of musicality in poetry, I am tracking and attending to the onset of thinking by means of play—a kind of lateral move in language that trusts the resources of language (and the accidents and heuristics of improvisation) enough to adventure into an uncharted acoustical space. Oddly enough, the specific space explored in *The New Spirit* is decidedly Heideggerian, including "*beckoned* listening" (16) and an even more direct reference (60):

> he called the language place
> the house of being   a dwelling place for time   & the life
> of consciousness in it
>
>
>   tenant   in it

The kind of micro-music, the precise particulars that engage me in *The New Spirit* are the minute modulations of sound and rhythm from "in it" to "tenant   in it".   Oddly, what I end up affirming in that process, in addition to an adoration of difference, is an anti-transcendental valuation of hearing (16):

> what can be heard
>   what can be now attended
>   to   *hear this*
>   the exact metaphysics
>   of your historical
>
> moment of listening
>   what does not change   is the

will or   disposition to listen
         what does change   is
which rhythms   which combinations of sounds   what music one
in his or her time   is inclined to listen
to
       perhaps *close* listening   but more exactly   *beckoned* listening
audition
               summoned from the criss-cross   of your
                       historical circumstance

What is insisted upon is not hearing as some transcendental
and ahistorical event, but hearing as precisely rooted in immediate
historical circumstance, in the particulars that at any given moment (in the listener's or reader's or writer's given moment) allow
some musics to be heard and others not. If you stick with poetry
long enough, you will certainly have the experience of coming to a
poetry that has been recommended to you for its musicality, and yet
that musicality is not something (at that time) that you can tune in
to. And several years later, that music does become something quite
appealing to you. Just as in the visual arts, "natural" or "realistic"
modes of representation—say, of the human face, or of a still life
arrangement—change over time (as we see differently), so too does
hearing (and thus musicality in poetry) have a history and a temporal and cultural particularity. A function of musicality in poetry is to
make manifest new modes of acoustical awareness that are essential
to one's given time.

Perhaps one somewhat unnoticed quality of the writing of poetry (and of sustained careful listening to it, along with a careful
writing about it) is the making clear precisely of the differences in
the ways we hear, the differences in the musics that capture our attention, the different acoustic pathways and suggestions available to
us in poetry (23):

       each   lives within a different hearing   given to each
that babel   attunes   our differential thinking / singing   choral
gathering of each genetic specificity
                difference   difference   difference
                       the common

denominator
                    in the name of specific rhythmic
                                        in the name of *is*

The metaphysical assertion here—a Derridean claim—is that difference itself is "the common denominator" and a crucial feature of our
singular experience of being. This insistence on infinite variability,
on infinite difference, goes to the heart of my dissatisfaction with
traditional scansion and most received forms due to their reliance
on a binary sense of syllable stresses (stressed or unstressed) and
the reliance on rhyme (which strikes me as perfectly appropriate in
Romance languages or other language systems with more common
instances of rhyme than English). Such a position with regard to
rhyme and meter gets taken up throughout *Days*: "exact & infinitely
variable particulars / of human specific rhythmic insistence" (#39)
and "*not* fixed rhythm / infinite rhythmic difference" (#44) and "actual rhythms being / like sky in / absolute variety" (#153).

    In *Days*, where each poem lives within an intensely concentrated
ten line limit, the focus is on a music of adjacency:

        attention intention a tension

        . . . .

        diversions die virgins divergence

        all along   song   tang   tongue (#10)

Or

        day's eye

        to daisy &

        dasein

        thus has

designs upon

you   (#129)

In *The New Spirit*, there are instances of the kind of concentrated musicality (what I think of as high bond density [see page 35 of *The New Spirit*], or a close proximity of similar soundings) that typify *Days*. For example, in section 8 of *The New Spirit*, the insistent play on "three little words" and the transmutation of this unit of composition into "when the saints," "bags and trane," "in that number," "*baruch atah adonai*," "love what is," "lush southern sound," "*shma yisroel adonai*," "three word suite," "hear o israel," "lord our god," and finally back to "when the saints," presents a kind of rhythmic/verbal compositional unit that gets highlighted visually by the three-word construction (nine words per line) on page forty-six. Thus in *The New Spirit* there is a lyricism of song and number ("in that number"), which represents a continuation of the fascination with numbering in *Days* (where each poem lives within two different numbering systems [the calendar date as in a journal; and the consecutive numbering system, with deletions, for all of the *Days* poems] and where the overall epigraph for the book, from Psalm 90, is "Teach us to number our days / that we may get a heart of wisdom"). At times in *The New Spirit*, as in "half off   to damn deaf / soft fall   to   falderol" (62) and "short order   short circuit   shirk it   the shirt you designed" (21), the kind of stuttered percussive music of slight modulation that appears frequently in *Days* makes a cameo appearance.

But more typically *The New Spirit* reaches toward a larger, less definite, less concentrated somewhat symphonic operation. Or perhaps the better analogy is with an extended Coltrane solo. Perhaps all of *The New Spirit* can be thought of as a suite, like Coltrane's *A Love Supreme*, or as a composition in the manner of one of Coltrane's many extended versions of "My Favorite Things." Scattered throughout *The New Spirit* there are key phrases that recur and that have the feel of a recurring melody, with "when the saints" and "*teshuvah*" (meaning a turning, or a return) being the most prominent of these. The one repeated extended melody in *The New Spirit* occurs twice (40, 45):

        crossed wolf river   ran along a road of words

        listened in the forward movement   of john's blue train

        distance is time & miles minutes   crossed hobolochitto
            creek

        linguistic visitant   beloved decadent protectorate
            & crossed it again

        & then the pearl river

Though the stanza itself has very little in the way of didactic meaning (except to suggest a narrative or a geographical movement, a
journeying), I suspect that listeners feel the passage's return as a
returning friend, as a familiar home, as a cherished restatement of
a known melody, much like the brief return of the familiar core
melody in the more extended improvisatory versions of Coltrane's
performances of "My Favorite Things." Perhaps the reference to
Coltrane's "Blue Train" also points toward the general importance of
a forward-moving energy (by means of attachment to musicality as
the guiding force of the poem—"'led on / by music' 'in the middle of
my life' necessity" [40]), a trust in the kind of yearning made possible by the specific path of Coltrane's years of performance, practice,
composition, and improvisation.

    The effort in *The New Spirit*, then, is ultimately loving—an ef-
fort to compose another love supreme (63):

            the tune   a love supreme

        not a known condition

                what *is* that particular love

The overall composition of *The New Spirit* becomes both a seeking after a new composition of a new love supreme and an inquiry
into what that might be. Of necessity, since it is a poem being composed in the early twenty-first century (and not a music of 1965), it

will be, in keeping with its attunement to *difference*, different than Coltrane's sacred composition, *A Love Supreme* being a composition that, to the best of our knowledge, Coltrane played all the way through only twice, once for the recording session, and once in concert in the south of France.[15] The musical space entered into in the composition of *The New Spirit* is "not a known condition," just as "toward the / middle   trane played ahead of any sense he already understood" (35). Thus Coltrane provides a model, but not a constraining model precisely because he chose to play "just ahead of any sense he already understood." That is the risk and propulsion (and in Heideggerian terms, the ad-venturing) encompassed in a poetry driven first by sound. If this loving music contains a specific hope, it is to join the saints in procession, in a transformative ritual (65):

and when the saints

cacophonous   raucous

soulful stomp   winding through the quarters

grief gone over   into ecstasy

"magnified   and   sanctified"

The commitment, then, in such a poetry is to sound and to musicality as a guiding force. In the concluding words of *The New Spirit*, "sounding it out   as you go" (70). And that is what we do and how we live, beginning with the advice as we first learn to read words to *sound it out*, and ending with the final sounds we make

15 For additional information on Coltrane's *A Love Supreme*, see Ashley Kahn, *A Love Supreme: The Story of John Coltrane's Signature Album* (New York: Viking, 2002); and Lewis Porter, *John Coltrane: His Life and Music* (Ann Arbor: University of Michigan Press, 1999), especially pp. 231–249. In 2002, Impulse released a deluxe 2 CD set featuring the Coltrane Quartet's 1965 studio sessions (including a couple of alternative takes), as well as the only live performance of *A Love Supreme* (in late July 1965, in the south of France, in Antibes).

as we go (out). For the world we live in and our particular singular instance of being, we have an opportunity to take a sounding, to learn to listen to the sounds of our time, and to offer up our thinking/singing, a particular and idiosyncratic sounding that takes its part in a larger and often unapparent choral offering, a collective that we participate in by virtue of our peculiar human residency in and determination by language. The sounding by means of poetry is perhaps our best and most serious play, our playing with the instrument and exploring the possibilities of and in language.

(January, August 2006)

Spirit

Returns:
Innovative Poetry and
Questions of "Spirit"

Language is the other in man; it constitutes him as man *himself*. Man does not *have* language in the sense of possession or property[.]...[H]e is not its master (on the contrary; language operates a strange dispossession, attracting man—within himself outside of himself). This is the motif of "prescription" (*Vor-Schrift*). Language is the essence, the inhuman essence of man; it is his (in)humanity.
—Philippe Lacoue-Labarthe, *Poetry as Experience*.

The history of poetry in our century is only superficially the history of the struggle to make it new. More enduring is the struggle to regain the definition of poetry as spiritual ascesis.
—John Taggart, "The Spiritual Definition of Poetry"

The poet Louis Zukofsky writes in *Barely and Widely*: "God is / but one's deepest conviction— / your art, its use." Just because it is a use of one's deepest conviction, I consider Poetry not to be a literary achievement or an affect of gentility (tho gentleness has its part in the real) and particularly not a commodity of cultured taste, but to be a process of the Process that is the culture or tillage of souls that there might be and is a spiritual reality.
—Robert Duncan, March 1, 1959.

Of course "spirit" is a topic that should produce squeamishness. In poetry, it is one of many areas that have been compromised by a contaminated, habit-ridden rhetoric. Like "personal expression" or an ego-based lyricism or linear personal narrative, "spirit" has become a too easily learned mainstream craft. In the case of "spirit," the commodification via advertising and pop culture is all too apparent, whether under the rubric of "New Age" or the more blatantly commodified forms of "inner world" self-improvement programs and retreats. But in each of these areas, an avant-garde or innovative poetry might indeed be throwing out the baby with the bath water if these topics and concerns are altogether avoided simply because of the obviousness of a contaminated rhetoric. [1]

Yes, there are other problems with "spiritual" (or inward) poetry in addition to a contaminated rhetoric. If we think of Rilke's poetry as a prime example—and how can it *not* be that—there is a troubling persistence of a priestly role. In his poetry we find last vestiges of European royalty—a dying era of patronage and of castle-hopping. We read there a kind of ethereal metaphysics that wishes for a negation of history and historical circumstance, as if a timeless spiritual conversation were a replacement for dailiness, as if a poetry of "spirit" amounted to a particular "purification" of language and its concerns.

When we think of the major strands and activities of contemporary innovative poetry, particularly American poetry, we perhaps think first of investigations of the operations of language, of critiques of meaning and new modes of meaning-making, of a poetry of exploded or multiple subjectivity, of collage principles of incorporating disparate elements into the poem, and of new forms of the poem. But innovative poetry of these past fifty years is also—and perhaps retrospectively will be seen as *principally*—giving us tremendously rich new work in the areas of "lyricism" and "spirit." The evidence for a growing interest and accomplishment of new poetry of "spirit" is considerable. I think of earlier work by Robert Duncan and Ronald Johnson (or, outside the US, Paul Celan, or bpNichol [especially the seven volume *Martyrology*]), but more particularly of recent writings such as Fanny Howe's *Selected Poems* (2000), Nathaniel Mackey's Song of the Andoumboulou (in *Eroding Witness* [1985], *School of Udhra* [1993], and *Whatsaid Serif*

---

1 First published in a considerably abridged form in Facture 2 in 2001.

[1998]), John Taggart's work (especially *When the Saints* [1999] and *Crosses: Poems 1992–1998,* Patrick Pritchett's *Reside* (1999), Paul Naylor's *Book of Changes* (1999), my own *The New Spirit* (2000)[2], Norman Fischer's entire body of work, particularly *Precisely the Point Being Made* (1993) and *Success* (2000), Jerome Rothenberg's body of work—especially *Seedings* (1996) and *the book, spiritual instrument* (ed., 1996), Allen Ginsberg's *Death & Fame* (1999), Armand Schwerner's *Selected Shorter Poems* (1999), Andrew Mossin's most recent poetry—including *Shelley Drafts* (2000) and the *ARC* series (2000), Norman Finkelstein's *Track* (1999), Susan Howe's *The Noncomformist's Memorial* (1993), Ivan Argüelles' work beginning with *"That" Goddess* (1992), Andy di Michele's *Black Market Pneuma* (1999), Jake Berry's *Brambu Drezi* (*Book I* [1993] and *Book II* [1998]), Jack Foley's *Exiles* (1996), Michael Basinski's *Idyll* (1996), Jim Leftwich's publications with *Juxta*, Gil Ott's *The Whole Note* (1996), Philip Whalen's *Overtime: Selected Poems* (1999), Robin Cooper-Stone's first collection of poems, C. D. Wright's *Deepstep Come Shining* (1998), Ed Roberson's *Voices Cast Out to Talk Us In* (1995), and Afaa Michael Weaver's *The Ten Lights of God* (2000), to name just a few.

What I am attempting to outline in this essay is an ongoing, active process of writing an innovative spiritual poetry—a quest to write something other than a formulaic poetry of Emersonian correspondence. In "Nature," Emerson offers a set of axioms which have, to a large degree, governed American conceptions of spiritual poetry—particularly those grounded in Nature as a storehouse (or factory) for symbols:

> Nature is the vehicle of thought, and in a simple, double, and threefold degree.
>
> 1. Words are signs of natural facts.
> 2. Particular natural facts are symbols of particular spiritual facts.
> 3. Nature is the symbol of spirit.
>
> 1. Words are signs of natural facts. The use of natural history to give us aid in supernatural history; the use of the outer

---

2 The *New Spirit,* written in 1999–2000, published 2005 by Singing Horse Press.

creation, to give us language for the beings and changes of
inward creation. (31)

The current endeavor, then, is to do something significantly different
from Robert Bly's version of the deep image. As deep image poetry,
from 1963 on, became a popular mode of epiphanic writing, that is
where and when a habitual, formulaic rhetoric developed. (For the
first effective critique of that "contaminated" rhetoric, see Robert
Pinsky's *The Situation of Poetry* [1976], particularly the sections on
"The Romantic Persistence" and "Conventions of Wonder.") Bly and
company, as Pinsky saw twenty-five years ago, elaborate a too simple
sense of one-to-one mapping—an image making of outer for inner,
which finally becomes a repetitive poetry of dumb wonder. A formulaic rhetorical poetry masquerading as contemporary revelation.

One way to revitalize the life of contemporary spiritual poetry is,
as Ed Foster has done, to reinterpret Emerson and the varieties of an
Emersonian inheritance. In re-examining Emerson's own process of
reconceiving the nature and example of Nature, Foster concludes:

> Instead of reading nature like Swedenborg as a series of
> hieroglyphs, Emerson came to see it as a process: "The uni-
> verse is fluid and volatile," he wrote in his essay "Circles";
> "[p]ermanence is but a word of degrees." It was the particu-
> lar function of the poet, Emerson believed, to disclose this
> perpetual process and make it manifest in words. The self
> had intuitive access to universal fact, and this was the source
> of great writing: "[t]he condition of true naming, on the
> poet's part," he wrote in "The Poet," "is his resigning himself
> to the divine aura which breathes through forms, and ac-
> companying that." (16)

Foster's emphasis on natural *process* and on the poem and poem-
making as embodying that spiritual/natural process, allows him to
trace an unexpected Emersonian lineage, one which includes, among
others, Gertrude Stein: "Another version of Emerson's poetics was
devised by Gertrude Stein, whose essay "Poetry and Grammar"
(1935), as Harriet Scott Chessman argued in *The Public Is Invited
to Dance*, is "a twentieth-century response to Emerson's 'The Poet,'"

'[shifting] the focus from the poet's relation to divine nature to the poet's relation to language itself, in which a form of divinity resides, not wholly beyond words, but within them'" (16).

Or, we may simply think of the writing of a new spiritual poetry as, in the words of critic Megan Simpson (in a talk January 28, 1999, University of Alabama), the writing of a "spiritual realism." I hear this term as resonating with Lyn Hejinian's comment in *My Life*: "So from age to age a new realism repeats its reaction against the reality that the previous age admired" (104). And, as Hejinian adds, "Realism, if it addresses the real, is inexhaustible" (101), and "To goggle at the blessed place that realism requires" (109).

Or, we may situate the current writing of "spirit" by re-visiting the controversy elicited by the publication of *apex of the M*, a journal first published in Buffalo in 1994, supported by various faculty of the Poetics program, and which gained considerable notoriety for its polemical initial editorial statement which, among other things, questioned, "Why, in a society in which communication between human beings is constantly discouraged and threatened, does a participatory valorization of this disintegration become the primary mode of many of the arts?" (5). Most of the reactions to the editorial position of *apex of the M* focus on the political elements of the editors' statement. Marjorie Perloff, for example, writes to the Poetics List (a list-serve which includes an international array of approximately 600 more or less participant/subscribers and which is moderated at SUNY-Buffalo):

> … but I must say I was dismayed by the manifesto "The Contextual Imperative," put out by the editors.
>
> Certainly, the post-language generation has every right to want to move in different directions—that's only logical—but the slight on the L poets vis-à-vis politics seems entirely misguided. The editors write "language poetry, in reproducing and mimicking the methods and language of contemporary capitalism, ultimately commits itself to the same anonymity, alienation, and social atomization of the subject in history that underlie capitalist geo-politics." And they go on to compare the language poets to Reagan, Bush, and Quayle!

> Come on now! Ron Silliman, Barrett Watten, Bob
> Perelman, Charles Bernstein, (the most "political" of the L
> poets) reproducing and mimicking the language of contemp
> capitalism? Just the opposite was/is true—these poets have
> worked very hard and put themselves on the line to break
> down language so that it couldn't function as the voice of
> "contemporary capitalism." (*Poetics@*, 92)

In Perloff's remarks, we can see a well-reasoned critique of the editors' apparently hyperbolic political critique of the foundational
language poetry use of fragmentation to disrupt a presumed "transparency" of communication. We can see as well the raw nerve—an
expected element of the ritual of generational replacement?—that
the editors hit with their critique of the language poets' "increasing conventionality of 'innovation,' leading to the socially inept
dead-end of autonomous forms, [which] remains unscrutinized as
an agent of potentially universal indifference in a world more and
more determined in its course of anonymity by the same break-up
of language that experimental poetry in particular glorifies as a mode
of resistance" (6). That conformist nature of "innovation" has, increasingly, been a topic of critical debate—one of the most cogent
critiques being Nathaniel Tarn's "Fragment of a Talk on Octavio Paz,
Anthropology and the Future of Poetry" (Mexican Cultural Institute
of Washington D. C. and the Library of Congress, October 1999,
and posted in the electronic magazine *Jacket* #9). Like the criticism launched by the editors of *apex of the M*, Tarn's critique begins
with a condemnation of a conformist "innovative" writing. He cites
Octavio Paz's "*Corriente Alterna*":

> If imitation becomes mere repetition, the dialogue ceases
> and tradition petrifies; if modernity is not self-critical, if it is
> not a sharp break and simply considers itself a prolongation
> of "what is modern," tradition becomes paralyzed. This is
> what is taking place in a large sector of the so-called avant-
> garde. The reason for this is obvious: the idea of modernity
> is beginning to lose its vitality. It is losing it because moder-
> nity is no longer a critical attitude but an accepted codified
> convention[.]

Tarn's own analysis includes his description and diagnosis of a process of writing "as a prolongation of experimentation usually leading
further on from collage and montage into ever increasing fragmentation and eventually into a degenerative disease which, adapting an
already common usage, I call 'disjunctivitis.'" (In a similar vein, Lew
Daly, one of the editors of *apex of the M*, writes of "an ossified focus
on the signifier" [Scroll, 84].)

But the *apex of the M* editors were, in addition to their perhaps
too early attention to the ossified aesthetics of disjunctive "resistance," equally concerned with calling attention to a turning away
from "spirit" in poetry (at a time when, as the contents of the six
issues of their magazine demonstrates, there were a number of poets writing a compellingly new poetry of "spirit"). In the reactions
to the *apex* editorial, most of the replies focused on overt political
claims and on the gnarly issues of generational replacement. One of
the few respondents who addressed the issue of "spirit" was James
Sherry, who, in criticizing the *apex* editors, relies on Wittgenstein:
"The quotation which I have overused from Wittgenstein helps my
explanation. 'If we speak of a thing, but there is no object that we
can point to, there, we may say, is the spirit'" (Poetics@, 94). Sherry
concludes his critique by noting that "the most egregious and annoying part of the M is how they have forgotten the lessons of the
enlightenment exposing the weakness of spiritual allegiances and its
institutions. But I guess we have to 'pay to keep from going through
all this twice'" (95).

My own initial assessment of the importance of the *apex of the
M* editorial appears as the Conclusion to Volume 2: Readings of
my *Opposing Poetries*. In that conclusion, I grant the validity of the
claim that "certain formally 'innovative' gestures lose their force
and become the means of a conformist, imitative practice lacking
in the oppositional energies suggested by Charles Bernstein's definition: 'poetry is aversion of conformity'" (182). When writing that
Conclusion in 1995, I also saw that the M editors—with their claims
about "spirit"—had indeed pointed toward "one possible contrastive
basis for such a poetic inheritance [which] may focus on the place of
the sacred in poetry" (182). The M editors argue for an innovative
poetry which *includes* the "sacred":

> We would also want to open in the pages of this journal the
> question as to whether there can be a purely secular form of
> alterity, of whether the relationship with the other can ex-
> ist independently of an acknowledgement of the sacred. Of
> course in utilizing the word sacred, or the word spirit, we
> run the risk of being misunderstood.... It should go without
> saying that we invariably and without hesitation separate our
> use of the words sacred and spirit from conventional reli-
> gious systems. (6)

My own conclusion (five years ago) was that

> There are a great number of formally innovative poets for
> whom the issues of spirit and the lyrical fall *within* their
> practice, even while that spirituality and lyricism may be
> practiced in an ambivalent or self-questioning manner.
> Clearly, the work of poets such as Susan Howe, Rachel Blau
> DuPlessis, bpNichol, Nathaniel Mackey, Lyn Hejinian, and
> Charles Bernstein engage such issues, as does the work of
> earlier poets such as Robert Duncan, H. D., and George
> Oppen. (183)

I continue to think that the *apex of the M* editors were on to
something important—though it is perhaps still unclear whether
tension over claims of "spirit" constitutes a generational marker
(contrasting L and M generations), or represents a conceptual site
of tension *within* current avant-garde poetry/poetics. (Or, more
likely, a mixture of both possibilities.) As a supplement to the first
issue of *apex of the M*, M Press published Lew Daly's *Swallowing the
Scroll: Late in a Prophetic Tradition with the Poetry of Susan Howe and
John Taggart* (1994), a book which extends and clarifies some of the
claims made by the *M* editors—a group which, in addition to Daly,
included Pam Rehm, Alan Gilbert, and Kristin Prevallet. Daly proclaims his interest in Howe and Taggart "as a call for reformation"
(7) and as attention to a body of poetry that "among the young will
come to pass as an irreconcilable but revitalizing rift, perhaps one
among many, within the avant-garde" (8). Daly finds the writing
of Howe and Taggart to be "wildly religious poetries, as profoundly

anomalous as they are traditional, as irreverent as they are devo-
tional, as resolutely at odds with current trends in the avant-garde
as they are with those in the mainstream as well" (9). Daly describes
their poetry as having "a radical regard for spirit and prophecy"
(10) as well as occupying "the precarious place of poetry in a radical Protestant tradition, or, more generally, in a prophetic tradition
of the written word. In the early Protestantism of the kind to which
these poems may be ascribed originated the very possibility of modern counterhistory" (10).

What remains to be considered, at present, is not merely an assessment as to whether or not the *M* editors, in their attention to an
ossified poetics and their renewed emphasis on "spirit" as a key element in a poetry of alterity, were "right." Their critique may in fact
point to a "spiritual" legacy—in the poetry and poetics of Robert
Duncan, H. D., Ronald Johnson, Jerome Rothenberg, Armand
Schwerner, George Oppen, and others—that has been repressed or
partially erased as well as to an undervalued (nearly invisible) "spirit"
writing of the present which, particularly in recent years, may be
coming to fruition.

In *Poetry as Experience*, Philippe Lacoue-Labarthe links discussions of "spirit" to a certain *zeitgeist*, to a sense of culmination and
re-commencement of fundamental modes of thinking. In talking
about Hölderlin and Heidegger, Lacoue-Labarthe writes that

> They give voice to what is at stake in our era (*dieser Zeit*). A
> world age—perhaps the world's old age—is approaching its
> end, for we are reaching a completion, closing the circle of
> what the philosophical West has called, since Grecian times
> and in multiple ways, "knowledge." That is, *techné*. (7)

Lacoue-Labarthe analyzes Heidegger's thinking as situating itself so
that "such thought must re-inaugurate history, reopen the possibility of a world, and pave the way for the improbable, unforeseeable
advent of a god" (7).

Like Lacoue-Labarthe, I find that my own thinking about "spirit," the task of thinking, and the nature of current existence inevitably leads back to a renewed reckoning with Heidegger's writing. But some of the key terms of Heidegger's thinking are ones that I have to consider, at best, skeptically, such as the return or advent of "a god." Perhaps the heroic and progressive possibilities for thinking itself must be questioned as well if we wish to free ourselves from the heroizing self-interest at the heart of western European metaphysics. The contemporary spirit-poetry that I am attending to in this essay is more modest and tentative in its claims (than a Heideggerian heralding of the return of a god) while still developing or re-turning to a dialog with the Other.

Such a tentative quality, in fact, is in keeping with Jacques Derrida's reading of "spirit" in Heidegger's writing. In *Of Spirit: Heidegger and the Question*, Derrida finds Heidegger's theses regarding "spirit" and thinking to be characterized by "their interminably preparatory character" (12). The same may be true of much contemporary innovative poetry as it engages "spirit"—my own *The New Spirit* and Andrew Mossin's recent writing come to mind immediately. It is as if much contemporary "spirit" poetry constitutes a preface. And perhaps that prefatory quality is due to a deeply felt sense of our *zeitgeist*—our own time, in the history of "spirit" and the history of our dialog with the Other, as a "between" time or a time of emerging possibilities.

Nevertheless, Lacoue-Labarthe's own sharply worded sense of the late twentieth century does, for me, ring true:

> The extermination gave rise, in its impossible possibility, in its immense and intolerable banality, to the post-Auschwitz era (in Adorno's sense). Celan said: "Death is a master who comes from Germany." It is the impossible possibility, the immense and intolerable banality of our time, of this time (*dieser Zeit*). It is always easy to mock "distress," but we are its contemporaries; we are at the endpoint of what *Nous*, *ratio* and *Logos*, still today (*heute*) the framework for what we are, cannot have failed to show: that murder is the first thing to count on, and elimination the surest means of identification. Today, everywhere, against this black but "enlightened" background, remaining reality is disappearing

in the mire of a "globalized" world. Nothing, not even the purest, most wrenching love, can escape this era's shadow: a cancer of the subject, whether in the *ego* or in the masses. To deny this on pretext of avoiding the pull of pathos is to behave like a sleepwalker. To transform it into pathos, so as to be able "still" to produce art (sentiment, etc.) is unacceptable. (8 – 9)

Within the stress and seeming finality of such a *zeitgeist*, what is poetry to do? Or, as Lacoue-Labarthe wonders, "What is a work of poetry that, forswearing the repetition of the disastrous, deadly, already-said, makes itself absolutely singular? What should we think of poetry (or what of thought is left in poetry) that must refuse, sometimes with great stubbornness, to signify?" (14).

That is, in fact, an intriguing and volatile nexus: a contemporary poetry that refuses simple acts of habitual signification, while at the same time that poetry seeks to keep open the possibility of taking part in an ongoing "spiritual" conversation.

John Taggart's writing constitutes a serious example of an independent lyricism and a stubbornly spiritual investigation—stubborn because John's work has been central to "experimentalism," and "stubborn" because he has taken his own direction, one drawing on the work of Oppen, Duncan, Zukofsky, Olson, Melville, and others, but in a way that calls into questions the seriousness of Language writing by foregrounding the major questions of poetry that such experimentalism, in its purity, may have forgotten. As Mark Scroggins argues, Taggart's poetry

has avoided both the talky, conversational poetics of the poetry workshop and the hypertheoretical technicalization of the art advocated by the proponents of Language poetry. Instead, he has with uncompromising single-mindedness pursued a poetics of both musicality and vision, exploring through his work aspects of the spiritual—even religious—that have almost disappeared from contemporary verse. (337)

Taggart's work was at the center of the *apex of the M* controversies, but due to the quirks of the publishing world, we have not had adequate access to the best of Taggart's poetry of the past ten years. A major collection of his poetry, *Crosses*, has languished for years in the "forthcoming" category of Sun & Moon Press. That major book is still not available.[3] But recently Talisman House Publishers issued *When the Saints* (1999), a book-length memorial to sculptor Bradford Graves.

Taggart's poem is a "space of provocation" (10), and poetry is where we register the differences and nuances of wish, desire, and need. Poetry provides what's needed. Literally, "lines are words put in combinations / a poem is a combination of lines / to write a poem is to make a discovery" (11). But to move forward, "combinations must be broken" (11), and the poem, as a site of regeneration, is equally a site of breakdown: "to find the unknown / find the one room of the chapel // make the roof to fall in" (13). The poem presents a possible way for "the question of making a progression through ashes / to an unknown destination" (20). Taggart's poem proposes a recurring set of terms—the fundamental keys and chords of his harmonic arrangement. As I hear it, several of the recurring terms are the words *problem*, *poem*, *question*, *memory*, and *song*. In "Chicago Breakdown," a series of observations (that Taggart calls "journal notes written in the wake of a new long poem *When the Saints*") given as a talk in Chicago in late 1999, Taggart offers a prose improvisation upon the poem's key terms:

> To have a problem, as a poet, is to know you don't have a poem, to be without or before a poem. But a problem has value precisely as it involves a question. My question: memory, whether a song can be extracted from memory. And not just any song, a new song. (2)

And this is where and how Taggart's poetry rebukes a possible superficiality in much "experimental" poetry. Though Taggart's own forms are new forms, he insists—as in the lineage of an older, "romantic" or "metaphysical" or "spiritual" poetry (such as Duncan's

---

3 *Crosses: Poems 1992–1998* did finally appear, in 2005, from Stop Press.

or Oppen's)—on keeping on the track of what is essential.[4] In *When the Saints*, the poem returns to a fundamental consideration, a ground of fundamental petitioning: "the question is what do I need / what do I need I need to make up my mind" (26).[5] But make up his mind about *what*? And how does one go about making up his mind, particularly in a poetry committed to questioning, to song, to memory, and to breakdown? And how is "what I need" linked to making up my mind? Do I need to make up my mind about death? About the death of Bradford Graves? About beauty? About what there is after death? The poem as the place of such questing/questioning is a costly place:

> You pays your money and you takes your choice. The poem, the *consequence* of those choices. This is the economy of poetry. A poem can be expensive, perhaps has to be expensive. The currency is attention, a progressive fineness of attention as it may be. Attention to what? To what you need: the next word which is always a word. The/a, a fineness of attention. ("Chicago Breakdown," 5)

If the poem's currency is attention—and here, I'm reminded of Paul Celan's underlining in Walter Benjamin's essay on Franz Kafka a quotation of Nicolas Malebranche: "attention is the natural prayer of the soul"[6]—we must wonder, attention *to what*? In Taggart's *When the Saints*, attention turns "to what you need." As the poem is in the

---

4 As Mark Scroggins affirms, "[Lew] Daly is correct in seeing Taggart as one of the few poets of the postwar period who has been committed both to exploring a spiritual vision and to pursuing an innovative poetics" (343).

5 Taggart's sense of "the question" reminds me of Derrida's analysis in *Of Spirit: Heidegger and the Question*, where he remarks that "he [Heidegger] *almost* never stopped identifying what is highes and best in thought with the question, this 'piety' of thought" (9). Derrida, in a footnote, quotes Heidegger: "For questioning is the piety of thought" (117). Taggart's *When the Saints* tracks a similarly "pious" and essential thinking-as-questioning.

6 See Lacoue-Labarthe's *Poetry as Experience*, p. 64. See also John Felstiner's *Paul Celan: Poet, Survivor, Jew* (New Haven: Yale University Press, 1995), 163–164.

process of being made, what is needed is always "the next word." In "Chicago Breakdown," Taggart fine tunes our notion of attention, from something generic to "a progressive fineness of attention as it may be." That is precisely the sense, I think, in which poetry constitutes a spiritual discipline. Poetry, when we pay up in an intensive experience of reading or of writing, constitutes a cultivation of fineness of attention—to the word, to the next word, to the key questions, and to the song-like qualities of such thinking. To learn and to nourish that fineness of attention is, in Keats's terminology, the soul-making quality of poetry.

Taggart's own cultivation of fineness of attention has produced a particularly haunting mode of lyricism, in a manner that is at once self-restrained, that has a solidity to it (as one would expect in the presence of "the necessary"), and that feels self-evident. In its slowly building, overlapping, self-modifying statements, there is an odd collision of lyricism and statement. The units of Taggart's composition—at the level of the phrase or the line—are not (as I hear them) in and of themselves particularly lyrical or obviously or flashily beautiful in their musicality. But the cumulative effect of sustained attention to a long poem, such as *When the Saints*, is a tremendously lyrical experience. It is the odd construction of this macro-lyricism that is the mark of Taggart's peculiar song. As one of Taggart's most important forebears, Robert Duncan, states, "In declaring that there is a Poetry, a man in order that there be a poet seeks to open his mind and heart to be a dance floor where a new, an Other, life may come to dance in this world. A poem is news of an other life" (113). And such news is not particularly a mode of personal expression. As Duncan concludes, "a poem is a service of the Divine," and a poet "writes in the office of the Poet in order that there be a poem, and if he claim personal honor for the act he usurps the honor" (112).

In Taggart's poem, it is the music that leads us on,[7] as he is "led on by music / charged to obey // in the middle of my life" (57). It

---

7 As a general observation about Taggart's poetry, Mark Scroggins suggests, "His [Taggart's] is a poetry that has questioned and sought to plumb the relationship of the human and the spiritual in ways that have analogues, not in twentieth-century poetry, but in the music of John Coltrane and Carlo Gesualdo, or the paintings of Edward Hopper, Mark Rothko, or Hans Memling" (337).

is a charge—at once, a cost, a compulsion, a rush, a command—to be sure that "obedience is to necessity // to what is needed" (57). In part, what is needed is "the next word" and "a new song" that would allow some way for Taggart to remember Bradford Graves and to be adequately attentive to his death, for grieving involves dissatisfaction and incomprehension, and "your soul / is known by its dissatisfactions" (59). Part of "what is needed"—particularly in poetry today—is fineness of attention (and *sustained* attention) to what is needed.

In the fourth and final section of *When the Saints* the various melody lines begin to fuse, so that the work of poet and sculptor find some commonality: "the art is cutting / cutting what has been already cut // cutting into and around / the art is recutting the cut" (64). So that many modes of making—from the precise cutting of the gardener, to the cuts of musical production, to the poet's inscriptions, to the sculptor's cutting of slabs of stone, and the refining cuts that each makes—begin to assemble themselves together. The large slabs of stone, particularly in work such as Bradford Graves' large stone xylophone pictured on the cover of *When the Saints*, become akin to Taggart's own "rough cut from the language quarry / rough cut slab of words" (65)—a metaphor not simply wished for or reached for, but utterly accurate to the mode of assembly that Taggart has worked in for many years. In either case, it is easy enough *not* to hear the particular music of the sculpted work or the written work—to be stone deaf to either or both. But the truth is "stone / not without tone / when struck deep tone and deep tones / marvelously distinct and deep tones" (67). And the truth is that Taggart does not pander to his listeners/readers. In fact, we are not necessarily being addressed. When Taggart ends with the declaration, "taken and changed," "thank you this is a new song / saying thank you" (72), we end in a Heideggerian space where "thinking" and "thanking" are kindred spirits. We are still left wondering at "thanks" for what and to whom? Perhaps the procession of saints—from Coltrane to Rilke, from Sainte Colombe to Charlie Parker—who have made this "new song" possible, though part of the way of that path is "cutting / the quotation / free from the quotation" (65).

Taggart's giving thanks also points toward the peculiar mode of memory achieved in *When the Saints*. What is needed is a new song that enables seeing, that allows the poet to sense and behold the per-

son (Bradford Graves) who is no longer present. That sensing and
beholding—for friends who are artists—takes place in a reinvigo-
rated attention to the work. As Taggart writes in his Introduction for
To Construct a Sculpture (a series of notes by Bradford Graves which
accompany photos of his sculptures):

> The memory doesn't bring our friends back so much as it
> allows us to see them. Perhaps to see them with a sudden
> and revealed clarity. Perhaps to see them as, frankly, we
> never saw them when they were with us. And if we see, what
> we see is not a thing of memory, not the past but rather
> the present.... And, if we see, this is also not a matter of
> memory. It stands before us in a sudden and revealed clarity.
> Stands before us as our friends' work and as itself. It is an
> unexpected gift, an unexpected clear gift. (6–7)

When the Saints offers thanks for the gift of a new song which enables a renewed vision.
      In *When the Saints*, Taggart retells a classic Bird story:

> after a concert
> Charlie Parker was asked
> how much he cared about the critics
> the critics who know so much
>
> about as much as birds
> he said as birds care about ornithologists (51)

Underlying the joke, though, is a serious concern: for whom is the
music made; and, analogously, for whom is the poem written? In
Taggart's case—his poetry has existed at various border zones (at the
edge of experimental poetry, but more lyrical in nature, more "spiritual" in nature; even within lyrical poetry, the units of Taggart's
lyricism are longer and not standard) and his physical location (at
Shippensburg State and in rural Pennsylvania) has been somewhat
remote—that question, of poetry to and for whom, is an important
one, and perhaps one of the (his?) soul's dissatisfactions. One answer, from Ed Foster, is that "poetry ... is responsible to itself and in

every other context answerable to none" (10) is somewhat extreme in its purity, but it is an answer that hints at the seriousness of address in Taggart's writing. Those addressed are the saints ("to the saint to the other saints" [72]), the key musicians, the makers of similar harmonies, readers and listeners at some future date, and the dead with whom one is (increasingly) in conversation. One other pure answer to the question of poetry to and for whom would be the Hebrew word *leeshma*—for its own sake. As Taggart concludes, "word is found in what comes after" (5), and the issues of specific address, of the poem and poet's participation in a socially mediated matrix of institutions, certifications, and circulations, are after-effects that should not impinge upon the moment when the poet is able to "do the do" (4).

When the Saints stands as evidence of Taggart's career-long pursuit of a new spiritual poetry. In the case of this new long poem, that activity, like Paul Naylor's *Book of Changes*, is linked to a personal and poignant loss. In "The Spiritual Definition of Poetry," Taggart argues that "the history of poetry in our century is only superficially the history of the struggle to make it new. More enduring is the struggle to regain the definition of poetry as spiritual ascesis" (23). That particular corrective emphasis (upon "spirit" over and above "innovation") marks Taggart's implicit and explicit critique of Language writing. But his prescription for how poets are to regain poetry as a spiritual discipline—

> There are two ways to secure this definition [of poetry as spiritual ascesis] for poets who would write from the visionary imagination: (1) arduous study of and complete immersion in mythic and spiritual literature; (2) a like immersion in language. (23)

particularly in its second dictum, suggests why Taggart's work remains read and valued as part of (or proximate to) the enlarged context of Language writing. But crucially for Taggart, the poem itself—and I would suggest that his generalization applies as well to *When the Saints*—is not strictly speaking something that the poet alone makes or controls: "Form (content) is not imposed upon lan-

guage but received from it. It chooses you" (24). Hence, Taggart's
thankfulness at the end of *When the Saints*.

Returning, then to Derrida's *Of Spirit*, perhaps "spirit" bears
some kinship to *sunyata*. Derrida—and bear in mind Derrida's
thinking of "spirit" (in *Of Spirit*) is always within and through
Heidegger's particular on/off meditation on the term—claims that
"rather than a value, spirit seems to designate, beyond a deconstruction, the very resource for any deconstruction" (15). As many others
have claimed—including James Sherry by way of Wittgenstein—
"spirit" becomes a kind of "not"-term:

> The word relates back to a series of meanings which have a
> common feature: to be opposed to the thing, to the meta-
> physical determination of thing-ness, and above all to the
> thingification of the subject, of the subjectivity of the subject
> as supposed by Descartes. This is the series of soul, con-
> sciousness, spirit, person. Spirit is not the thing, spirit is not
> the body. (15)

In a particularly interesting phrase, Derrida writes of "spirit" as related to "grasping of self as grasping of non-self" (26). Aside from the
obvious hay that can be made of such writing's relationship to actual
and caricatured "eastern philosophy," it is this very "not"-quality of
"spirit"—indeed, "spirit" as "the very resource for any deconstruction," that is, as a powerful corrosive element to withdraw unquestioned content—that contemporary poetry of the "spirit" struggles
to align itself with in a truthful manner. Derrida writes of a notion
of "spirit" that would evade vulgar conceptions of "who" and of
"time" (20). Poetry, particularly a lyric poetry (which, by virtue of its
brevity exhibits and aligns itself with a powerful consciousness of finitude and mortality), seeks in drawing itself in proximity to "spirit"
to embody—perhaps beautifully—a space that is itself a critique of
vulgar embodiments and overly simplified (and simplistically expres-
sive) subjectivities.

From my perspective, one of the most compelling and instructive cases today is that of Norman Fischer, a poet closely linked to the inception of Language writing and a Zen Buddhist priest (recently retired as co-abbot of the San Francisco Zen Center and Tassajara Springs). In *Jerusalem Moonlight*, a travel book and meditation based on Fischer's first visit to Israel, Fischer pauses to write a brief personal account of the rise of Language writing:

> I used to try to write prose but that ended with my involvement, for many years, with Zen meditation. I found my experience was getting very slow and deep and impossible to describe; I found it no longer possible or desirable to divide the life up into the time of life and the time of writing about the time of life; and in any case the writing was never describing the life. And I could not keep on doing it that way so I had to find other ways of doing it and I found ways that pleased me and said what needed to be said. I was lucky to find other writers of my generation in the same dilemma I was in and together we made a way of writing that pleased us and said what needed to be said, and many of my friends wrote about how we did this, wrote literary theory and criticism, started magazines and institutions, and some even got degrees and took over English departments in important universities. The enemies of what we wrote thought it didn't make any sense, didn't express normal human feeling, the stuff that poetry had always been about. But I think it expressed all that but expressed it just a bit more honestly and accurately, taking into account the fact that words have their own lives too and that the people that we are cannot so simply be defined. (24 – 25)

I find Fischer's account interesting for several reasons. He introduces (from his own viewpoint) a spiritual continuity as part of the development of Language writing, though it is a mode of "spirituality" that does not have its basis in description. There is, as well, an

implicit sense of such "new" writing as constituting a truer form of
"realism"—that is, of being a writing more consistent (than the more
prevalent univocal personal poetry) with the complexities and contradictions of contemporary identity and consciousness. The common point of departure for Fischer and company is a dissatisfaction
with a writing that presumed to "describe life" and an intensified
sense of the importance (and intractable otherness) of words themselves. What interests me in writing this essay is that I feel that we
are today, in 2000, at another such hinge-time, when the interest in
"words-as-such" has, to a large degree, played itself out, when formal innovation and the mere evasion of the mistakes of mainstream
poetry is finally not enough to satisfy a range of poets. In Fischer's
narrative, the story of Language writing's inception (and of Fischer's
own innovative poetry) gives way to a more fundamental consideration of the value of writing:

> I find a peacefulness in the aloneness of writing now, it is its
> own validation, apart from communication, it is in this sense
> holy, the speaking, the setting down of words, itself a kind
> of redemption, if I can use these words here in Jerusalem, it
> is the humanness of us, our curse and at the same time our
> blessing. We describe the world to ourselves, inevitably, in
> the words we use to talk to ourselves and others; to make
> that description is what it means to praise God, which we
> must do, and in the doing of it we inevitably become con-
> fused, and knowing that we have to have religion, to try to
> work our way out of it. (25)

What Fischer has done over the past twenty-five years or so is to
build a writing practice that is absolutely consistent with his fundamental assumptions about meditation:

> Meditation is not a special state. It's an aspect of mind all
> the time that can be emphasized or heightened at certain
> times by chance, or intentionally. It involves a focusing or
> clearing of the mind onto a single point and then finally no
> point at all. This kind of clearing out, or attention, is called
> "kavanah" in Hebrew, and has always been the main point

of prayer in Judaism. Only we've gotten preoccupied with other things and have forgotten about it.

The trick about meditation is that it's not instrumental: if you are trying to get something out of it that intention prevents the deep clearing of the mind. Since meditation involves this giving over of intention to non-intention, to what is deeper than your intention or what is your real intention underneath your intention, it is always a religious act. It is not a technical thing. (J, 133)

In his earlier poetry, there are numerous instances of intelligent descriptions, pronouncements, and an emerging phenomenology of consciousness. Fischer points out that "'In reality' is a phrase whose referent is a specific problem of human thought or language" (17, P). Or, the moment of writing, entering into writing: "It is like this, a feeling inside that breaks up into words that do not convey thought" (12, P). Or, "This is the burden of my thought: to feel but not go anywhere" (25, P). Or, more ambitiously, on the relationship of habits of thinking to our construction of an understandable and familiar external world:

> Above all we do need to allow ourselves to look squarely into the face of the gargantuan ugliness that is existence, to face this, digest it, and realize that for all its shock value it is in fact only a product of our thought, speech, and imagination, the resolution of opposites. The red sweater that is in fact blue. The mountain that is a lake. The deeply held tolerance of this condition not as a joke trick or indignation but out of reverence. If we had not had a great deal of practice and instruction in putting on our shirt we would have had no idea how to do it. (14, P)

In *Success* (2000), poems selected from Fischer's one year exercise of composing twenty-eight lines every day, Fischer achieves a lucid casualness, a quality of wisdom that retains humor, contingency, and dailiness. Here is Fischer's complete entry for Monday, May 7:

Early morning plane
Remembered later though on this day
It is now, how words work
And back again
Related to what's known
Is a spacious garden it uses less water
Than a lawn
We need to know about
Nearly anything
We need to hear about it
This means know in the biblical sense
To love it anyhow
To really affect it
And to make something of it
"It" being perhaps
What's faced at a time like this
And therefore never really lost
All of culture works against it
Adjunct to the culinary arts
Which have always existed
Wherever you have a high culture—
There's so much to think about!
Even now an ambivalence
Because what you want
Once you get it
Is not it—
That "it" again ...
Probably it's the wrong answer (27)

Fischer's poetry in *Success* is very much a poetry of statement,
though the statements have a great deal of twisting and turning to
them. Even so, this is unusual poetry for someone associated with
Language writing; it is decidedly a poetry of *voice* (and in *Success*,
that voice is often singular) though a highly skeptical voice that
undercuts its own tendencies to be conclusive. Fischer's writing
(like my own) is an example of a productive return—of an innovative poet returning to a poetry that once again permits the use of
a singular voice, that allows for non-ironized statement, and that

takes on "big" questions and issues again. It is, then, an important poetry as the poet passes through the strictures of a "pure" avant-gardism to write—like Taggart in *When the Saints*—quite simply what is needed.[8]

Postmodern modes of fragmentation offer some ways out of the repetitive posturings of the self-expressive poem. As Fischer's brief analysis (in "Modernism, Postmodernism, and Values") makes clear, the postmodern, though, also carries with it the prospect of its own self-cancelling (rapidly metastasizing) irony. As its own kind of negative theology, such ironic writing would have the virtue of not engaging in certain contaminated and habitual rhetorics. But the merely ironic, in spite of its initially refreshing correctness, may also prevent the poet from engaging "what is needed." That is, such writing may be "correct" in what it does *not* do, but it may, as its own habits fall into place, become unable to address the questions and issues that motivated the activity (of writing poetry) in the first place. This potential liability is what Fischer, in writing about the postmodern, calls "perhaps a confusion of purpose under the weight of wit and skill" (113). If a credible writing of "spirit" is taking place in our time—in the work of poets such as Fischer, Taggart, Naylor, Berry, and others—such work, in order not to fall prey to earlier hieratic, subjective heroizing postures, must still address the "big questions," but must do so in a manner that does not stem merely from the self-expressive and the anecdotal.

In a decidedly unfashionable way, in *Success* Fischer is even willing to think and write about "God":

8 During the Fall of 1998, in response to my reading of *Jerusalem Moonlight*, Norman Fischer and I wrote back and forth several times. I explained to Norman that I felt that in my own poetry I had been moving away from an "avant-garder-than-thou" position, and that I found myself less restricted in my writing and more able to address what felt necessary. Norman wrote back: "yes i think i am in the same place you are—not needing to be so pure in the poetry, but now, after all that, just seeing how to say what is true, with all of that behind us—with us and in us" (E-mail, Norman Fischer to Hank Lazer, October 15, 1998). Fischer's remarks indicate an important balance: an ability to get to a more direct treatment of what matters, combined with an ongoing internalization of the "pure" do's and don't's of an actively innovative writing. That balance is part, I think, of the importance and exemplary quality of Fischer's poetry.

God strangled us in the crossed wires
Not out of any malice but in imitation of Lenny Bruce
His right hand man and a major influence
Just because we've got a face
We think we can figure everything out,
Drive through to a purpose: No.
God's the song in thinking, in that key,
So it's free, floating, reflective,
Creates the world, transforms the world (13)

To engage the "God-term" in poetry today is admittedly a problem, but Fischer and others suggest that poetry and thinking suffer from a greater impoverishment if that term is avoided, censored, or erased. Fischer's own engagement with the term bears some kinship to a position that Robert Duncan articulated (in a talk that he gave to the Telegraph Hill Neighborhood Association, March 1, 1959, and used the next day as well in his reading at the San Francisco Poetry Center):

> The poet Louis Zukofsky writes in *Barely and Widely*: "God is / but one's deepest conviction— / your art, its use." Just because it is a use of one's deepest conviction, I consider Poetry not to be a literary achievement or an affect of gentility (tho gentleness has its part in the real) and particularly not a commodity of cultured taste, but to be a process of the Process that is the culture or tillage of souls that there might be and is a spiritual reality. (113)

Fischer (in "Do You Want to Make Something Out of It? Zen Meditation and the Artistic Impulse," an essay that concludes *Success*) affirms Allen Ginsberg's claim that poets are "practitioners of reality, expressing their fascination with the phenomenal universe and trying to penetrate to the heart of it" and that "poetry is a 'process' or experiment—a probe into the nature of reality and the nature of mind" (121). But Fischer's own statement on the importance of poetry involves a tone that is at once humorous and deflationary while still affirming the serious Ground of the activity: "For me this sense of making poetry or art as an heroic and grandiose undertaking whose cost and goal is everything sounds about right—providing you don't get too excited about it, seeing it as anything more or less than any human being is doing, or would do, if he or she reflected for a few minutes about what is a worthwhile and reasonable way to spend a human life" (121). It is this mixture of humor and affirmation—akin perhaps to Kenneth Burke's "comic frame of acceptance"—that I find so attractive in Fischer's writing. Though Fischer's thinking is marked by a radical contingency, he affirms that "Yet what you do / Absolutely matters" (35), so that the fact of radical uncertainty, of the inability of thinking to rest in fixed conclusions, does not undermine the ethics of daily choice and action.

In his daily thinking, Fischer exhibits a nimbleness—somewhat similar to what I have called in Rae Armantrout's poetry a "lyricism of the swerve":[9]

> What's the basis of the rules of conduct?
> Not that they hem you in
> But that they flow like nectar
> Naturally
> From the clear heart
> It's what you want to do
> What gives you joy
> There are problems only
> From the human point of view
> But humans aren't human
> Only sometimes
> And never
> No problem but the one you think about
> One moon
> Or half a moon
> Formed by a bare branch
> Behind a mountain
> And talking for a thousand years
> Will never show this
> Though we have to talk
> More or less like we have to sleep
> Or eat or go to the toilet

9 Chapter Three in *Lyric & Spirit*

That's the secret about everything:
It's marvelous, interchangeable
It's high and it's low if you ask who says so
It's me (40)

Such a turn in thinking occurs with an interruptive line such as "But humans aren't human;" such a line becomes a productive obstacle to habitual or confidently consecutive thinking. Fischer affirms a classically Zen Buddhist position that critiques the limits of "intellect." At times, he will write lines that have that much caricatured *koan* quality to them: "Love what is good / As if bumping into furniture" (65). But Fischer, as he explains, is extremely wary of adopting "a Zen perspective":

> what I have been saying is a Zen perspective on art, although I have a strong resistance to the idea of a Zen perspective on anything[.]... So take the words Zen perspective please with a grain of salt, and understand them as shorthand for a way of looking at the world that is essentially unmade and undefined. (129–130)

Fischer's poetry does not, then, settle into conclusions, nor are his statements unaccompanied by a humor that carries with it a sense of the provisional or momentary scope of the conclusion's value. There is an inviting, non-doctrinal quality to Fischer's spirituality. That quality coincides with what Rodger Kamenetz, in *The Jew in the Lotus: A Poet's Rediscovery of Jewish Identity in Buddhist India*, calls Buddhism's open door: "Buddhism offers portions of its practices and teachings for a person to experiment with. You do not have to believe in Buddha or Buddhism to meditate on the breath—you merely have to give it a try. This is the charm of Buddhism's open door" (230). In fact, the statements in Fischer's poems can be understood simply as part and parcel of the *pleasure* of thinking:

Yet thinking has nothing
It needs to do
In that case
Other than to enjoy itself

And purify the ground
Making it smoother
So people don't trip so much
And accidentally smash into one another
Causing an endless chain of trouble (72)

This non-instrumental sense of thinking is perhaps the principal hinge in Fischer's long-standing relationship to Language writing and to a wide range of innovative poetries.

In his thinking/writing, Fischer is after an embodiment of momentary consciousness: "What is to be done? What is this moment after all?"(131). Fischer's emphasis is similar to Lacouc-Labarthe's statement of the existential and "spiritual" nature of the poem, and of the poem's peculiar positioning: "The poem (the poetic act), in this mode proper to it (dialogue), is the thought of the present's presence, or of the other of what is present: the thought of no-thingness (of Being), that is to say, the thought of time" (65). Like Derrida's concept of "spirit" as a resource or base for deconstruction, Fischer's sense of art-making is as a kind of un-doing that clears the ground:

> Art making is an anti-making. It is an anti-making because it is a making of what is useless—this is what makes art art, that it is useless, that it doesn't do anything, that it is something inherently unmade and this is the source of its liveliness. (122)

In it unmade and accidental nature, art begins to "rhyme" with several other key terms:

> This has been the job of this time: to point out directly and baldly that doubt and accident lie at the heart of what art has always been. And in doing this one comes close to the boundary between art and life and immerses the boundary itself in doubt and accident. The words art and life become quite indistinct and imprecise. One could substitute for both the word reality, or being. (128)

Thus, from Fischer's perspective, "the job of all art or living is to appreciate and authenticate what is" (128). And thus, the best of his poetry is often celebratory, as in the concluding poem of *Success*:

> New Year's Eve
> Bonfire smokes
> Anything hard and easy to end
> A year, a book, a life
> Time ends in its midst
> In front of total strangers
> Dropping the conclusions easily
> Like so many raindrops or pebbles
> The edge of the book's
> The middle of the tongue
> Not so much in any meaning
> As in the physical action of flesh
> And the effort and intention
> The feeling conveyed as sure as
> Breath
> No ideas but in words
> Poems built up tall
> Fall down again into heaps of rubble
> At the end of any life or civilization
> What I have to offer is
> The presence of these things
> I can see and hear
> Raise them up by virtue of
> My singing to them having been moved
> By them
> And in this way
> Give birth to everything
> That never ends (118)

In his celebration of art and world and being, Fischer recognizes that one's experience of art is radically unstable. A work of art "may strike you as profoundly moving one day, and completely beside the point the next day" (123). Thus our interaction with the poem mirrors the inconstant, unstable nature of our relationship to being, reality, the world, and "spirit." As in meditation, not all experiences of attentive breathing yield to an experience of intensification; so with the experience of reading or of engaging a work of art—or, for that matter, of engaging any given present moment. In reading, we have an experience of spiritual striving:

> No one reads poetry or at least
> No one reads my poetry
> Not even me
> And there is a reason for this
> And it is
> That it would be impossible
> For anyone to read what is written
> They are only reading
> Air
> Somewhere other
> Than here
> Where the needlepoint of reality
> Pierces the interstices of the poem
> But this is not the poem (50)

Like Stein's Oakland, Fischer's poem—like "reality" or "the world" or "spirit"—is a particular site where, when we take up fully attentive residence, there is no there there. That is the peculiar mixture of rootedness in the materiality of word, text, and world and a profound sense of the emptiness of these and all entities that energizes Fischer's poetry.

⁓

One of Derrida's more interesting conclusions—again, by way of Heidegger by way of Hölderlin—is to identify "spirit" with thinking, gathering, and with what is:

> In its metaphysical concept, inasmuch as it gathers, spirit is, par excellence, thought, thinking itself (*Denken*). It is properly (*eigentlich*), it is truly spirit inasmuch as, thinking the essential, it gathers—which it does by *thinking itself*, thus

finding itself at home, *close up to itself (zu Hauss)*. ... The hymn [Hölderlin's] poetically meditates spirit as what is; and what is assigns to every entity the sending or the mission of its Being. (76)

For Derrida, "spirit" is supposed as "that which *gathers* or in which what gathers is gathered" (76). It seems to me that what is gathered in that place and action of gathering is an intensive summoning into the thinking of being. (My own phrase is "thinking / singing," placing as I do a high priority on that thinking engagement as properly—as a kind of tribute and imitation—being beautiful.)

The enigmatic non-presence of the divine—as described by Lacoue-Labarthe—has obvious "rhymes" with the concept of *sunyata*: "God shows or reveals himself in the same way as the sky's pure opening—the 'abyss,' as Celan would say; as the ceaseless ebb, on and right against the whole surface of the visible, the invisible from which the visible streams" (116–117). To approximate the divine—to be proximate to and with the invisible (that enabling and sustaining realm of the invisible in Rilke's poetry, for example)—remains one of poetry's most sacred possibilities. In Lacoue-Labarthe's phrasing—"that he is evident as the invisible is evident, withdrawn into the visible *as* its visibility" (117). Poetry marshals its peculiar forces—particularly the invisible force of breath (*ruach*)—as a key partner in making manifest that invisibility. That particular charge or obligation, that duty, is part of why poetry is so often (wrongly) critiqued as being too indirect and as unable to "say what it means." As Lacoue-Labarthe concludes, poetry's peculiar form of truth, the mode of "realism" appropriate to it, is linked inextricably to this affinity with the concealed revelation of the divine:

But the more he sends himself into "the sky's aspect," which is unknown to him, the more he "reveals" himself as invisible. Thus Heidegger can say: "The poet calls, in the sights of the sky, that which in its very self-disclosure causes the appearance of that which conceals itself, and indeed *as* that which conceals itself." (117)

Poetry is, and sacredly so, most direct in its indirection and in its habitual concealment, in its very refusal to "mean" directly. Knowingly, the poem is a hymn to the unknowable—poetry as an approximation and an intimation.

~

The writing, then, that I am examining in this essay often involves an element of "return" or "re-engagement"—of the "spiritual," of certain fundamental questions of being, and of "romantic," or metaphysical, or mystical elements of poetry and poetics. For me, a small but important book in that "return" is Paul Naylor's *Book of Changes*, a series of poems that, in the wake of the death of Naylor's mother, arises from the necessity of a re-engagement of the personal.[10] As with Norman Fischer's emerging re-engagement of the spiritual in poetry, Naylor's *Book of Changes* is of interest because such writing takes place *within* a writing-practice community that does *not* take the form of the writing as a given or received element. The form of the writing is as "meaningful" or declarative as any other element. Naylor's renewed "personal" writing occurs within a social and aesthetic context of deep skepticism and longstanding critique of an established (or habitual, or mainstream) rhetoric of "personal expression."

In *Book of Changes*, Naylor engages in a writing through practice with the *I Ching*, in part as a means of studying a recent claim for an embedded narrative in the sixty-four hexagrams. Naylor writes, "I am drawn to the sense of necessity narrative writing brings to the text, a sense of chance guiding a major moment of change, so I decided to write through those first thirty hexagrams consecutively in order to consult the oracle about the invasion death was leading in my life" (Preface, p. 1). In fact, Naylor's series of poems occurs at

---

10 For another noteworthy re-engagement of the personal, see also Susan M. Schultz's "Happiness Project" and related writings: *From "Memoir"* (Honolulu: Tinfish Limited Edition, August 1999) and *Memory Cards [the happiness project]* (Prague/New York: Twisted Spoon Press/x-poezie, 2000).

an interesting intersection of seemingly contradictory impulses—at once, through "borrowed" materials and a writing through procedure, "impersonal" and, due to the occasion that provokes the poems, the death of his mother, highly "personal" and emotionally charged. In his "Preface," Naylor tends to emphasize the "impersonal" half of this dialectic:

> These poems may strike some as too quiet for their occasion, perhaps too impersonal for such a personal subject. But quiet is a condition of listening, and making a monument of my feelings wasn't what I was after. I simply wanted to understand the natural fact of death from a view I've long held as true. For me, a person is not a piece of eternal private property, sealed off and saved from the impersonal forces of nature and death. A person is part of, not apart from, nature. From this perspective, nature is anything but impersonal. The *I Ching* informs us about what—not who—we are: energy ordered by chance and necessity in an ongoing process where everything and nothing is lost. That's the other view that broke through as I listened, and what little I understood became these poems. Fragments they are—but fragments of a whole unassigned in advance, unfolding as change arranges us in its wake. (Preface, 2)

One might call this a "spiritual" perspective (on death, on being, on personhood); it certainly involves a shift in perspective on the person in the world—on the person as an aggregate of energy and form involved in a natural process of re-arrangement.

The poems themselves exhibit qualities of an Eigner-ish syntax and a Creeley-ish concentration of the short lines. The third of the hexagrams, "Birth Pangs," reads

> thunder
> then rain cleans
> the wound death gives
> birth to change
> leaves us still
> in thought

As in Creeley's best work, the twists and swerves invoked by
the line breaks re-order our understanding of what goes with what.
What we have then is an incremental thinking, a gripping down and
a coming to grips with. So that we return again and again to re-read
and re-think "the wound death gives / birth to change," in part to
wonder at the boundaries of that process and when (where and how)
one process gives way to the next. As Naylor's brief poem has it, we
are both "still" (i.e., continuing) in that thought, and also stilled or
stopped or held—brought up short—in that thinking.

The poems—which seem to me to function best when understood in the personal context established in the Preface—offer somewhat oblique but also very moving memorials to the poet's mother,
as in the seventh hexagram, "The Army":

> of the dead from whom
> we hear so little
> water runs below
> the earth's surface
> washing recollection away
> of what once was her

Naylor writes about choosing, through the *I Ching*, "to deal with
my mother's death in my life and in these poems" (Preface, 1). In so
doing, in important ways he loosens the implicit do's and don't's of
experimentalism, choosing in the process to write a poetry that may
address "the dead," "the earth," and other "forbidden" big terms. In
the eleventh hexagram, "Peace," Naylor writes,

> begins with breath
> drawn in slowly
> released to arrive
> where one is
> known as home
> she's there

Merging meditative practice—the zazen of sitting meditation comes
to mind—with a sense of location, Naylor's *Book of Changes* may be
contained within the line "released to arrive." It is that intersection of

conclusion and arrival (which also is "where one is") that characterizes the occasion of the series of poems and its concomitant articulation of faith—a faith that professes to be a description.[11]

If Naylor's poems constitute a thinking about absence, then they
are also a bodying forth of a precise phenomenology of the turns in
thinking, as in the twenty-third hexagram, "Freeing Yourself":

> from what was never
> the question but how
> to live without
> an insistent I
> hear the mind
> murmur

That precise phenomenology tracks a motion of thinking (and an
emotion of thinking) by means of the resources of lineation and
arrangement upon the page. Naylor, writing through another's
text and writing in an awareness of the individual life as subject to
chance, writes of the necessary dissolution of the self within larger
forces and more encompassing continuities. The poems themselves
are part of the consolation that allows "how / to live without."

The memorial that Naylor provides for his mother at once arises
from a personal occasion and becomes a more general investigation.
As in Naylor's concluding hexagram, that more general investigation—of what flexibility an "experimental" poetry must grant if the
poet is to engage the issues and events that matter; of how the words
of another may in fact provide a means of personal emotional expression (without "making a monument of my feelings")—does not,
however, negate sentiment:

> sudden as fire burns out
> nothing lasts or is lost
> a pheasant flies
> east at sunrise
> passing in
> time

---

11 Naylor's *Book of Changes* strikes me as a pertinent example of
Megan Simpson's provocative term "spiritual realism."

Naylor's effort throughout has been to articulate the processes of
a person within the processes of nature—to write an "objective"
nature poetry (one that, importantly, is written in a form that he
characterizes as "fragments of a whole unassigned in advance") that
is simultaneously highly personal and emotional while continuing to
occur within a community of poets and poetics that values highly a
heuristics of form.

Robert Duncan no doubt represents an extreme affirmation—
certainly within the valorized lineage of mid- and late-twentieth century innovative poets—of belief, faith, and mysticism. In a classically
Emersonian (i.e., the early Emerson) position, Duncan writes,

> And from childhood I have been seeking the lore of that
> other life, with a faith that everything that is realized here *is*
> there, and real only there—thus I call it the real world; that
> everything we do here, each act, the actual world, is a sign,
> an omen of the real, and an enactment of its reality, as the
> actual words in actual script or print on the actual page are
> signs of a real spiritual world. (113)

Duncan's position is echoed in a wide range of writers, from Plato to
Edmond Jabès. Among contemporary innovative poets, Duncan is
unusual in the directness of his affirmation of a functioning, active
concept of the divine, of his sense of his own life as a tangible participation in a larger entity:

> Paracelsus tells us again: "As soon as a child is conceived, it
> receives its own heaven." I have my own life and my own
> time because I am utterly mortal; it is indeed by the virtue
> of these boundaries of birth and death which are the grace
> of God that I have this tenancy of my self. Thus I know that
> I am not the Poet. As a "poet" I am only an instance and
> instrument of the Poet that I imagine—that is, Who is real,
> and Whose work is immortal Poetry, is Reality. (114)

What I am interested in is our ability, and /or inability, to come to grips with Duncan's ardent spirituality (as a repressed aspect of the poetics we inherit from Duncan and others).

Similarly, Jerome Rothenberg's work—crucial to an expansion of the "literary" and of the range of poetics that contemporary poets engage—is foundational for contemporary innovative work, but the grounding of his poetics in "spirit" (and shamanism) constitutes another aspect of a discomforting or repressed nexus. From the outset, Rothenberg's development of an ethnopoetics depends upon a relationship to "spirit." He writes about what

> ...I & others had recently been speaking of as *ethnopoetics*. Still more there was a recognition that any exploration of language that took us into what I came to think of as areas of deep culture (wherever found) was at the same time a descent into the domain of deep mind, or, if I can say so without blurring the issue, into the domain of *spirit* as such. (7)

In his "Pre-face (1996)" to the collection *the book, spiritual instrument*, Rothenberg identifies dual resources that lead him to the title-concept:

> There were two widely separated guides who brought the connections together in my mind: the Mexican (Mazatec) shamaness María Sabina & the pivotal French symbolist poet Stéphane Mallarmé. Unlettered & speaking only Mazatec, Sabina conceived the key to Language & to her own Language-centered chanting in the form of a great Book of Language or as "little luminous objects that fall from heaven" to be caught "word after word with my hands." Both of her images rhymed for me with others that had come to us principally from Mallarmé—the latter as if it prefigured the typographical castings & recastings of his master poem, *Un coup de dès*; the former his vision of the book as "spiritual instrument... the [single] Book that every writer worked at even without knowing... the Orphic explanation of the Earth, which is the poet's only duty." (7–8)

For Mallarmé—and his phrase, "Le Livre, Instrument Spirituel," is as concise a summary as I know for the renewed textual spirituality that I am tracing in this essay—"everything in the world exists in order to end up as a book" (14). To work on that Book, what is required? Mallarmé answers, "the hymn, harmony and joy, grouped as a pure unity in some lightning circumstance, of the relations between everything. Man is entrusted with seeing divinely, because the bond, at will and pellucid, has to his eyes no other expression than in the parallelism of the sheet" (14). As in Fischer's sense of the text and of reading as a site of access to "spirit," Mallarmé concludes that "through reading, a solitary tacit concert presents itself to the spirit that regains, at a lower volume, the meaning— ... the act of thinking" (19).

A noteworthy and eccentric example of writing "spirit" anew is the multifaceted body of work produced by Jake Berry. A musician,[12] visual artist, and poet, Berry's location in Florence (Alabama) as well as his rare travels mark his work as part of a tradition of intensely individualistic exploration—part of a lineage that might run from William Blake to Frank Stanford. An active correspondent, and a poet whose work has received considerable circulation internationally (through the zine-world, international postal art shows, and small press / independent publication), Berry's work bears kinship to that of southern visionary folk artists, religious visionaries, traditional blues/folk musicians (including Bob Dylan, with whom Berry has played). Perhaps the most sustained inheritance for Berry is a fusion of Christian traditions—from his Church of Christ upbringing (Berry's father is a minister [as well as an engineer])—gnostic Jewish

---

12 Jake Berry's CDs include *Shadow Resolve* (Front Porch Records, 1997, which includes "From a String of Perals," "Keys to the Kingdom," and "Lightning Scars"), *Trouble in Your House* (by Bare Knuckles, with Wayne Sides; Front Porch Records, 1998; includes "Dark Side of Heaven" and "St. John of the Cross Blues"), and *Roses on the Threshold* (Front Porch Records, 2000; includes "After the Veil," "Lazarus Bound," and "After the Storm"). Berry's lyrics are of extremely high quality and address issues of vision and "spirit" that are quite pertinent to the poetry.

traditions, ancient Egyptian religion, and Voudoun, enriched by Berry's readings in myth-based poets such as William Blake, Charles Olson, and Michael McClure.

Berry's major ongoing work is *Brambu Drezi*,[13] an epic work of poetry and visual text (which also lends itself to performance).[14] In *Brambu Drezi: Book II* (1998), Berry begins,

---

13 At the time that I wrote this essay, two books had been published: *Brambu Drezi: Book One* (Port Charlotte, Florida: Runaway Spoon Press, 1993), and *Brambu Drezi: Book II* (Berkeley: Pantograph Press, 1998). In November 2006, Station Hill published a new edition of *Brambu Drezi* which included books one, two, and three. In November 2007, Berry began posting some preliminary versions of Book Four in a DVD video format.

14 There are videotapes available of two particularly noteworthy, mul-timedia performances of portions of Berry's *Brambu Drezi*. On November 14, 1997, Berry staged a one hour performance (including dancers, musi-cians, video installation, visual art) at the AB Theater at The University of Alabama. On December 4, 1998, for Joe Speer's weekly TV show (in Nashville), Berry recorded portions of *Brambu Drezi* for public cable TV broadcast. (Subsequently, in February 2007, Berry performed portions of *Brambu Drezi*, again at the AB Theater at the University of Alabama, with dancers and jazz musicians Tom Wolfe and Chris Kozak.)

And darkness opened
       drifts in
              viscid air   (boundless light

              conception's shadow
       profusion from the exodus chamber
                                                        genus loci

       the joy of appearing   .

                        UMGATHAMA

crosses take root in the sun
driving it from its sepulcher
                     (govi)

   frequencies collide
   bone white mares   All worlds are projections
              torn screaming neck deep   of a beautiful agony
   from zodiac tar

       We have formed
       a compact
       with discord

              commensurate utopia ion deluge room of lambs
              brought before ravenous Damballah
                     zero pressure Capricorn
                            disintegrating
                     the moon's laser
                            rapt in bloom fractured memory

This beginning to Book II of Berry's epic poem contains many of the
essential elements of his poem. The opening "And" is, as Berry's epigraph announces, "a hinge." The text itself will be a site of colliding
sources and perspectives as well as an intersection for heightened and
conflicted emotions, with the poem itself being the recurring experience of "a beautiful agony." The poem pivots about key moments of
glossolalia, including the annunciation of UMGATHAMA. Berry
indicates that "glossolalia, speaking in tongues is the result I suppose of an experience of overwhelming awe. This would be the most
fundamental religious experience" (56, interview with Jim Leftwich).

Berry's own relationship to that central word UMGATHAMA is a complex, elusive one:

> ...I have no concrete idea of its meaning. I am not sure one is intended or necessary. The word arrived as a result of hypnogogic vision. As I lay on my bed one evening, Charles Olson stood over me repeating the word "UMGATHAMA" with great force, but not anger. The urgency in his voice suggested he was bringing a message, but one from a poetic realm and therefore a word of power, an address of the holy, which is how it continues to arise throughout BRAMBU DREZI. I was surprised that Olson should be the messenger since I had read only small portions of his work, being particularly impressed by "In Cold Hell, In Thicket." (53)

The poem, from its beginning, will rely on words that stretch our sense of sense-making, though, as with UMGATHAMA, those key words point to irresolvable but multiple sources.[15] Also, from the very beginning, the visual elements—from the layout of the phrases to the drawings—are an integral part of the poem. The right hand shadowy filament—a kind of emerging or devolving genetic strand—recurs throughout the text in a variety of ways.

The next three lines of the poem point to an important source:

> loa racine raged across the highlands
> green mantle shrouding cathode zombies
>   dolmen transubtantiator   wichasha wankan

The term "loa" is crucial to understanding Berry's poetics, particularly in an epic poem that is so radically released from mastery, where the poet clearly exists in subordination to a greater reality and where the poem is released from the performance and will of one's individual intentions. Maya Deren in *Divine Horsemen: The Living Gods of Haiti*, her foundational book on Voudoun, explains,

---

15 See Jim Leftwich's excellent commentary on UMGATHAMA (essay and interview with Jake Berry; pp. 56–58; *Brambu Drezi: Book II*).

The loa, whose function is to direct the enormous primal
mass of the material universe into patterns of intelligence
and benevolence, are involved in a great and endless labor. It
is their moral energy which animates this huge bulk of matter, and so, since that energy is constantly expended, it must
be constantly replenished. And this is man's duty: to feed the
loa, to insure the constant flow of the psychic energy, to as-
sure the moral movement of the universe. (209)

The loa are forces that the poet summons—forces that "ride" the
poet and that possess him and, at times, the poem. Deren writes of
the importance of the loa:

To be made aware, once more, that man is of divine origin
and is the issue of and heir to an uncounted multitude of
hearts and minds; that at the root of the universe the great
imperturbable principles of cosmic good endure; and that
even under his torn shirt, his hunger, the failures of his wit
and the errors of his heart, his very blood harbors these
monumental loa—is to experience the major blessing with
which possession rewards men's dedicated service. (248)

The poet as a gateway to a *multitude* of forces and beings is a foundational premise for *Brambu Drezi*, as is the reality (and peril) of
possession, an experience that is often marked in Berry's text by glossolalia and by the way that the text constantly remains outside the
control of its author.

When I began my own reading of Deren's *Divine Horsemen*, I
was struck by a worldview utterly compatible with that of *Brambu
Drezi*. When I asked Jake about my observation, he wrote back:

You're absolutely right to be reading Deren along with
Brambu II. I read *Divine Horsemen* a year or two before starting BD2, so it was a fresh part of the psyche, near the surface,
and she has continued to be there. The last lines of the book
in fact are in part inspired by her film *Meshes of an Afternoon*.
Voudoun seems to have all the right elements with little or
none of the kind of moral strictures that the heavy orthodox-

ies have. And it remains beautifully balanced between magic
and religion and makes magic of everything it touches. I
hope always in *Brambu* that the "I" is not only another, but
one of a multitude, so that the ego is a player but only one
of many more or less equal players. Polytheism comes closer
to daily human experience than monotheism, but even in
voudoun the one, Bondeye, remains God, but the loa are the
divine beings we have contact with. In Jewish mysticism we
have all the various names of God, Elohim, Adonai, YHVH,
etc, which became the Tree of Life in Kabbalah; Catholicism
has its saints; Tibetan Buddhism a host of Bodhisattvas. The
transcendental reality is there certainly enough and it must
inform everything, since everything is its expression and
vehicle, but there are many details and these take on bodies,
sometimes human bodies. Possession is just a natural completion of the human drive toward the divine, and the divine
toward human. I could babble on about this for hours. Best
to let *Brambu* do the speaking since it is the experience and
not just words about it.[16]

Deren describes the loa as the means of encounter of the human
with the divine. The ceremonies, songs, and drum beats are "like
lines thrown out, to become the cables of the bridge upon which
man would cross that chasm [between the human and the divine]",
a divide that Deren says that "no man can straddle" and that is "present, as physical fact, in the amnesia which makes even the sense of
the loa inaccessible to the very 'horse' which bore him. *To understand
that the self must leave if the loa is to enter, is to understand that one
cannot be man and god at once*" (249). In *Brambu Drezi*, the recurring incidents of terror and dissolution, alternating with episodes of
possession and vision, are completely consistent with Deren's analysis
of the experience of possession:

> Thus the possessed benefits least of all men from his posses-
> sion. He may even suffer for it in material loss, in the some-
> times painful, always exhausted physical aftermath. And to the

---

16 E-mail from Jake Berry to Hank Lazer, August 2, 1998.

degree that his consciousness persists into its first moments or becomes aware of the very end, he experiences overwhelming fear.... It is toward the achievement of this—toward the forcing open of the door to the source—that the entire structure of Voudoun is directed. The serviteur must be induced to surrender his ego, that the archetype become manifest. (249)

Thus the second page (and a quick look reveals that the *page* is a pertinent unit of composition) of *Brambu Drezi: Book II* indicates

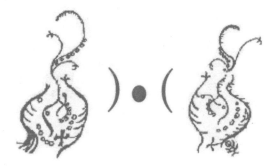

<u>mouth</u>
  black   sibylline infusion

        epistrophes
        brujo / hermit

                                  Nova Cygni_1992

brambu langage
  AHG PRIMINCIA SABAYI meniso SABAYI isosyn
(santhgroi scau awi-spuh sungvis nahgway
  frlanmus) ISHNUI AMA (hawol alahmae
eelezay shadnre neevah unapwa)
      UMGATHAMA

Berry's note glosses "langage" as "the sacred language used in Voudoun ceremonies, the "Brambu" as a qualifier here, meaning the sacred tongue (or part of it) of this particular body of work" (53).[17]

17 Jake Berry's work can be seen and heard as participating in a tradition of art-work that goes by various labels such as self-taught, "outsider" art, or visionary folk art. For example, Berry's work—particularly in its interplay of script and visual imagery—bears some kinship to that of Howard

Berry's poem is full of references that mark Voudoun as an essential realm of terminology, experience, and ritual. As with the Olson
dream-delivered term UMGATHAMA, dream-experience is one of
the poem's recurring modes of possession:

                                                                begin the planter
mal(sanguinary)stain   straighter than carbon
your ichthycloset   horse shaper
    remnemonish wave
in pleurisy of evolute ragadin

                        "cochiciery", he spoke
                thundranamus fray torn banter spiked
                        jangling nimbostrativicta
                                jangling
                            raining ridiculous
                                blow

In a note, Berry explains the source of the term "cochiciery" (which,
in the note, Berry spells "cochiery"): "'cochiery'—word spoken to

---

Finster, JB Murry (and his mystical script), and the gourd-writings of
Reverend Perkins. (See *Howard Finster, Man of Visions: The Life and Work
of a Self-Taught Artist*, J. F. Turner, New York: Knopf, 1989; *Outsider Artists
in Alabama*, Catalogue a Project of The Alabama State Council on the Arts,
compiled by Miriam Rogers Fowler, 1991; and *Baking in the Sun: Visionary
Images from the South*, University Art Museum: University of Southwestern
Louisiana, 1987.) Berry's work can also be placed in the context of more
traditional "textual" writings such as the work of Hannah Weiner or
Antonin Artaud, or in the context of various book-makers represented in
A Book of the Book: Some Works & Projections About the Book & Writing
(edited by Jerome Rothenberg and Steven Clay, New York: Granary Books,
2000), particularly Aleksey Kruchonykh and Adolf Wölfli. For those interested in a more detailed study of Berry's compositions, The Sackner Archive
of Visual and Concrete Poetry (and accessible at www.rediscov.com/sack-
ner.htm, and located in Miami) has a substantial collection of his work,
including the complete manuscripts for *Brambu Drezi: Book I* and *Brambu
Drezi: Book II*.

me by Sun Ra, the jazz composer/performer, in a dream. It was to
be my new name he said. I was unable to understand what he said
at first and had to go back to sleep and back into the dream and ask
him to repeat it. The word I have used is as close an approximation
as I was able to bring back" (54).

As with page thirteen of *Brambu Drezi: Book II*, what we often
get, as in Blake's illuminated manuscripts, is an active interplay of
text and drawing:

magpies scatter & return
cyclical as dervish
"It means tornadoes," she said smiling
"whole herds of them
grazing rooftops and mamal soul.
We begin with carnival."

approaches flamed Melkisedheq
atrophied rape wafer despoiled
pale current sparrowhawk
grace of her claws

                                                moal

specilist green with posture
the four corners region encrypted now
held as lien against the glacier's retreat
slow movement through the barricades
even spirit is detained by
the heavy circumstances of blood

He came to a place where 12 men had been hung
from 12 spiked rods   grain
over each of them a television flickered   heart jar
their images at various ages, through the
perfunctory rites of passage, private indulgences
and significant dreams
       gown
         splendor
         abstantial
         river   gesture
           neuropsalm
         screamer
"I know the secrets of the ways fo the lord,
    their paths and signs…

oblivion be my redeemer
oblivion my shelter
oblivion the message of my blood
oblivion is the name of the Lord
      oblivion my redemer
        oblivion my stallion
        oblivion the message of my blood
          oblivion is the name of the Lord"   valences

In this passage, the central word "encrypted" points both to-ward what is entombed and what is coded. The drawing suggests a DNA-like strand of encryption—a kind of governing helix-like structure that bears a generative relationship to the surrounding text. The drawings at times look like the line drawings of Klee or Miró, though they also suggest science textbook illustrations. The page itself often becomes a crowded space—of words and illustra-tions—what Bataille would call the world of excess, of spiritual de-tritus, of a flood of images and words, what Berry calls "soul trash" (17). Throughout *Brambu Drezi: Book II*, there are ever-shifting per-spectives, the "holy" and the "tawdry" readily changing places, with a fallen or debased world and word readily at hand ("Word become venom" [24]) as in the recurring pop-perversion of the spirit world/ word. So that while Berry's poem is definitely a "spiritual" text, it is also "brutal as scripture" (25) and the product of a consciousness ex-isting under great tension and pressure ("'I've got a brainful of light-ning / ready to blow'" [25]). Thus the text itself occurs at the edge of an explosive, disintegrative intensification.

~~~

Clearly, some of the problems today in "writing 'spirit'" rhyme with Jewish prohibitions against representations of the divine. Lacoue-Labarthe locates a similar strain in Celan's writing, "the in-terdiction against representation; or, rather, they [Celan's poems] are haunted solely by the unfigurable or unrepresentable" (41). He concludes that a Celan poem, which Lacoue-Labarthe identifies with "the interruption of language" (49), "must clear a way between si-lence and discourse, between mutism's *saying nothing* and the *saying too much* of eloquence" (56). Lacoue-Labarthe conceptualizes Celan's poetry as "the interruption of the 'poetic.' At least, as it is defined as a battle against idolatry. All 'real' poems, all that are effectively poems, seem to aim at nothing other than being the place where the 'poetic' collapses and becomes abysmal" (68).

While I agree—by way of writings such as Nathaniel Mackey's (in *Discrepant Engagement*) on the importance of the stutter and the stammer, or the numerous examples in Susan Howe's work—that there indeed is an interruptive quality of poetry, I react somewhat

skeptically to what I perceive as a Euro-existential macho posturing
on behalf of the terminal or the abysmal or the unsayable. Indeed,
poetry is, oddly and sequentially, an active critique and rebuke of the
"poetic." And if this hypothesis is true, then the very formulations
of the poem that are Celan's or that belong to the first generation of
language poets are themselves rhetorics that move from being 'real'
poems to becoming 'poetic," by means of assimilation, familiarity,
commodification, fashion, and historical determinations. Lacoue-
Labarthe sees poetry as battling with "art" (or with the "poetic"):
"what poetry wants to rid itself of is the beautiful. The poem's threat
is the beautiful, and all poems are always too beautiful, even Celan's'
(69). But perhaps poems, such as today's writing of "spirit," may
resist being "too beautiful" if the poem's beauty remains inextricable
from difficulty or if the beauty is such that it is able to retain (over
time) a strong quality of "otherness" and of the "unassimilable."

Lacoue-Labarthe explains, "This is just what justifies the idea
that poetry is the interruption of art, that is, the interruption
of mimesis. Poetic art consists of perceiving, not representing.
Representing, at least according to some of the 'ancient rumors,'
can only be said of the already-present" (67). Perhaps this formulation points to the situation of an innovative poetry on the track of
"spirit." It would be a poetry that is, in its own new ways, indeed "realistic"—that is, true to the phenomenology of experiencing "spirit,"
in all the ambiguity and imprecision of that experience, in its peculiar "otherness" (here, decisively *not* an "otherness" that has anything
much to do with the particularities and differences of personal/eth-
nic identity). It is a poetry that may nonetheless partake of the beautiful—"the singable residue" (23)—but one that risks the incarnation
of a potentially reinvigorating mixture of uncertainty, desire (a desire
to believe?), and a feeling of proximity.

Lacoue-Labarthe's *Poetry as Experience* moves toward a particularly critical triangulated relationship for man, language, and god:

> Language is the other in man; it constitutes him as man
> *himself.* Man does not *have* language in the sense of pos-
> session or property[.]…[H]e is not its master (on the con-
> trary; language operates a strange dispossession, attracting
> man—within himself—outside of himself). This is the motif

of "pre-scription" (*Vor-Schrift*). Language is the essence, the inhuman essence of man; it is his (in)humanity. (96)

By virtue of man's peculiarly intimate relationship to language—and particularly in language's ineluctable otherness—man is drawn into a relationship as well with the divine:

> Thus language can be considered man's origin. Not as God is[.] ... But as that by which man is necessarily related to the other, and thence to the wholly other, so that God is not language, but its supposition, or at least what irresistibly draws it. (96)

While drawing language (and man) toward it, the divine remains—as in basic Jewish edicts—unnameable and outside of language. In fact, the divine is precisely that which remains outside of presence: "It is precisely because the being reveals itself as nothingness, no thing, that the God (someone, *einer*) reveals himself as "not one" or "none" (*keiner*), and from there as "no one" (*Niemand*). A no one whom it is (still) possible to address (you, *du*)" (80). It is this address that poetry ventures. The history of poetry—of some strand of Poetry—can be viewed as successive modes of address and successive approximations. It is equally important to note that these successive deeds are not linear, not "progressive" (certainly not progressively wiser), and not steady in seeming importance, centrality, or pertinence to Poetry. In part, that is why I am writing this essay: to respond to an intense feeling that *now* is one of those times in which some significantly interesting modes of address (again) become possible and are occurring.

⌒⌒

In my own poetry, "turning" is an essential feature—hence, the centrality in *The New Spirit* of the concept of *teshuvah*. The term "verse" itself is linked to turning—as is the way that a poem, as we read it, turns back to begin again at the end of each line. "Turning" can also be a kind of "swerving," particularly in a lyric poetry such as Rae Armantrout's where the shifts in direction (and the very slipperiness of what any poem is "about") constitute a beautifully investigated metric.

In Lacoue-Labarthe's analysis—principally within a poetic lineage of Hölderlin through Celan—"turning" has more to do with the retreat of the divine:

> the "withdrawal" of the divine in Hölderlin, the "categorical turning away" of the god (the Father, who is the "father of time") that draws on the essence of Greek tragedy, is in no way related to any of the figures of God's death. "Retreat" is not death; it is, on the contrary, what preserves the god and separates the human from the divine, what retraces the limit of finitude [.] (77)

The poem, then, is a radical and intensified turning toward that which we are not, toward that which may have retreated, and toward that which is fundamentally other. The poem's tropism—its very turning toward this "not"—constitutes a peculiar quality of address. As Lacoue-Labarthe asks and wonders,

> mightn't it be that a poem which thus maintains the possibility of prayer—at its outer limit, to be sure—is the sign that a link, and perhaps a necessary link, exists between prayer and poetry? That poetry in its essence is prayer, and conversely that every prayer is a poem? (79)

Admittedly, such claims are hard to listen to and hard not to ridicule. But such dismissal, it seems to me, is rooted in a "vulgar" or simplistic notion of prayer. What Lacoue-Labarthe has in mind—and what I am seeking to make manifest in a range of contemporary American poetry—is a prayerfulness that is part of the task of thinking, fully engaged in skepticism (about its own nature, necessity, desirability, and ways of proceeding, as well as about its history of self-serving quasi-priestly self-glorification), and decidedly exploratory (rather than summational) in its activity. As Lacoue-Labarthe suggests, "the sole archives of the divine are poems, and an address to the god, more than any other kind, requires a conversion in language or an entirely different attitude within it" (79). That particular explanation, in my opinion, goes a long way toward answering why an innovative or experimental poetry might now be well situated for a renewed adventuring of the "spiritual."

At its outer limits, the poem becomes a site for investigating (and at times celebrating or singing [as well as signing]) that complex nexus of human being, language, and the divine (as a not-being), being the province of the human as "the one who exists at the being capable of attesting presence and absence in general" (L-L, 95). As address and in the minutely calibrated "singing" (or infinitely nuanced lyricisms), "the faculty of language, the ability to name, is in reality intimacy itself, the intimate differentiation of the being" (L-L, 95 – 96).

———

Lacoue-Labarthe offers an interesting etymological consideration of poetry as "experience":

> I propose to call what it [poetry] translates "experience,"
> provided that we both understand the word in its strictest
> sense—the Latin *ex-periri*, a crossing through danger—
> and especially that we avoid associating it with what is
> "lived," the stuff of anecdotes. *Erfahrung*, then, rather than
> *Erlebnis*. I say "experience" because what the poem "springs
> forth" from here—the memory of bedazzlement, which is
> also the pure dizziness of memory—is precisely that which
> did not take place, did not happen or occur during the
> singular event that the poem relates to without relating: the
> visit[.] (18)

Though his description has in mind a specific context—visits by Celan to places associated with Hölderlin and Heidegger—Lacoue-Labarthe's description has a more general applicability. The description is close to Heidegger's own sense of ad-venturing in language—of risk involved in the adventurous nature of questioning and thinking. In much contemporary poetry, there is talk of valuing "risk-taking," but that term tends to mean the (mimetic) expression of highly personal or intimate experiences. But such experiences are precisely what Lacoue-Labarthe dismisses as "anecdotes."

In a passage that points toward the seriousness and the profundity of such "risking" and ad-venturing, Derrida, by way of Nietzsche, writes:

> No, Nietzsche does not disavow or deny spirit, he does not avoid it. Spirit is not the adversary (*Wildersacher*) but the scout (*Schrittmacher*)—it draws and, once again, *leads* the soul whose path it breaks. When it opposes soul, i.e. life, when it does this harshly, this is in favor and not to the detriment of life. (74)

If the poem is a province for the "spiritual," it is not then today imagined as a site for re-counting an anecdote. In fact, the particular phenomenological space of the poem is one that embodies conflicting measures of saying and not-saying. It is a space charged by what cannot be said and by what can only be approximated. To say, as European poets and metaphysicians are prone to do, that such poems "take place at the limits of language" still strikes me as a romantic posturing and as at best a half-step away from self-serving heroizing. Nevertheless, the poem as such is a place charged with contra-dictory orders and impulses regarding presentation and protection, clarification and occlusion. That is, a complex (and somewhat historically governed) ethics of representation. As Lacoue-Labarthe describes it:

> But the poem's "wanting-to-say" does not *want* not to say. A poem wants to say; indeed, it is nothing but pure wanting-to-say. But pure wanting-to-say nothing, nothingness, that against which and through which there is present, what is. (20)

Thus, today, there is an increasingly significant body of renewed writing of "spirit." This poetry is no longer principally an anecdotal recounting of "spiritual" experiences and lyricized epiphanies, but a poetry ad-venturing in language the complex, elusive location that we bear (and bear witness to) in our intimate and proximate relationship to alterity.

(2000)

Works Cited

apex of the M #1 (1994). Lew Daly, Alan Gilbert, Kristin Prevallet, and Pam Rehm, editors. "State of the Art." Pages 5–7.

Berry, Jake. *Brambu Drezi: Book II*. Berkeley: Pantograph Press, 1998.

———— E-mail correspondence. To Hank Lazer. August 2, 1998.

Daly, Lew. *Swallowing the Scroll: Late in a Prophetic Tradition with the Poetry of Susan Howe and John Taggart*. Buffalo: M Press, 1994.

Deren, Maya. *Divine Horsemen: The Living Gods of Haiti*. Kingston, NY: Documentext, 1953.

Derrida, Jacques. Of Spirit: Heidegger and the Question. Trans. By Geoffrey Bennington and Rachel Bowlby. Chicago: University of Chicago Press, 1989.

Duncan, Robert. Address to Telegraph Hill Neighborhood Association. March 1, 1959. *Chicago Review* 45, 2 (1999): 112–114.

Emerson, Ralph Waldo. "Nature" (1836), in *Selections from Ralph Waldo Emerson*, ed. Stephen E. Whicher. Boston: Houghton Mifflin, 1960.

Fischer, Norman. *Jerusalem Moonlight: An American Zen Teacher Walks the Path of His Ancestors*. San Francisco: Clear Glass Publications, 1995.

————. "Modernism, Postmodernism, and Values." *Poetics Journal* #7 (September 1987): 114–116.

————. *Precisely the Point Being Made*. Oakland & Minneapolis: O Books & Chax Press, 1993.

————. *Success*. Philadelphia: Singing Horse Press, 2000.

————. E-mail correspondence. To Hank Lazer. October 15, 1998.

Foster, Edward. *Answerable to None: Berrigan, Bronk, and the American Real*. New York: Spuyten Duyvil, 1999.

Hejinian, Lyn. *My Life*. Los Angeles: Sun & Moon, 1987.

Kamenetz, Rodger. *The Jew in the Lotus: A Poet's Rediscovery of Jewish Identity in Buddhist India*. New York: Harper Collins, 1994.

Kuszai, Joel, ed. *poetics@*. New York: Roof, 1999.

Lacoue-Labarthe, Philippe. *Poetry as Experience*. Trans. By Andrea Tarnowski. Stanford: Stanford University Press, 1999.

Lazer, Hank. *Opposing Poetries—Volume 2: Readings*. Evanston: Northwestern, 1996.

Mallarmé, Stéphane. "Le Livre, Instrument Spirituel" ("The Book, Spiritual Instrument"). Trans. By Michael Gibbs, pages 14 – 20, in *the book, spiritual instrument* (eds. Rothenberg and Guss), New York: Granary Books, 1996.

Naylor, Paul. *Book of Changes*. Lambertville, NJ: Quarry Press, 2000.

Rothenberg, Jerome and David Guss, editors. *the book, spiritual instrument*. New York: Granary Books, 1996.

Scroggins, Mark. "John Taggart." *Dictionary of Literary Biography 193: American Poets Since World War II (Sixth Series)*, edited by Joseph Conte. Detroit: Gale Research Press, 1998: 335 – 344.

Taggart, John. "Chicago Breakdown." (essay/lecture/journal notes) Fall 1999. 17 pages. Unpublished manuscript.

———. "Introduction," pages 5 – 7, in *To Construct a Sculpture*, by Bradford Graves. Brooklyn & New York City: Meeting Eyes Bindery & Poetry New York, 1999.

———. "The Spiritual Definition of Poetry," in *Songs of Degrees: Essays on Contemporary Poetry and Poetics*. Tuscaloosa: University of Alabama Press, 1994: 14 – 24.

———. *When the Saints*. Jersey City: Talisman House Publishers, 1999.

Tarn, Nathaniel. "Fragment of a Talk on Octavio Paz, Anthropology, and the Future of Poetry." *Jacket* #9 (1999/electronic journal/ Australia): http:/www/jacket.zip.com.au/jacket09/

Sacred Forgery and the Grounds of Poetic Archaeology: Armand Schwerner's *The Tablets*

The final edition of Armand Schwerner's *The Tablets* arrives as a valuable, important book, extending and challenging our conceptions of poetry, reading, certainty, completeness, and instructing us in the value of humor and the centrality of various modes of not-doing. The National Poetry Foundation has done a beautiful job of producing this book, giving it a properly large page-size format, pricing the book reasonably, and including an excellent, helpful CD recording of Schwerner's superb reading of a great many of *The Tablets*.

The Tablets exists at a timely and seemingly timeless intersection of the written/visual and oral/performative. It is a profoundly moving and flawed project, at once greatly humorous, learned, and outrageous. When I call Schwerner's great work "flawed," I do so with the awareness that *all* writing is inevitably flawed. But, as part of my taking this work seriously, I do wish to consider what I see to be some of the limitations of Schwerner's work as well as the great accomplishment of it.

The Tablets is, among other things, a key book in the work of a particular generation—a group of writers/thinkers that includes David Antin, Jackson Mac Low, Jerome Rothenberg, and Dennis Tedlock. These writers extend the encyclopedic impulse of modernism—the beginning globalism of Pound and Eliot and Olson—to make (in Robert Duncan's words) "a symposium of the whole," and an ethnopoetics pursued with a rigor, intelligence, curiosity, and passion that has changed forever the scope of poetry, particularly in the United States. Set beside the anthologies, translations, and books of poems by these writers, much contemporary poetry, particularly the poetry of official verse culture, is readily seen to be minor, narrowly conceived, and claustrophobic in its scope and ambition.

Schwerner began work on *The Tablets* in 1968, and, as Arthur Sabatini notes, Schwerner's career "is a paradigm of the way, during the past three decades, poets and poetry have become enmeshed in the many forms of discourse and performance that characterize contemporary art" (DLB, 243). In an interview with Ed Foster, Schwerner describes the incident that triggered the conception of *The Tablets*:

> ...the thing that spawned the beginning stages of that work occurred when I was a graduate student working in the Columbia Library. At the end of one of the long stacks I stuck out my arm to rest it on one of the shelves for a moment, looked at what I was covering and there was a large format edition of Samuel Noah Kramer's translation and transliteration from the Sumerian. I interpreted my experience as an omen. I have never forgotten the power of that initial charge. Charge in both senses, both electricity *and* the responsibility for a task I hadn't yet formulated. (T, 43)

For me, *The Tablets* opens up tremendously and extends its scope of consciousness in crucial ways with *Tablet XXVII* (the final Tablet) and with the concluding section, *Tablets Journals/Divagations*. Finished in the last year of Schwerner's life, *Divagations* constitutes one-fifth of the final book. Perhaps it is fitting that a book such as *The Tablets*, with its key figure of the Scholar/Translator, would conclude with such a superb commentary on a commentary, an extended meditation less ruled by the governing conceptions of the rest of the work itself. For me, this Apocrypha becomes the heart of the text itself, where we learn most passionately and exactly what is at stake in *The Tablets*. Schwerner was quite aware of the significant departure and "violation" involved in adding the *Divagations* (which first appeared in the Atlas Press 1989 edition of *The Tablets*, and now appears in a much more extended version in the new National Poetry Foundation edition):

> For so many years, I'd been deeply convinced that everything should go into the poem, that there should be no need for external divagations. And then, years after that profoundly

held belief, I added "Divagations," a long section of citations
and commentary as an appendix to Tablets I – XXVII. (T, 30)

The *Divagations* section gives Schwerner an occasion to ask
fundamental questions and to state fundamental premises (of the
work and of human being). Schwerner asks, for example, "is man
the only animal that laughs?" (129). That laughter is, of course, an
essential feature of the knowledge embodied in *The Tablets*—and
it is an action that anyone who hears Schwerner read aloud will
inevitably come to know (as I did when I first listened to a tape recording of *The Tablets* in 1972). Schwerner writes *The Tablets* in a
manner consistent with a key maxim: "the greatest daring is in resisting what comes easily" (129). Though, as I will argue throughout
this essay, that *via negativa* ultimately limits the pleasures available
in *The Tablets*, I don't mean to suggest that Schwerner should have
been striving for a sustained lyricism throughout. But his scrupulous
avoidance of various modes of "accomplished" composition severely
limits the modes of beauty allowed to take up residence in the text.

   While Schwerner asserts that "there is no nuclear self," in
Divagations there *is* one, even if and as it is a self that recognizes
the multiple and complex nature of selfhood. In places, Schwerner
is simply wise, as when he defines "Poetry as that playful and difficult activity which is a part of the life-effort to heal the self…"
(132), or when he suggests that "The Space inside the poem is the
necessary precondition for a perception of infinity" (133). It seems
to me that it is *Divagations* that enables such directness—a mode
of sporadic insight and (unmediated) didacticism which is *not* an
option in *The Tablets* (proper) due to the many layers of filtration
essential to the form of the work and to the partial nature of the
voices/scribes of the work.

   Schwerner is deeply concerned in his thirty-year work *not* to
make certain mistakes—mistakes that often (through arrogance
or egotism) characterize the most ambitious modernist works that
precede *The Tablets*. Even as he invents and investigates the ground
of human spirituality and ritual, Schwerner seeks in his work "the
avoidance of spiritual fascism" (T, 32). He has a fundamental ethical commitment to an epistemological incompleteness and to a
truthful inconclusiveness:

The Tablets are involved in wave after wave of denial about any significance in all the looking, checking, interpreting, which their own Scholar/Translator apparently embodies. Not only is there no there there, but the very bases for the ideas and constructions of joke or woes or civilized particularizations, these founder endlessly. No Kung-Fu-Tse behind the Poundian arras, no Anglo-Catholic deep thumpings to sadden the reader into a melting sense of loss to be overcome by the music of eternal verities behind the sucking sounds of the Waste Land. All is ego and all founders, although the Tablets' humor and litanies and erotic intensities go on in their susurrations on page after page of text. (T, 31)

Schwerner's great work constitutes a serious challenge—achieved, ironically, by an archaeological method of digging and probing—to the myth of depth. As Brian McHale wonders,

Sink a shaft into the psyche, the Freudian counsels, and in its depths you will find buried truths. Cut a trench into the ruins of the Unreal City, the middens of Gloucester, a northern bog, says the poet-archaeologist, and you will uncover our culture's mythic substrate, its authentic history, the ancestral mummy whose face you will recognize as your own. This myth of depth is itself one of the foundational fictions of (post)modern culture. But, whispers the trickster-archaeologist, what if the deep truths are really just another story? What if the ruins are only stage-sets or scale-models? What if the mummified face is really just another Piltdown skull, planted there for you to find? (T, 89)

Schwerner, as trickster-archaeologist, has, from the outset, built in that element of fabrication as essential to the documents, texts, pictographs, and rituals that we investigate in *The Tablets*. Of the various protagonists who inhabit *The Tablets*, Schwerner says,

The reader doesn't know whether they're telling a truth or their truth or aspects of social verity or as it were inventing parts of a world; you don't know whether they're the object of scribal emendations; you don't even know whether the whole sequence has any kind of verifiability. But the work doesn't exist in a realm of fantasy; there's too much deep structure of familiar archaeology and paleography for that easy course, and thus the work is continuously subject to anchoring constraints. (T, 35)

Schwerner concludes that

> In spite of the unverifiabilities the human figures are *there*. So the reader's constantly "inter," and as the Tibetan teacher Gampopa says, "irrigating one's confusions." And that's I think, the most consistent climate from which the need to write poetry comes. In any case mine. (T, 35)

For me, though, the activity of "irrigating one's confusions" is, in part, an *individual* story. Hence, my intense appreciation for the importance of *Divagations* in giving us another (more commonly individualized) location for the need and the activity of the text. As Brian McHale suggests,

> In place of a "direct" encounter with the past, there is a Chinese-box puzzle, in place of a primordial scene of archaeological insight, a game of hide-and-seek, in place of "knowledge," uncertainty, speculation, make-believe and trompe l'oeil effects. These are the kinds of epistemological cul-de-sacs into which the narratological structure of *The Tablets* leads us, and in which it abandons us. (T, 88)

But the primary artificer—the trickster-archaeologist-poet—does not stand apart from that experience of entering an epistemological cul-de-sac. *Divagations* gives us an opportunity to feel and see and hear Schwerner in that cul-de-sac too. His text, then, with the addition of *Divagations*, becomes a construction from which he too does not stand apart.

Above all else, *The Tablets*, as a conceptual site, represents Schwerner's deepest attempt to find a usable form—one that could

accommodate what he knew (and what he didn't know), one that
would be true to consciousness as we experience it. He writes,

> The modern, accidental form of Sumero-Akkadian tab-
> lets provides me with a usable poetic structure. They offer,
> among other things, ways out of closures—which I find
> increasingly onerous—as well as the expansion of the syn-
> tactical girdle of English. They also invite spontaneous pho-
> netic improvisations. The uses of the past, by means of these
> found archaic objects, are thus more than ironic and other
> than nostalgic. The context of sober translation creates a
> mode suitable for seductions by the disordered large which is
> the contemporary, and the narrative, which is out of honor
> in the most relevant modern poetry. The context also makes
> me feel comfortable in recreating the animistic, for which I
> have great sympathy [.] (134)

In fact, this may be a major contribution of modernism-extended by
Schwerner's generation: a serious quest for (invented) usable forms. I
think, for example, of Antin's talk-poems, or the various manifestations of Jerome Rothenberg's anthologies (as well as his marvelous
"total translations"), and John Cage and Jackson Mac Low's variously
constructed forms. This era of modernism-extended (from 1950 to
the present) may indeed be characterized by a quest to create non-
trivial forms that are responsive to a broad range of discoveries (in
many fields) and to extend the range of knowable poetries. These
practitioners of, to use David Antin's comprehensive term, "the language arts" make varieties of poetry that may offer a fit embodiment
of the complexities of human consciousness. Antin in particular
directs our attention to the centrality of collage as a formal principle
in the art of this century. Works such as *The Tablets* seem to me to
make the case for formal inventiveness itself—with collage as one
key technique but not necessarily as the most central—as the primary inherited activity (as much as any particular thematic or philosophical premise) from works such as *The Waste Land*, the *Cantos*,
Paterson, and from the serial formal inventiveness of Gertrude Stein.

    In the promotional materials that accompany *The Tablets*, a
claim is made for Schwerner's work in relation to other great twen-

tieth-century modernist poem-projects: "Worked on by Schwerner for over 30 years, *The Tablets* bears comparison to other great experimental sequences of our century: Pound's *Cantos*, Olson's *Maximus* poems, Williams's *Paterson*, Duncan's *Passages*, Zukofsky's *"A-".*" While one might be tempted to argue with the list of "greatest hits," arguing for the inclusion of works such Ronald Johnson's *ARK* and George Oppen's *Of Being Numerous*, it is more important to observe that Schwerner's *The Tablets* demonstrates a profoundly different relationship to "source" materials. Also, in overcoming some of the ego-based "deficiencies" of earlier great modernist texts, there is in *The Tablets* a Buddhistic reticence, an ethical not-doing, that is both admirable and a serious limitation on Schwerner's work. Perhaps there is a valid desire not to fall prey to a kind of masculine, display-bravura (as found especially in some of Pound and Olson's writing). But Schwerner's ego-reticence, which, to some extent, gives way in *Divagations*, combined with his distrust of poetic craft-on-display, means that there are far fewer (recognizably) "beautiful" passages in his major work than in those of his modernist precursors.

Oddly, Schwerner's encounter with and presentation of "archaic" materials is in perfect harmony with (and even somewhat dependent upon) contemporary technology. As Arthur Sabatini suggests, "a convenient and not wholly irrelevant analogy for Schwerner's poetry, writings, and performances is a hypertext program for computers" (DLB, 244). Schwerner's work embraces this odd conjunction of the pictographic past with the hypertextual present, and his method of textual creation makes substantial use of the layout and design capabilities of the computer. As Sabatini concludes, "that one would need a hypertext program (or its image) to return one to the original energies of the body, voice, song, spirit, writing, and the performance of the self and others is an irony for which there is not resolution—except, perhaps, in the always elusive realm of poetry itself" (DLB, 252).

Schwerner differs in essential ways from his modernist precursors in his use of and relationship to source materials. He observes:

> Eliot and Pound structured ironic and tragic commentaries by confronting past and present. Why not go further, I

thought, and recreate the past itself, in a series of subjectively ordered variations suggestively rooted in the archaic? (134)

Schwerner adds another layer to his work through "the further invention of a scholar-translator," a "fictive but oppressively present self" (134). The combination of an imagined limitation upon the archaic text (in translation) and the limitations of the at times annoying scholar-translator constitute, in my opinion, the heart of the conceptual flaws of *The Tablets*. While Schwerner's conception allows him to avoid certain "errors" of his modernist kin, his own grand project (prior to the composition of *Divagations*) is, in different ways, hamstrung. Even so, Schwerner is aware of a prime virtue of his imagined, archaic text and its ongoing interpretation-as-text. Quite clearly, *The Tablets* embodies and illustrates a fundamental question: "To what degree is any poem a translation, or a thereness?" (134).

At the heart of Schwerner's project is a refreshing seriousness, a passion for a kind of metaphysical and ethical honesty. There is, as well, a subdued or somewhat covert sense of crisis that energizes the work. Schwerner believes that "Poetry, as game, as act of faith, as celebration, as commemoration, as epic praise, as lyric plaint, as delight in pattern and repetition—poetry is in trouble." To which he adds, "Not any more trouble than the Earth, concepts of nobility and self-lessness, senses of utility, hope" (135). For Schwerner, as for many other adventurous late twentieth-century poets, our writing is situated within a serious crisis of representation. But Schwerner's sense of that crisis is much more encompassing than the aestheticized version that, in the name of a now old and quite standard but ever self-proclaiming "new" fragmentation, calls attention to the limitations of a self-expressive, conventionalized "realism." For Schwerner too, the cooptation and corruption of language (by advertising and other modes of manipulation that cast into doubt one's ability to trust words) poses a threat and leaves him longing for "a new language, one that we cannot speak, may not be able to speak, unseizable, pro-literating like the elementary particles in physics: no end to it: uncertain statistical places left from which to look at the negative-muons which are told by their uncertain traces" (136–137).

For Schwerner the complexity of adequate representation gets framed not so much in terms of an adequate picture or object but of an adequate medium for representing the dynamic interplay of mind and reality. For him, the central questions (and they are the defining questions for *The Tablets* as well) are:

> How will the mind work? By the eidetic confrontation of the "real"? The real changes. By feeling through Cassirer's moving elaboration of the primitive ethos as "the consanguinity of all living things"? Intermittently at best, and with the edges of despair for being so irrevocably far. The real changes. (136)

A concluding passage of Tablet XXVII gives us a complex, ritualized version of that world-language-person-mind interchange for which we are a point of intersection:

> so this world is the one
> it constitutes our food language-food we eat and we are
> translatable let's say equidistant from every point or we are
> a bloody loin of soul like them that's all right language-
>   cannibal bait (123)

Like the complex inter-relationships that the passage registers and that *The Tablets* make manifest, this particular passage is susceptible to many different readings as we decipher, interpret, translate, pull apart, reconstitute, and give voice to what goes with what.

It is, then, an odd faith that Schwerner brings to the poem, and to his poetic project: "Poetry is a body invested with rhythmic cells; it is neither the Way nor the object" (137). Particularly if one can resist the lure of using the poem as a site to display one's (personal) craft, mastery, or grace, the poem may become a treasured site for discovery. As Schwerner puts it, "The voices: the maker does not know the identity of a voice or many voices. They speak to him in a way he later discovers. The locus appears later" (136).

It is difficult for me to write about *The Tablets*. The gravity of the work, its seriousness, its high ethical endeavor, and its representation of nearly a lifetime's engagement all make any mode of evaluation (an inevitability of the assignment to write a review) one that ought properly to keep in mind those dimensions of the text under consideration. It doesn't help that the book's cover consists of a large photo of Armand Schwerner; the eyes of the author stare straight at you. For those of us who knew Armand and who are ourselves engaged in writing poetry, there is something of an accusation and a challenge in *The Tablets*. We feel too the inevitable sense of finality that accompanies this edition of *The Tablets*—an edition supervised and completed by Armand just prior to his death on February 4, 1999.

And yet that is the way it should be. Poetry is (among many things) a serious endeavor. That element of accusation should not be shirked. It is all too easy merely to become active in poetry: to read incessantly; to write steadily; to send poems out; to publish. In Armand's long work, I feel something akin to the call to self-accounting that I encounter in reading certain great works such as Thoreau's *Walden* or the end of Rilke's "Archaic Torso of Apollo" with its last line, perhaps emblematic for all truly serious works of poetry, "you must change your life." I want, then, to be fair to Armand and to the nature of *The Tablets*.

In criticizing Armand's work—in pointing to what I consider to be the text's limitations and deficiencies—I am not (merely) wishing that it had been or *should* have been otherwise. All of our writing has its limitations and its inevitable deficiencies. If any work of poetry were truly sufficient, it would be the *final* work. Perhaps all poems and all books of poetry are a working toward something. But I do, nonetheless, in the spirit of fairness and seriousness, wish to describe the parameters of self-imposed limitations that I encounter in *The Tablets*.

———

A governing anxiety of Armand's text stems from his own claim that "all concepts are misconceptions" (139). Such a position will inevitably produce a reticence about many modes of action, though concepts and forms can always be advanced as necessarily provisional and incomplete, or as ironized deeds (perhaps further ironized by the interpretive overlayering of the only partially insightful Scholar/ Translator). Armand creates a large text that exists within an ancient dialectical tension: "The archaic pre-Christian antinomies of *kenosis* and *plerosis*, emptying and filling, characteristic of early Middle Eastern civilizations, served largely as a generalized and suggestive context" (138). I suppose that what I'm saying throughout this review amounts to little more than a complaint that *kenosis* got too much of an upper-hand.

Clearly, Armand is perfectly aware of the hazards created by the recurring "interruptions" of the Scholar/Translator:

> The pain I felt when I interrupted a lyric song by any of my unknown archaic speakers by intercalating—or rather by finding necessary the presence of—the S/T's discursive, often apparently irrelevant comments, often wrongheaded inventions which nevertheless brought the reader into a consideration of the essential ambiguities of syntax, grammar and translation, a kind of undependable groundlessness of appearance. I remember part of me would almost agree with a hearer's wish that I omit the S/T's commentary as unnecessarily clotting; I'd almost want to accede. But precisely such ambiguities, left somewhat to integrally radiate, is useful work done. The thing is, I wanted not to separate the song from the entropic world. This *and* that. (157)

Armand, then, retains an ethical and decisive commitment to the "realism" of the Scholar/Translator's interruptive function. My own critique is not directed strictly at the interruptive nature of the Scholar/Translator. The fact that *all* modes of writing in *The Tablets*—the Scholar/Translator's *and* the "original" imagined/fabricated archaic texts—are filtered through a preconceived limitation and a predetermined inadequacy leave me hungry for the more author-empowered text that constitutes the concluding *Divagations*. I am interested finally in hearing *Armand* write and think (at *his* fullest—for even that fullness can be assumed to have its own qualities of incompleteness and emptying). Armand is a better poet than *The Tablets* shows. I know that that is a viewpoint that would have drawn

his contempt—as having missed the point and nature of the text's
creation. But, for me, too much of the intelligence and beauty of *The
Tablets* exists *outside* the text itself—in the form, ethics, and wisdom
of its compositional methodology—and not enough in the text itself,
not enough in the primary text itself.

Having raised this objection, let me hasten to add that I am
perfectly respectful of some of the sources and reasons for Armand's
textual decisions, including Armand's fundamental subverting of
any writing that would have an unmediated status as the "primary"
or "original" text. *The Tablets* is very much a thinking about thinking. Like his friend David Antin—particularly in *Meditations* and in
the three decades of talk-poems—Armand too draws on the work of
Descartes, Montaigne, Pascal, and La Rochefoucauld as key prede-
cessors. Like Antin, Schwerner explores how we think, and Armand
is interested in making a writing that does not present thinking in
a merely decorous, trivially accomplished, trivially "well-crafted," or
formulaic manner.

There is immense glory in what *The Tablets* is. As Armand puts it
in one of the most essential fragments: "…crossroads where biology,
philosophy, linguistics…intersect" (147). For me, that intersection
is greatly enhanced by the extraordinary meditation of the concluding (though not conclusive) *Divagations*. Among other things,
Divagations is an intimate and tremendously intelligent meditation
on a writer's life. Armand is beautifully lucid and honest about the
forces at war within him: "There's a negative force within me that
wants to stop writing this, to go elsewhere, to leave as in every ses-
shin I've ever suffered through, almost every group I've involved myself with" (144). Rather than valorizing the isolato or critiquing the
superficialities of group identifications, Armand analyzes unsparingly
his own complex (and mostly unfulfilled) needs for recognition:

> The work on *The Tablets* was not the result of a "divine
> madness"; it involved clear thinking in radiant context of
> self-confidence and aloneness. Somehow, in some rock-
> bottom way I didn't care about the introjected authorities
> in my mind, the success-ghosts, the lyrics of reward-mon-
> gers—I cut through them. But I assumed there would be a
> worldly reward, a permanent order of recognition, a clear

and continuous placement of my work in the critical adum-
brations of the establishing world. To live awaredly in that
world, no longer envisaging myself as say Emily or Melville
in his last 30 dog years, is the outer mandala, the inner
and secret ones potential. Fear's part of all mandalas; my
fear of being out-there comes from a tactician's pettiness.
Awareness of literary politics is not the same as craven submission; since I'm not craven, but thirsty for *la gloire*, I've
sometimes elected withdrawal. (144–145)

In spite of my criticisms, *The Tablets* and Armand Schwerner
clearly merit *la gloire*. Armand has said that his poetry "embodies the complex and obdurate persistencies of soul-making" (DLB,
250). Arthur Sabatini concludes that "*The Tablets* are spectacu-
larly representative of Schwerner's learning and understanding, as
well as his artistry, joy, and fearlessness" (250). At times, as I read
Divagations, I feel like the adequate Scholar/Translator that I have
longed for throughout *The Tablets* emerges in that final section.
Perhaps the more annoying qualities of the Scholar/Translator get
on our nerves because, in truth, the reader's consciousness is more
similar to that S/T's fumbling efforts than to the more comprehensive (though ethically self-limiting) consciousness of the poet
himself. As Michael Heller observes, "The Scholar/Translator seems
to be performing *our* work, *our* questing, seeking to becalm himself
by creating some form of tranquilizing story, some encompassing 'translation' of the archaic culture under hand which will give
him certainty by explaining the present" (T, 84). The final voice
of *Divagations*—what I think of as the ruminations of a super-
Scholar/Translator—offers readings and conjectures, interpretations
and contextualizings that are wise, beautiful, and provocative. What
emerges with this final publication of *The Tablets* is a kind of double
palimpsest which includes the source-text and its multi-layered
markings and translations along with the written over journey of
Schwerner's own remarkable career. As Sabatini concludes, "there is
an intimate, felt voice throughout the text and an inescapable depth
created by Schwerner's pursuits in this primordial, archetypal, spiritual, and artistic journey. In this dual sense, *The Tablets* are a pa-

limpsest that reveal all the technical skills, themes, and intellectual concerns of Schwerner throughout his career" (252).

The Tablets represents one of the most important documents— called "poetry"—in the latter half of this century. It is a composition that is, in the words of the Scholar/Translator, a "sacred forgery" (98). It is also, as Michael Heller concludes, "one of the great ironic workings of the scholarly quest for self-knowledge, a masterwork of what we might call 'experimental scholarship'" (T, 83). For me, with the addition of *Divagations*, the flaw or error of an overly absolute erasure of self-immediacy gets beautifully corrected. Schwerner concludes by locating himself with us in the epistemological cul-de-sac of his great work. *The Tablets* thus takes its place beside a range of important poetry-archaeologies of this century which "play out some highly important, real, revelatory skirmishes of soul and dream and cultures" (T, 31). Finally, it is a work that merits and rewards our extended consideration.

Works Cited

All passages for which there is only a page number (but no abbreviation) refer to Armand Schwerner, *The Tablets* (Orono, Maine: The National Poetry Foundation, 1999).

DLB = Arthur Sabatini, "Armand Schwerner," *Dictionary of Literary Biography* 165 (Detroit: Gale Research, 1996): 242–253.

T = *Talisman: A Journal of Contemporary Poetry and Poetics* #19 (Winter 1998/99), Armand Schwerner Issue (pages 30–116), particularly Edward Foster, "An Interview with Armand Schwerner," 30–44; Michael Heller, "The *Philoctetes* and *The Tablets*," 82–85; Brian McHale, "Topology of a Phantom City: *The Tablets* as Hoax," 86–89.

The Art and Architecture
of Holding Open:
The Radical Yes of *Architectural Body*

> But there is a turn with mortals when these
> find their way to their own nature.
> —Martin Heidegger, "What Are Poets For?"

In Stanley Kubrick's film *2001*, an ape-human picks up a long piece of bone and, with dramatic drumming music in the background, begins to use that bone as a tool, the ape-human completely absorbed in the ecstatic experience of using the tool to pound and to smash. A fragment of bone—in slow motion—drifts upward, and the camera cuts from the floating bone fragment to a space ship heading outward in space. In terms of human development, Kubrick shows us the absolute continuity of this lengthy time sequence. Once humans become tool users, there is an absolute and direct line that can be drawn from that initial use to the space ship. No new fundamental development in human consciousness is required to get from moment A to moment B; the first gesture of tool-using extends directly and logically to the flight of the spacecraft.

What might be the next primordially formative change in the nature of human being? Arakawa and Madeline Gins' *Architectural Body* places us in the midst of such a tradition of philosophical thinking. It is a question that is central, for example, to Heidegger's thinking and to Rilke's poetry. In *Sonnets to Orpheus*, Rilke's poem-series of fifty-five sonnets (written in February 1922), the poet asks us to "will transformation" (II, 12, l. 1); the means of doing so involves a renewed knowing, entering, and confronting of death:

> Be—and at the same time know the condition
> of not-being, the infinite ground of your deep vibration,
> that you may fully fulfill it this single time. (II, 13, ll. 9–11)

As Rilke describes it, ours is a history of daring and of venturing, moving out of loosened clay to a sketching of the gods, and, as Rilke suggests, moving toward a possible fulfillment of the terms of being human through a self-surpassing change:

> We, a generation through thousands of years: mothers
> and fathers, more and more full of the future child,
> so that someday, surpassing, it may overwhelm us, later.
>
> (II, 26, ll. 9–11)

Heidegger, in "The Origin of the Work of Art," sees history as "the transporting of a people into its appointed task as entrance into that people's endowment" (77). Arakawa and Gins ask us to reconsider—indeed, inaugurate us into a reconceived version of—our species' endowment. They offer us a new sense of our founding by providing a new foundation for our thinking about what we are.

Heidegger's reading of Rilke (in "What Are Poets For?") turns our thinking about the foundation of the human toward the technological—a domain and an activity that both Rilke and Heidegger understand as tragic and as obscuring the foundations of our relationship to Being. Heidegger, reading Rilke, finds "a hint from the rising technology, directing it [human attention] toward those realms from which there could perhaps emerge a surpassing of the technical—a surpassing that would be primordially formative" (112). That is precisely what Arakawa and Gins point us toward: a *next* fundamentally different mode of human being.

For Heidegger, and for Arakawa and Gins, an inquiry into the nature of our being involves simultaneously an inquiry into the nature of our dwelling here. In "Building Dwelling Thinking," Heidegger establishes the proximity of those inquiries by etymological means:

> *Bauen* originally means to dwell. Where the word *bauen* still speaks in its original sense it also says *how far* the nature of dwelling reaches. That is, *bauen, buan, bhu, beo* are our word *bin* in the versions: *ich bin*, I am, *du bist*, you are, the imperative form *bis*, be. What then does *ich bin* mean? The old word *bauen*, to which the *bin* belongs, answers: *ich bin, du*

bist mean: I dwell, you dwell. The way in which you are and I am, the manner in which we humans *are* on the earth, is *Buan*, dwelling. (147)

Heidegger's investigation of *bauen* leads him to conclude that it means "to remain, to stay in a place," and that

> To dwell, to be set at peace, means to remain at peace within the free, the preserve, the free sphere that safeguards each thing in its nature. *The fundamental character of dwelling is this sparing and preserving.* (149)

Whereas for Heidegger dwelling essentially means "the stay of mortals on the earth" (149), for Arakawa and Gins—who have a similar understanding of the intimate relationship of building, dwelling, thinking, and being—the assumption of "mortal" as an essential feature of human being is a mistaken one. While they might share Heidegger's conclusion that "thinking itself belongs to dwelling in the same sense as building" (160), they think *building* and think *dwelling* toward the possibility of a primordially formative turn wherein *mortal* is no longer a governing presupposition.

How might we build or shape ourselves toward that emerging possibility? For Arakawa and Gins, that process of building—of self-lathing or of self-milling—begins as a rhetorical activity. We must build up our optimism; we must acknowledge our pessimistic, defeatist foundation:

> Without doubt, the human race had hideously acquiesced in regard to its own abysmal fate.... So unquestionably mortal are we that we have even come to call ourselves mortals, for God's sake.... A bunch of defeatists all. (xiv)

Arakawa and Gins choose and build their words carefully. They do not write "without a doubt"; they write "without doubt". And that is our problem: as a species we have been without doubt—we have proceeded "unquestionably"—along a defeatist path that assumes rather than engages our mortality. In a moment at once humorous and audacious, Arakawa and Gins suggest that we have done so "for God's sake."

Like that other great American manifesto of how to live, Henry David Thoreau's *Walden*, Arakawa and Gins' *Architectural Body* goads us, confronts us, cajoles us, persuades us. They ask us to examine and to re-think our most basic governing assumption: the terms of our own mortality. Like Thoreau, who wrote, "men labor under a mistake" (5), they conclude "that the whole crowd has it all wrong" (xiv). And like Thoreau, who wrote in *Walden* that "man's capacities have never been measured; nor are we to judge of what he can do by any precedents, so little has been tried" (10), Arakawa and Gins' insistence that we rethink our basic understandings of our existence has a contagious exuberance that derives from their awareness that we have not considered, from a non-defeatist viewpoint, who or what we might be.

Throughout their careers, as is amply shown in the retrospective (and prospective) *Reversible Destiny*, Arakawa and Gins have been engaged in training our methods and awareness of perception. *Architectural Body* constitutes a continuity and culmination of that project, the ultimate reconfiguring being one that fundamentally changes the nature of our being: "Three decades ago, by wedding the word *reversible* with the term *destiny*, a supposedly set-in-stone sequence of events, we announced a war on mortality. Reversible destiny was our first step into a crisis ethics" (xviii). In a fundamental sense, that activity—at times, as an instance of "defamiliarization," at others, of "transgressive" or "Socratic art"—lies at the heart of the making of art. Arakawa and Gins have moved from more specifically focused individual, discrete works of art to an architectural surround to an entire city as the scale and scope of their activities in perceptual training.

Architectural Body begins with a specific address: the book is addressed to and dedicated to "transhumans." It is a book addressed to what we will or might become. The logical outcome, or the outward projection, of Arakawa and Gins' work is a re-casting or re-configuring of human life. This new structuring of our life amounts to an autopoiesis. If we, of the present, are transitional—beings on the way toward a transhuman existence—then a work that urges us forward becomes the most essential kind of avant garde art, perhaps even a final avant garde, a horizon imagined, constructed, and inhabited that allows us passage into that (imagined and then realized) primordially formative change.

We are already edging toward that change. We are already becoming an increasingly prosthetic form of the human, extending our range and abilities through non-carbon complements, through digitized, compact surrogates, supplements, and enhancers. Arakawa and Gins take the dramatic step of thinking through this gradualism at its base, which, of course, means a confrontation with our mortality and our assumptions about the terms and ethics of existence.

To re-energize our living and its possibilities, and to counter an implicit or assumed defeatism, Arakawa and Gins ask us to consider "how to be most fully at the service of the body" (xi). The answer involves a seriousness of intent and a newly imagined outcome.

Architectural Body takes its place as a central philosophical text (as well as a manifesto or provocation). It is a work in the spirit of Heidegger's recurring insistence that we re-think our knowledge and lack of knowledge regarding the fundamental term "being." Similarly, Arakawa and Gins ask us to confront the fact that as a species humans must return to "the nature of itself as the central problem" (xvii). Linked to Heidegger's insistence on a renewed awareness and understanding of "being," Arakawa and Gins add, "Figuring ourselves out must include determining what coheres as sentience" (xii).

As Heidegger established a critique of western metaphysics—as a philosophical tradition built upon an incomplete and repressed non-understanding of "being"—Arakawa and Gins, similarly, require us to begin by confronting the fact that we do not know what we are:

> Who or what are we as this species? Puzzle creatures to ourselves, we are visitations of inexplicability. What is in fact the case? We must surely go to all possible lengths to find out what we exist in regard to....We, the members of this species, have thus far failed to come up with a set of explanatory statements that could be universally countenanced as the definitive figuring out of ourselves. (xii)

We are figures sited in figuration who need figuring out. The figuring out will be artful. How we have learned to make and to inhabit art will help us in this figuring out. As we will see, the ability to exist in a state of negative capability will assist us in the requisite courage to admit what we don't know and to imagine (and, ultimately, to construct) what we might be. Autopoeisis as a key architectural skill should invoke what we have learned and are learning about the more finite construction of poems.

"The nature of itself as the central problem" (xvii)—in asking that we think, with *urgency* and with *emphasis*—about the nature of our species, Arakawa and Gins decisively open us toward the draft of a new premise, initially posed as a question: "What if it turned out that to be mortal was not an essential condition of our species?" (xviii).

While such thinking is relatively rare within the traditions of philosophy and art (with the exception of the imagination of *the work of art* [rather than the artist] achieving immortality), it is a line of thinking quite fully realized in the genre of science fiction. Notable instances include Arthur C. Clarke's *2001* (the concluding entry into a new realm of being) as well as his earlier *Childhood's End* (with much more attention paid to the emotional repercussions for the parents' generation as they witness the next generation make the transition to a radically changed mode of being), as well as the more recent writings of Octavia Butler (particularly *Wild Seed* and *Mind of My Mind*).

The concept of the landing site becomes a key point of intersection through which Arakawa and Gins are able to link their lifelong artistic work with a philosophical project of re-thinking the nature of human life (in our intimate and perpetually reciprocal relationship to our surroundings). The landing site names the place of our ongoing (and often unacknowledged) perceptual activity, the site by which and in which we imagine and construct our being and our being-in-the-world:

> ...a landing site is but a neutral marker, a simple taking note of, nothing more. When how the world is apportioned out is translated into landing sites, all stays the same, touched but

untouched. A person parses the world at any given instant
into particular distributions of landing sites... (6)

The landing site is "a heuristic device ... capable of reading what
else has been and is being apportioned out" (9). Think of the landing site as constituting a feedback loop, a location and a method
for achieving self-awareness (of our processes of self and self-world
construction), and as the locale for refiguring what we are. It is via
the landing site that Arakawa and Gins' thinking "rhymes" with
the making and experiencing of experimental or innovative art.
Defamiliarization—a seeking after states of intensified awareness of
consciousness and of our perceptual activities and assumptions—invokes an opportunity for new possibilities—for a heuristics—of the
fundamental terms and experiences of human being.

　　The landing site—as it becomes a place for learning an attitude
toward perception, a location for developing a craft of open attentive
awareness—is positioned in Arakawa and Gins' thinking for a maxi-
mum (though muted) resonance with our relationship to particularly
challenging works of art. Arakawa and Gins focus our attention on
learning to hold open that particular moment of intensified nonresolvability—a phenomenon common both to aesthetic experience
(our experience of certain works of art) and of those rare instances
when we step back from and observe and analyze our emerging perceptions and orderings of the external world:

> A landing-site configuration forms, as a heuristic device,
> when the continual symbolizing of a symbolizing creature
> ... becomes slightly muted or is put on hold for a bit [.]...
> A neutral stance asks that nonresolvable issues be kept on
> hold—fluidly and flexibly on hold—right out there in the
> world where they occur; it asks as well that they be held
> open and be made to open still further to yield additional
> information about what is at issue. (22)

Such a phenomenology—of sought for and maintained openness,
of an appreciation of the importance of the moment of nonresolvability—indeed bears a close relationship to the frame of mind
sought in *zazen* (Buddhist sitting meditation) and an uncanny rela-

tionship as well to the poet John Keats' description and definition of negative capability: "that is, when a man [sic] is capable of being in uncertainties, mysteries, doubts, without any irritable reaching after fact and reason."[1]

As Arakawa and Gins develop their sense of the landing site experience—a development which draws on their many years of art-making—the phenomenology that emerges extends a level of detail highly pertinent to the experiences of poem-making and of reading or entering the emerging constructed world of the poem as a new language grid:

> Here is what architecture means to us: *a tentative construct-ing toward a holding in place.* Walk into this building and you walk into a purposeful guess. The built world floats a hypothesis or two as to how and by what the apportioned out comes to be everywhere, the everywhere. (23)

So too is the poem—particularly of the open field variety practiced over the last fifty or more years by poets such as Robert Creeley, Larry Eigner, Robert Duncan, Ronald Johnson, Susan Howe, and many others—a testing out of a fabricated design of words, of words in white space, of a form of plausible and unique assembly. The poem itself—the new poem, the poem that risks or ventures a new architecture—is an essential building, a version of Heidegger's lan-guage as the house of being, a place within which we are encouraged to enter and hold open an alerted and attentive consciousness in a site of nonresolvability. As Arakawa and Gins describe it—a descrip-tion equally applicable to the architectural project of *Architectural Body* and to the deliberate construction of the open field poem—the architecture or hypothesis (or poem) "constructed to exist in the tense of *what if,* it presents itself as intentionally provisional, replac-ing definite form with tentative form, the notion of a lasting struc-ture with that of an adaptive one" (29).[2]

---

1 John Keats, Letter to George and Thomas Keats, December 21, 1817.

2 For a detailed study of "a myth of immediacy located in the making of the poem" (411), see my essay "Poetry and Myth: The Scene of Writing, Thinking As Such," Chapter Twelve in *Lyric & Spirit.*

The word *stanza*—a key unit in the poem's construction—means *room*, and the poem as house resembles the house described in *Architectural Body*: "This house is a tool, a procedural one … [that] examines and reorders the sensorium" (30). It is the site for invoking that examination and potential reordering. The poem, perhaps like Arakawa and Gins' house, invokes that Socratic or meditative (or negative capability) activity by means of altering our relationship to time and to the ordering of our perceptions. To say that the landing site experience is marked by a slowing down of temporal experience only begins to hint at the fundamental changes in perceptual processing that occur. The implicit closeness of architectural site and text becomes explicit in *Architectural Body*: "If architectural procedures serve as the words of a built discourse, then tactically posed surrounds, combining these procedures as they do, are its phrases, sentences, paragraphs, and texts" (57).

Arakawa and Gins thus choose to reorient architecture, from permanence or durability as a guiding feature to a preference for the provisional, the hypothetical, the heuristic, and the tentative: "we have chosen tentativeness as organizing principle in our practice[;] …it is necessary to construct architectural works that reflect bioscleave's intrinsic tentativeness" (49). Such reversal of the nature of architecture points toward the fact that "thus far only nomads have held architecture to be as a matter of course tentative" (49).

Architectural Body reads like a guide book offering not simply exhortations but advice on how to seek, promote, and maintain that landing site experience of a holding open:

> *Do not mar tentativeness. One ought not to try and hold onto what one cannot hold onto. How to swim in tentativeness. How to hold tentativeness in (its/your) shape. Do not be greedy: do not try to hold onto too much. What holds or registers as tentativeness, that great on-to-the-next…* (84 – 85)

Reiterating the base of architectural activity, Arakawa and Gins establish their investigative procedures as at once philosophical, aesthetic, and ethical:

> Performing an architectural procedure, a person launches
> an inquiry-on-the-go into her own constituent factors.
> …Architectural procedures disclose, highlight, and explicate
> the tentative steps by which an organism maintains herself as
> a person. (73)

As with innovative art (which breaks the spell of habit and of the
"natural"), Arakawa and Gins link their mode of heuristic architecture to a life of inquiry and to a process refiguring the terms of our
lives, presenting

> Architecture as the supreme context for the examined life,
> a stage set for body-wide thought experiments. With archi-
> tectural procedures prodding the body to know all that it
> is capable of, this becomes an intrusive and active stage set.
> The body must either escape or "reenter" habitual patterns of
> action—habitual actions that have customized life into only
> a few standard patterns. Upon the body's mastering new pat-
> terns of action, bioscleave emerges reconfigured. (62)

The hope, perhaps utopian, perhaps realizable, of such activity is for
a renewed and renewing questioning of habit and of defeatist assumptions: "Exhorted and cajoled by their town, by virtue of being
gently constrained by its features and elements, to perform architectural procedures, people work and play at figuring out what in the
world they could possibly be" (61).

The recurring tone of *Architectural Body* is one of audacious optimism. Like *Walden* where Thoreau announces, "I do not propose to
write an ode to dejection, but to brag as lustily as chanticleer in the
morning, standing on his roost, if only to wake my neighbors up"
(84), Arakawa and Gins' book is similarly a call to humanity to wake
up: "Once people realize that the human race has not yet availed
itself of its greatest tool for learning how not to die, they will cease
being defeatists in the matter" (xi). The book is an invitation for us
to reinvent ourselves: "It will be a way to undo, loosening to widen
and re-cast, the concept of person" (xi–xii). Arakawa and Gins write
with a reassuring calm and confidence. They believe and they ask us
to believe that "the architecture we speak of in this book is within

our species' reach" (xi) and that we can "reconfigure supposed inevitability" (55). Their book constitutes nothing less than "an open
challenge to our species to reinvent itself" (xviii).

Thoreau wrote *Walden* to inspire others to live their own version
of a deliberate life—to suck the marrow out of life, to question fundamentally how to go about living so as not to give away our time in
labor without purpose, to realize that the possibility of a rich life did
not depend upon a level of elaborate material possessions. Thoreau
realized that the chief enemy of an intense, realized life was our own
laziness, our own defeatism, our own persistent doubt that such a life
could be ours. Thoreau hopes to awaken us into an infinite wakeful-
ness: "We must learn to reawaken and keep ourselves awake, not by
mechanical aids, but by an infinite expectation of the dawn, which
does not forsake us in our soundest sleep" (90). Arakawa and Gins
realize that as a species we may be "oblivious to its own desperate-
ness" (xvi)—a kind of species-level version of Thoreau's "the mass of
men lead lives of quiet desperation" (8). But there is an equally pernicious individual level of despair that Arakawa and Gins confront
head on: our tendency, in the face of their own optimistic absolute
Yes, to say no to the greatest of our own possibilities. They assert:
"That mortality has been the prevailing condition throughout the
ages does not mean it will always have to be" (xv). They hope that
their own insistence, belief, and plan of action will inspire the rest of
us to resist our own habitual negativity:

> The effort to counter mortality must be constant, persistent,
> and total. The wish and will to do this must be in the air we
> breathe, having been built into the places within which we
> live and breathe.... We believe that people closely and com-
> plexly allied with their architectural surrounds can succeed
> in outliving their (seemingly inevitable) death sentences!
> (xv – xvi)

To counter our habit of saying No,[3] Arakawa and Gins insist that we
consider their Yes: "That life must not be extinguished, yes, that is

---

3 In making the connection between *Architectural Body* and Thoreau's
Walden, I am principally remarking on similarities of tone and of rhetorical strategy. But a more detailed comparison would also note that *Walden*

our teaching" (xviii). *Architectural Body* represents the building of a
radical Yes: "Can it be, then, that in architecture we have the means
to construct awareness on a new basis? Oh yes, that is what we have
begun to believe" (56). The book ends, appropriately, provisionally,
pointing toward its own and our continuation, an ending that quite
rightly has no concluding period:

TO BE CONTINUED…

To what else life will be able to originate as because of what
architecture will have become (100)

I suspect that each reader of *Architectural Body* struggles with a
recurring desire to say "no, this isn't possible; we can't *really* do
that.…" But Arakawa and Gins keep returning us to the fact that
we *don't know* what we are, and they keep asking us to reconsider
our deep-seated negative presupposition that we *must* be mortal
and that somewhat mortality itself is an essential feature of human being. *Architectural Body* instructs us in the art of construct-
ing tentativity—of building a holding open as a crucial element of
transforming human consciousness. The most important construction by Arakawa and Gins is the building of a place in our reading-
thinking-imagining-projecting consciousness for a line of thinking
that begins "what if.…" They describe their project as "revved and
revving; an amassing of the provisional; a ubiquitous piecing together" (65). I hear "revved and revving" as echoing the French *rêve*
(dream). The terms "revved and revving" suggest both the dream-
like quality *and* a mechanical, logical truth: the machinery of that

concludes with an immortality story about an egg deposited in a tree many
years ago. The tree was made into a leaf of a table and stood in a farmer's
kitchen for over sixty years when the egg hatches and a bug gnaws its way
out of the wood. Thoreau concludes, "Who does not feel his faith in a
resurrection and immortality strengthened by hearing of this? Who knows
what beautiful and winged life, whose egg has been buried for ages under
many concentric layers of woodenness in the dead dry life of society… may
unexpectedly come forth[.]… Only that day dawns to which we are awake"
(333). At the heart of both books is a compelling and enthusiastic belief in
the possibilities of human life, particularly once we set aside our habitual
and limiting defeatism.

which is revved up; an *engine* of imagination; an engine that powers us toward what we *can* be. And *if* we can hold open the opening they have constructed, *Architectural Body* will mark the dawning of an age in which humans think of ourselves as perhaps not necessarily mortal, and then, perhaps, as immortal...

DREAM

dream we then
of every step
the home our

body made of
interface as we
objectify ourselves bit

by bit reprogram
splice heal redirect
reconvene what we

arc tcxture of
tense repaired   dream
we then &

sing of our
new relations to
time milling ourselves

to new specifications
dream we then
of every step[4]   (August 2003)

----

4 "Dream" is from *Portions*, a series of 54 word poems composed from May 2001 through October 2006. Many of the poems written from 2001 to 2002 occurred during the period of time that, as co-editor of the Modern and Contemporary Poetics Series, I was corresponding with Arakawa and Madeline Gins about drafts, revisions, and editings of *Architectural Body*.

Works Cited

Arakawa and Madeline Gins. *Architectural Body*. Tuscaloosa, Alabama: University of Alabama Press, 2002.

Arakawa and Madeline Gins. *Reversible Destiny*. New York: Guggenheim Museum Publications, 1997.

Heidegger, Martin. *Poetry, Language, Thought*. "The Origin of the Work of Art," "What Are Poets For?," and "Building Dwelling Thinking." Trans. by Albert Hofstadter. New York: Harper & Row, 1971. 15–88, 89–142, 143–162.

Keats, John. *Selected Poetry and Letters*. Letter to George and Thomas Keats, December 21, 1817. New York: Holt, Rinehart and Winston, 1969. 307–309.

Kubrick, Stanley. *2001: A Space Odyssey*. Warner Studios, 1968.

Lazer, Hank. *Portions* (poems). In manuscript. May 2001–October 2006.

Rilke, Rainer Maria. *Sonnets to Orpheus*. Translated by M. D. Herter Norton. New York: W. W. Norton, 1942.

Thoreau, Henry David. *Walden*. Princeton, New Jersey: Princeton University Press, 1989.

Meeting in the Book:
Reading Edmond Jabès through
Rosmarie Waldrop's *Lavish Absence*[1]

Rosmarie Waldrop's *Lavish Absence*[2] is an extraordinary mixture of reminiscence, a study of the writing of the poet Edmond Jabès, reflections on the nature of poetry and translation, and a somewhat autobiographical piece of writing that gives us occasional glimpses into Waldrop's own development as a writer. I find Waldrop's book to be extremely engaging. Often, it feels perfectly continuous with Jabès's own writing, becoming an extension of or a meditation in the same environment of thinking. *Lavish Absence* represents an appropriately cross-genre and unclassifiable piece of writing—an appropriate portrait and homage to Edmond Jabès, one of the twentieth-century's important writers of "the book," a poet who, fittingly, died reading a book.

Perhaps best known for *The Book of Questions*, Jabès is a writer of considerable ambition—not personal ambition nor individual accomplishment, but ambition in writing a poetry that is unflinchingly fundamental and of metaphysical and spiritual consequence. As Waldrop summarizes:

> Energy, matter. It exists, but it becomes "world" only in the book, in language, which is created by man and at the same time creates him. "You who are the one who writes and is written" stands at the beginning of *The Book of Questions*. Faced with an undecipherable world we set out to create language, a place where human discourse can arise, and we come to exist as human beings; where, at the same time, we

---

1 This essay originally appeared under another title. See acknowledgements page.

2 Rosmarie Waldrop, *Lavish Absence: Recalling and Rereading Edmond Jabès* (Middletown, Connecticut: Wesleyan University Press, 2002).

can maintain a relation to what transcends us, the undeci-
pherable, the ultimate otherness, and speak to it under the
name of God. (1)

Jabès's writing addresses and embodies the most fundamental aspects
of human being, particularly the paradoxical nature of the human as
a being housed within the possibilities of language and, most often,
the accidents and wonders of *a* particular language. A particular as-
semblage of the possibilities of language is the book. For Jabès, "The
world exists because the book does" (15).

Such a pronouncement about the fundamental relationship of
world and book seems to echo the thinking of an important French
predecessor, Stéphane Mallarmé, particularly the famous beginning
of Mallarmé's "The Book, Spiritual Instrument": "A proposition
which emanates from myself—whether cited variously as my eulogy
or as blame—I claim it as my own together with all those that crowd
in here—affirms, in short, that everything in the world exists in order to end up as a book.[3]" Jabès's conception of the book can be seen
as a dialog with and a critique of Mallarmé, as Jabès himself indicates
in a 1980 interview with Philippe Boyer. Jabès refers to the ground
of his book as

> the desert, that infinity where there is nothing. It's funda-
> mentally the white page. My questioning, my obsession
> with the book, may very well have been born from that
> white page, which becomes written. I never thought of a
> Mallarméan book, of a totality. To think of a book in ad-
> vance, as a project, is to limit it. The book for me should be
> without limits, like the desert, thus an exploded book. (126)

Jabès critiques and rejects the Mallarméan conception of a grand
project—the book-architecture that Mallarmé refers to in a letter

---

3 Page 14, included in *The Book, Spiritual Instrument*, edited by
Jerome Rothenberg and David Guss (New York: Granary Books, 1996).
"The Book, Spiritual Instrument," translated and visually interpreted by
Michael Gibbs, pp. 14–20. The passages subsequently cited from Philippe
Boyer's 1980 interview with Edmond Jabés are also included in this same
volume, pp. 124–134, translated by Jack Hirschman.

to Théodore Aubanel (July 28, 1866), in which he foresees the need
for "twenty years for the five volumes of this Work.⁴" But Jabès's
book *does* resemble Mallarmé's as a site capable of incarnating the
complexities of our being, though Jabès insists simultaneously on
the need for the book to be exploded, broken, and questioned. Jabès
locates that conception of the book in a Hebrew (not a French) tradition of the book:

> My books are for me both a place of passage and the only
> place where I might live. Isn't it surprising that the word of
> God should come from the desert, that one of the names
> of God in Hebrew should be PLACE, and that the book
> should have been lived as the place of the word by the Jews
> for millennia? But at the same time I don't accept the book
> as it is. I believe that the refusal is what one also finds in the
> Jewish tradition.
> The Hebrew people obliged Moses to break the tablets.
> The origin of the Book therefore comes to pass by a break-
> age. (Boyer, 129)

Waldrop, in *Lavish Absence*, does not really address the relationship
of Jabès's thinking about the book to Mallarmé's, focusing instead
more steadily on Jabès's Jewish sense of textuality, and on the implications and nature of the book. Waldrop writes,

> It is language, the book, that enables us to perceive—and to
> live. It is our universe to the point where we ourselves meta-
> morphose into the word. "I took you in as a word," the nar
> rator says to Yaël. And Jabès to Marcel Cohen: "We become
> the word that gives reality to the object, to the being." (15)

As Waldrop notes throughout *Lavish Absence*, Jabès places his faith
in the efficacy and accuracy of the fragmentary: "'The fragment, the
exploded book, is our only access to the infinite,' Edmond Jabès says
in conversation after conversation. And writes: 'Only in fragments
can we read the immeasurable totality'" (18). Here, perhaps, in a re-

---

4 *Stéphane Mallarmé: Selected Poetry and Prose*, edited by Mary Ann
Caws (New York: New Directions, 1982), p. 85.

jection of a totalizing book (or of a book that would achieve closure)
lies Jabès's fundamental difference from Mallarmé's conception of
the book, though the radically dispersed textuality of Mallarmé's *Un
Coup de Dés* should call into question any such simple conclusion.

Waldrop herself deserves considerable praise for her translations
of Jabés's writing, for making such an important writer available to
those of us who cannot read French fluently, and for the heroism
of her persistence. When she began to translate Jabès, the response
from publishers was hardly overwhelming: "I had translated about
fifty pages and sent them with a description of the book, to twenty
American publishers. All declined on the grounds that translations
had always lost them money" (5). Eventually, Waldrop translated
fifteen volumes of Jabès's writing. To her credit, Waldrop realizes the
inadequacy of any translation, and as she re-reads Jabès, she finds
key sentences that, thirty years later, she would have translated differently (now that her understanding, after thirty years' reflection,
has changed):

> I look at my translation: "The book never actually surren-
> ders." This now seems inadequate. The adverbial form weak-
> ens the statement, makes us read over it rather than pause to
> ponder its strangeness and implications. In 1973, I did not
> see this sentence as I see it today. This pleases me in as far as
> it shows my reading and interpretation are not frozen. (138)

Waldrop's consideration of the complexities of translation inevitably becomes a thinking about the nature of language. She understands and takes some pleasure in the fact that language—in translation, but also in the "primary" act of writing—exceeds our control
of it, and "that language is not necessarily a tool we can simply
'use'" (100). Waldrop's philosophy of translation resembles Walter
Benjamin's, concurring with his conclusion that a literary work's "essential quality is not statement or the imparting of information" (7).
For Waldrop, such understandings do not lead to the more customary laments about the impossibilities and woeful imperfections of
translation. For example, rather than seek a translation that perfects
an imagined harmonious relationship of sound and sense, Waldrop
realizes (and confirms by way of Giorgio Agamben) that poetry

often lives in the particularities of a disagreement or productive tension and discord between sound and meaning. Waldrop writes of Jabès: "His aim is not to invert the traditional hierarchy of *sense* over sound, but to establish parity between them, or, rather, to establish a dynamic relation between language and thinking, where the words do not express pre-existing thoughts, but where their physical characteristics are allowed to lead to new thoughts" (70).

Such thinking about language and the word leads, in part, to an endless process of commentary and interpretation: "'Our lot is to interpret an unreadable world.' 'In the beginning is hermeneutics,' repeats Jacques Derrida" (24). Hence, for Jabès the centrality of questioning: "The Jew has for centuries questioned his truth which has become the truth of questioning" (26). But an even more interesting consequence of Jabès's sense of the word is a profoundly compelling notion of the complexities, motions, and exhilarations of reading:

> "The name of God is the juxtaposition of all the words in the language," Edmond Jabès reminds Marcel Cohen. "Each word is but a detached fragment of that name."
>
> This Kabbalistic idea means that breaking open words and recombining their letters is neither just fun nor impious. It is not even just the Kabbalistic tradition of "traveling inside the word." For Edmond Jabès, this method "permits a rediscovery, a rereading of the word. One opens a word as one opens a book: it is the same gesture." More, it is creation in the sense of enacting the possible. (13)

Attention to the word leads to some remarkable perspectives: "According to Kabbalistic tradition this pure spiritual light of the first day *was*, but did not remain. Where did it go? Into the Torah. That is, into the word" (151).

Jabès's thinking about the nature of the word, though, inevitably leads to a consideration of his own complicated relationship to two key words: "Jew" and "God." Jabès—who lived his life in Paris in exile from his native Egypt—carries the notions of otherness and exile into what Waldrop calls "the double isolation of the *unbelieving* Jew" (3), a description that from my readings of Derrida's work of the past

twenty years also has important applications to Jacques Derrida. For
Jabès, the term "Jew" becomes a term of fundamental otherness:

> The Jew has been persecuted for being "other." But "other-
> ness" is the condition of individuation, the condition of be-
> ing set apart from the rest of creation in the glorious—and
> murderous—species of humankind and, in addition, set
> apart from our fellow humans as individuals, always "other."
>   Judaism: a paradoxically collective experience of indi-
> viduation. Exemplary of the human condition. (3)

Jabès's sustained, intensely spiritually engaged writing—of a professed nonbeliever, of a professed atheist—establishes, oddly, a
powerful relationship to the most fundamental issues and questions
of belief, of the divine, of our complicated and barely expressible
relationships to various abstractions that bear down on our lives with
an invisible intensity. His peculiar relationship to God is at the heart
of his writing:

> I ask Edmond Jabès:
> "You say you are an atheist. How can you constantly write of
>   God?"
> "It's a word my culture has given me."
> Then he expands:
> "It is a metaphor for nothingness, the infinite, for silence,
> death, for all that calls us into question. It is the ultimate
> otherness." Or, as he puts it later, in the conversations with
> Marcel Cohen: "For me the words 'Jew' and 'God' are, it is
> true, metaphors. 'God' is the metaphor for emptiness; 'Jew'
> stands for the torment of God, of emptiness." (11)

I find Jabès's writing—and Derrida's too—to be the most important religious writing of our time. Yet I find myself wondering
how that comes to be: how a non-believing Jew, an atheist, writes a
poetry (or, truly, a generically unclassifiable writing) that has such
a powerful capacity to engage and to instruct. Perhaps Jabès's writing demonstrates to us—in book after book—how inadequate and
crude terms such as "belief" and "non-belief" are, and that while

Jabès may be classified as being a "non-believing Jew" and an "athe-ist," the opposing qualities of belief are, throughout his writing, of equal intensity. Perhaps what matters, then, is the intensity (and credibility and the nuanced nature) of Jabès's relationship to these fundamental portals of "Jew" and "God," and in this regard his writ-ing is unsurpassed. I sometimes suspect (or entertain the thought) that for Jabès (and for Derrida as well) a direct or simple profession of belief, particularly a profession that assumed a static or definitive quality, would not only be a betrayal of the fundamentals of their thinking and writing and of their profound sense of thinking as al-ways being *in motion*, but also a violation of an orthodox interpreta-tion of the commandment prohibiting one to have or worship any false images of the divine. For such a fixity of belief carries with it the hazard of actually standing between one and one's relationship to the divine by becoming a sign or site or formulation that one mis-takenly substitutes for that engagement.

The qualities of exile, of otherness, of removal, of being beside that recur in Jabès's writing have their foundation (in addition to Jabès's personal, biographical experience) in Jewish history and in Kabbalistic interpretation. When Waldrop was talking to Jabès about the Kabbalah, at one point she reports,

> Edmond seems not to be listening. Then, after some si-lence, begins to talk about the concept of *simsum*, which arose in Lurianic Kabbalism around the time of the expul-sion of 1492. The creation occurs when God voluntarily contracts himself into nothingness to make room for the world to emanate from him. A projection of exile onto the cosmic plane. (128)

In a passage cited by Waldrop, Marjorie Perloff declares, "Language is the new Spiritus Mundi!" (87). Perhaps what writing such as Jabès's demonstrates, is that while indeed it may be true that the attention of poets has shifted to the operations and idiosyncrasies of language itself—and that language has become the site wherein spiritual relationships (or relationships generally to the numinous) have been enacted—we may also be gradually backing into renewed relationships with older modes of that Spiritus Mundi as we've found that a devotion to language as an end in itself has its own problems, limitations, self-indulgences, romanticizings, and evasions.

Waldrop's wonderful book entertains us as well, by taking this daunting poet and humanizing Edmond Jabès through the intimacy, care, and candor of her portrait of him:

> I had half expected a severe ascetic. I come to know a man with an enormous sense of humor, a man who loves food, tells jokes, who at the drop of a hat improvises parodies and skits, who plays the clown for his grandchildren. *Faire l'idiot*, he calls it. A man who cultivates lightness because he knows gravity? (5)

One important dimension of *Lavish Absence* becomes the intimate sense we get for Jabès's daily life. When Rosmarie and Edmond reflect on their first meeting, Rosmarie also suggests, "I guess we met in *The Book of Questions*." Edmond adds, "We are still meeting in the book" (57). Such dialogues allow us to realize that indeed through reading we *do* meet in books—with an intimacy and depth peculiar to the experience of poetry. An unusual and intimate (and often unacknowledged) friendship—not simply among the living, but also between the living and the dead—occurs in *this* book, and Waldrop's *Lavish Absence* offers an affectionate and thorough exploration of such a meeting and its continuing reverberations. The person that we meet in the writing is also a "person" that the writer meets there as well, for that written person is, of course, different (in nature, not simply different in opinions or voices) than the person-in-the-world. As Jabès notes, this difference occurs because "to write means 'to wait for words that wake our thoughts as they write us'" (119). And thus his views of the experience of writing bear an interesting relationship to poets such as Robert Duncan who often found himself to be a medium during the moment of composition. Thus, while poetry is often thought of as having a revelatory intimacy of autobiography, Jabès points as well to a self in erasure through writing, a self that is absorbed in writing, in the word, and in the book.

While my own reading experience (over the past twenty years) of Jabès's writing has been an enriching and very positive one, there are qualities to his work that many others, even partisans of innovative writing, may find off-putting. Jabès's work—particularly if read in large doses—runs the risk of coming off as overly "heavy" or too insistently "profound." There is an obsessive quality, too, as Jabès works and re-works a somewhat limited vocabulary and tone. The humorous and playful qualities that Waldrop finds so active in Jabès's daily and familial life are not so evident in his writing where his version of the religious runs the risk of becoming portentous, in spite of the somewhat comedic inventive structures of imagined midrash-like commentary that are so much a part of Jabès' self-modifying books.

Waldrop's *Lavish Absence* partakes, inevitably, of the elegiac—remembering, but also mourning the loss of Jabès, while noting as well his continuing presence in his books. In response to a friend's mentioning of a Chinese tradition of mourning for one year, Waldrop ends her book with the admission, "I myself have a messier sense of mourning, that it is perhaps never done altogether, that is, like memory for Aristotle, a delayed motion that continues to exist in the soul" (155). Waldrop's *Lavish Absence* becomes a multi-faceted demonstration of that messier process of mourning and remembering. It is a process that—like writing, or reading, or translating, or interpreting—cannot be completed, and it is precisely this irritating, engaging, pleasurable, instructive indeterminacy—this engagement without conclusion—that constitutes an attractive feature that allows and encourages an active, ongoing reading of Edmond Jabès's writing.

Poetry & Myth: The Scene of Writing, Thinking As Such

When I was an undergraduate at Stanford in the late 1960s, myth was an academically sanctioned portal for entry into the proper study of poetry. Yeats and Blake were major figures, as were Eliot and Pound. Just as one needed to be able to recognize references to Dante and Milton, the clever student needed to know a basic set of European myth-stories and characters. Many poems would be explained by professional critic-professors who would refer to an appropriate myth-story, whereby the poem could be understood as a kind of homeomorph, a re-telling of a mythological story with contemporary resonances.

This essay some twenty-five years later begins to trace my resistance to some versions of myth. My skeptical reading and writing of poetry involves questions about the status, necessity, nature, and value of joining poetry and myth. How does "myth" (functionally speaking) differ from "allusion"? Must a mythological poetry work through *those* proper names only? Is the mythic dimension the act of a particularly sanctioned mode of reference, or might the activity of poetry-making itself be understood as fundamentally mythological in nature? If mythic poetry can escape from the cookie-cutter version of mythic resonance, at what point does a broadened (or metaphorical) version of the mythic become so diffuse a category as to make worthless the thinking in such a category? If we take "myth" to its root word, *muthos*, mouthing, won't all modes of mouthing have something of the mythic to them? Is poetry a sacred or intensified mouthing? And does such a version of myth, as mouthing, negate the other address of poetry as *written* text?

Imagine a poet growing up, coming to his craft, in the late 1960s and early 1970s. Imagine that such a poet worked to heal the rift between philosophy and poetry—a rift energetically constructed

initially by Plato (as philosophers fought an earlier turf battle with
poets) and constructed again (especially by academic institutions) in
the 1960s and 1970s with the rise of university programs in Creative
Writing. Imagine a poet who thought of poetry and philosophy
as inseparable activities, as part of a more general project of thinking, of the exploration and manifestation of consciousness. Imagine
that such a poet began to read, enthusiastically, the work of Martin
Heidegger, and that the poet began to conceive of his work as existing within that philosopher's language-centered House of Being.

   Or, alternatively, and synonymously, as part of the single project
of writing as imagined by Shelley; or the extended conversation of
philosophy as articulated by Kenneth Burke, Michael Oakeshott,
and Richard Rorty; or, as practiced in the talk-poems of David
Antin; or, as in John Ashbery's more demotic version of these grand
collective enterprises: "The desire to have fun, to make noise, and so
to / Add to the already all-but-illegible scrub forest of graffiti on the
shithouse wall" (1976: 18). Or, as part of the grand collage, as suggested in the poetry of Robert Duncan and the art of Jess Collins.
Perhaps in such a poet's writing, the proper names and professionalized debris of Yeatsian mythological reference have virtually disappeared. Nonetheless, might we not imagine that the poetry remains
within an indirect but nonetheless foundational mythic dimension?

   Which set of references count as mythic? If Orpheus, Leda,
Abraham, Jacob, and Venus are replaced today by John Coltrane,
Thelonious Monk, Emily Dickinson, Henry David Thoreau, Louis
Zukofsky, and John Taggart, is the writing still mythic? To what
extent is the mythic a self-aggrandizing prop for the poet? Is the
mythic a compensatory claim for an activity thoroughly devalued
in the commercial, capitalist marketplace? Is the mythic other than
a rhetorical intensifier, a mode of claiming hieratic privilege by the
poet? *Is all such heroizing suspect?* Is the mythic, in particular, inevitably subject to a phallic aggressive heroizing, an inevitable subsump-
tion into the figures of Outward and Onward, figures of a (male)
quest? Or might pieces of the mythic be, as in other elements in the
modernist and postmodernist collage, parts that are equal to other
collaged elements in the assembled poem?

   If the contemporary poet feels uncomfortable with the trappings
of the sacred and of the priestly—not because the realm of the spiri-

tual is bankrupt, but because the self-serving nature of such unacknowledged rhetorical moves are suspect—what modes of definition
remain truthful both to the seriousness of poetry's play, and yet are
not so blatantly self-aggrandizing and (adolescently) compensatory
in nature? Can the poet be thought of as a perpetual activist, a construction worker, on behalf of a changing and ever-necessary new
realism? Is the poet's a heuristic role through which new modes of
consciousness may come into existence as a shamanism adequate to
our own day?

Perhaps I can best get at my uneasiness with most mythopoeic
writing by examining in some detail Robert Duncan's "The Truth
and Life of Myth" (1985). I admire Duncan's poetry a great deal; in
fact, my most recently completed cycle of poems, *Days* (1994–95),[1]
begins with a prefatory poem dedicated to Duncan:

>Poesis
>>*for Robert Duncan*
>
>oh great joy
>of early labor
>waking into day
>light exact plea
>sures commence &
>are commensurate with
>consciousness a room
>of words calling
>love among them
>turn to light

Duncan's essay begins with several epigraphs. One from Jane
Harrison's *Themis* proposes: "Possibly the first *muthos* was simply
the interjectional utterance *mu*; but it is easy to see how rapid the
development would be from interjection to narrative. Each step in
the ritual action is shadowed as it were by a fresh interjection, till the
whole combines into a consecutive tale" (1985: 1). My resistance to
the conventionally mythological begins with the observation that
the poem need not be *about* ritual action: the poem already *is* ritual

1 Subsequently published by Lavendar Ink in 2002.

action. The poem is not written *for* a ritual; its writing, *as* it occurs, *that* it occurs, is an instance (and an infinitely particular one) of ritualized making, a poesis.

Duncan writes, "The meaning and intent of what it is to be a man and, among men, to be a poet, I owe to the workings of myth in my spirit, both the increment of associations gathered in my continuing study of mythological lore and my own apprehension of what my life is at work there" (1985: 2). I can assent quite thoroughly to a version of myth-in-poetry as resonance, as an emotional reverberation, of awe, and of recognition. But I have a harder time when the mythological becomes aligned with a version of the quest, when the poet assumes the role of heroic, individualistic quester.

As I have experienced it, the poet's heroism, to the extent that a poet is heroic, is a heroism not of difference, nor of heroic individuality, nor of uniqueness. (And here I am in complete agreement with Duncan's insistence upon the poet's *un*originality.) Language itself, as a social and shared space, prohibits such possibilities (except as particular cultural and ideological distortions). The poet's deeds (especially in late twentieth-century America) are heroic as instances of active, exploratory intelligence *not* in the service of immediately useful commodification. The poet affirms the value of *play* as well as the activity of *cultural critique*. The poet affirms and takes possession of—as a *common*-wealth—our most valuable resource: language. In the poet's trust, that resource becomes a medium for unalienated labor.

Duncan writes, "For theosophists, psychoanalysts, and the converts of revealed religions, it is not the story that is primary but the meaning behind the story" (1985: 3). Such meaning is one danger for me of the mythic lens: an emphasis upon myth (as key, as story, as guiding shape) *can* be a denial of the immediacy of the *poem* and its specific differential contours, insofar as it gives an overemphasis to some single mythic reference which allegedly governs the story.

Duncan begins to write of a "myth of forms" (1985: 5), and here I begin to discern a mode of the mythopoeic wherein I have been practicing the art of poetry. Duncan's version of the myth of forms places poetry within a range of discourses on form:

> As the story told of stars and subatomic particles and story
> told of living organisms continue to reorient our possible
> knowledge of what is, the poetic imagination faces the chal-
> lenge of finding a structure that will be the complex story of
> all the stories felt to be true, a myth in which something like
> the variety of man's experience of what is real may be con-
> tained. (1985: 6)

Both for me and Duncan, such a myth of forms has little to do with
inherited forms of composition. But it has much to do with the
mythic or resonant act of *making*, of making new forms, of making
a new realism, of embodying forms that adequately incarnate the
mystery of form, the force of entropy, the complexity and inexplica-
bility of form. For me, there are many mythic figures of such poetic
form-making, from the handwritten incorporation of variability in
Emily Dickinson's manuscripts, to the many different formal projects of Gertrude Stein, to the vast design and indigenous ethnography of Ron Silliman's *The Alphabet*, to bpNichol's *Martyrology*, Louis
Zukofsky's *"A"*, Jake Berry's *Brambu Drezi*, and Jack Foley's *Exiles*.

My own grand project in form is a series of ten "books," *10 X
10*, each of which engages a different formal creation based upon
various incarnations of ten. The first of these to be published was
INTER(IR)RUPTIONS (1992b), a ten poem series of collage-po-
ems, incorporating layouts and materials from baseball batting av-
erages to critical theory, from fashion and interior design columns
to research in neurophysiology. *3 of 10* (1996) consists of three
more books in this project: *H's Journal, Negation*, and *Displayspace*.
H's Journal consists of ten chapters of 40 sentences each. The
sentences are numbered, and many of the sentences come from
Thoreau's own Journal (which, as I entered my fortieth year, I was
reading concurrently with both the passing of the calendar year and
the movement of myself and of Thoreau into our fortieth years).
There are many other H's who get a say in this *Journal*—Herman
Melville, Susan Howe, Lyn Hejinian—as I attempt a fairly intimate act of self-portraiture through the words and observations of
others, practicing my hand at a complex mid-nineteenth century
version of the sentence. In this work, the unit of composition is
the sentence, a resource and a shape that often gets lost in lineated

poetry. *Negation* consists of ten poems, each of which moves in two directions. The first letter of each line, read vertically downward, consists of a passage (on negation) from Hegel's *Phenomenology of Mind*. In the horizontal direction, the poem moves very rapidly, working without any pronouns, depending on the music and rapidity of association to create the poem's movement. *Displayspace* involves ten poems, with one form governing poems 1, 4, 7, and 10, and a different method of composition for 2, 3, 5, 6, 8, and 9. These latter poems alternate lines—one line of quotation, one line of "original" composition, the poems both associating and dissociating the two modes of address. Poems 1, 4, 7, and 10 each have ten sub-sections, with a very specific and complex formula developed for each of these ten sub-sections.

The compositional practices in *INTER(IR)RUPTIONS* and in *3 of 10* most definitely reveal my interest in incorporating prior sources, references, and materials in my poems. But in recounting these methods, I also am made aware of my discomfort with the mythological, a discomfort that may be little more than a personal prejudice against the capitalized versions of prior stories and against the capitalized *archetype* as a mode of reference. Nonetheless, I am quite actively involved in several mythic projects. One is my investigation of *the myth of fact*. My first big book of poems, *Doublespace* (1992a), itself an exploration of formal possibilities in a book that opens in two directions, has as an epigraph a line from Robert Frost's "Mowing": "The fact is the sweetest dream that labor knows." Facts, for me, have always been tied to dream, to labor, and to knowing. A key series in *Doublespace*, Law-Poems, includes many sections (presented verbatim as lineated poetry) from the Alabama Legal Code. Another mythic project that has engaged me for many years involves the poem as a mapping or incarnation of consciousness, what Louis Zukofsky called "thoughts' torsion" (1965: 73).

But to return to my specific wrestling with Duncan's writing on myth: as I circle back, I note that the first sentence of Duncan's essay points toward a version of myth that I find attractive: "Myth is the story told of what cannot be told, as mystery is the scene revealed of what cannot be revealed, and the mystic gnosis the thing known that cannot be known" (1985: 1). Here we have myth understood as an excess, an impossibility, an outer limit, a beyond—rather than as a mode of merely referential resonance, or as an explanatory subject-rhyme—understood as the potential to place myth-making in poetry as *a heuristic activity*.

Duncan tells us in the second sentence of his essay, "The myth-teller beside himself with the excitement of the dancers sucks in the inspiring breath and moans, muttering against his willful lips; for this is not a story of what he thinks or wishes life to be, it is the story that *comes to him* and forces his telling" (1985: 1). While I can assent reluctantly to this description of poetry as inspired, as forced, as coming to me (I say so reluctantly because of the capacity for self-aggrandizement and fakery that such a description allows), physically, I have always felt the onset of poetry to be coincidental with a kind of nervousness, an excitation, a sort of temporary minor trance. Or, to echo the language of my Law-Poems: in writing the poem, we obey a summons.

In re-encountering and re-considering Robert Duncan's particular enthusiasm for myth in poetry, I recognize a general uneasiness of many contemporary innovative poets (particularly Language poets) with myth. Within current experimental poetries, Duncan, somewhat like Charles Olson, is a difficult figure. Often, contemporary innovative poetries exhibit a textualized coolness, an ironized distance instead of the intense emotional directness of Duncan's poetry. While Duncan's poetry and poetics remain crucial to many innovative poetries today, particularly in the San Francisco Bay Area, the reception and continuation of Duncan's writing is often accompanied by an evasion of his active emphasis on spirit, myth, emotional intensity, his affirmation of the heart and of love, and his generally romantic version of the artist/poet. Here, I want to open up some of these differences, ambivalences, and resistances by focusing principally on the difficulties of assuming a continuity with Duncan's practice of myth in poetry.

Duncan writes, "The surety of myth for the poet has such force it operates as a primary reality in itself, having volition. The mythic content comes to us, commanding the design of the poem; it calls the poet into action …[.]" (1985: 13) That mythic content, for me, is *not* something nameable outside the poem. The mythic content of the poem is a topic which, as a good card-carrying avant-gardist, I usually resist discussing, and repress as a category of conversation. Here, I thoroughly value *this* opportunity to discuss and think through my somewhat allergic response to myth which for me represents the occurrence, the onset, the development, the manifestation and dwelling in the poem. For me, the mythic in poetry is the poem's trajectory of composition and the uniqueness of its making and thinking.

Duncan writes, "The poem that moves me when I write is an active presence in which I work" (1985: 15). *Yes!* And the poem, to the extent that the poet is capable, can offer a testimony to that presence, and make a site where others, including the poet as he or she is (after the instance of composition) subsequently other, may sometimes dwell, may actively think, engage, and, sometimes, depart again for other instances of creation. The primary myth within which I work is, then, a myth of making, of the profound resonance of the act of making, of the heuristic and instructive immediacy of writing. And this is a mythic dimension that merges with Duncan's description:

> Concentrating on the constructions of the poem, following the workings out of sound and content, in order to cooperate fully with what is given, … his intellect intent upon the ratios and movements of the poem he is almost unaware of depths that may be stirred in his own psyche. What he feels is the depth and excitement of the poem. The poem takes over. (1985: 18–19)

Here we have a myth of pure concentration, to the point of possession.

Duncan writes of "a melody of events"—and this may be where he and I part company. For me, that melody of events takes place *within* the sound and sounding of the poem, *within* the musical exchange of the words themselves. For Duncan, and for most myth-based poets, that melody of events has more to do with subject-rhymes, with chains of events, so that Duncan's full sentence reads: "The myth or pattern of elements in the story is a melody of events in which the imprint of a knowledge—knowledge, here, in the sense of a thing undergone—enters the generative memory and the history of man takes on tenor" (1985: 7).

I am talking about a difference in emphasis: the placement of *the story* (of the poem) in history, in prior chains of events, matters far less to me than to Duncan and to most modernists, such as Pound, Eliot, and H.D. For me, that generative memory/story derives from the particularity of *melopoeia*, from the particular incarnation of the given sounds and rhythms of *this* poem. Duncan and I share an enthusiasm: "The sounding is the love that moves the poet in language" (1985: 57). Or, as he writes in "The Structure of Rime II," "There is a melody within this surfeit of speech that is most man" (1993: 46). My own version of the mythopoeic is a language-centered, composition- (or creation-) based myth, *a myth of incarnation* that seizes upon (and sees and hears with) the making of the poem—not so much the specific stories as the medium itself, not so much the story being told as much as the telling of the story.

Or, to choose that portion of Duncan's articulation of myth that I am affirming, "Here, what I wanted to bring to focus was finally, as often it is for me in the poem, what is happening in the composition itself: the work of art is itself the field we would render the truth of" (1985: 48). Mine is *a myth of immediacy located in the making of the poem*, a myth of consciousness seeking expression in the poem, an expression coincidental with the poem, a myth of *poesis*.

Yet, as Duncan acknowledges, this myth of *poesis* rhymes too with a number of scientific investigations: "And science assumes that there is something to know but must always—I am thinking here of our contemporary theoretical sciences—be at work in the field of what it does not know" (1985: 50). Hence, an experimental knowing, a heuristic myth, which targets areas I *don't* yet know and can only know by venturing—a Heideggerian ad-venture in language—by a new act of making. My version of the poet does not seek eloquent and memorable expression for the already known. Rather, this poet I am attempting to be, fueled by a restlessness and by an adherence to a new summons, seeks to give being to dawning possibilities of human habitation in language. Duncan links such restlessness to living itself, as he cites the scientific writing of Schrödinger: "'When is a piece of matter said to be alive?,'" he asks, and answers: 'When it goes on "doing something," moving, exchanging material with its environment.' What interests me here

is…this picture of an intricately articulated structure, a form that
maintains a disequilibrium" (1985: 78).

Duncan reminds me that "Back of each poet's concept of the
poem is his concept of the meaning of form itself; and his concept
of form in turn where it is serious at all arises from his concept of
the nature of the universe" (1985:16). However, it may be worth
noting that even among poets, there are radically opposed concepts of the universe. One particular fork in the (conceptual) road
would oppose a decidedly cultural-historical-political materialism
(as in the writings of Ron Silliman) to a more metaphysical-philo-
sophical-mythic version of form (as in Duncan's writing). Insisting
upon his own *un*originality and his own derivativeness (in such
a fashion that is, nonetheless, quite original), Duncan remains
clearly a poet concerned with making and acknowledging his place
within certain traditions, while nonetheless seeking new forms for
the poem as a way of bodying forth the particularity of the poem's
immediate inception.

While Duncan's is a highly romanticized linking of *poesis* with
cosmic creation, for my own part, I am engaged by the complexity
of organization that he wishes to mirror, as in this statement:

> It has never seemed to me that the true form of a poem was
> a convention or an ideal of form, but, as in life, a form hav-
> ing its information in the language of our human experi-
> ence, as our bodies have their information in the life-code of
> the species, and our spirit in the creative will. The individual
> poem stirs in our minds, and even in our language, as the
> individual embryonic cells stirs in the parent body. The be-
> ginning of the poem stirs in every area of my consciousness,
> for the DNA code it will use toward its incarnation is a code
> of resources my life pattern itself carries; not only thought
> and feeling but all the nervous and visceral and muscular
> intelligences of the body are moved. Awakening—listen-
> ing, seeing, sensing—to work with the moving weights and
> durations of syllables, the equilibrations of patterns, the
> liberations of new possibilities of movement; to cooperate in
> the aroused process. Attending. From the first inspiration,
> breathing *with* the new breath. Man's myths move in his po-

etry as they move in his history, as in the morphology of his
body, all his ancient evolution is rehearsed and individualized; all of vertebrate imagination moves to create itself anew
in his spine. (1985: 16)

Duncan's statement is one of the primary formulations of "myth in
poetries" in our time. For me, it raises the importance of attaining
in our contemporary poetries an *adequate* formal complexity, one
which also allows for disequilibrium, difference, error, the stammer.
Adequate to *what*? Adequate to the complexity of matter as we know
it, to the infinite (and beautiful) combinings of DNA, of atomic and
subatomic particles, of letters and words. I might even choose to call
such a project *the perpetual remaking of realism*, and a desire to incarnate, temporarily and specifically, consciousness as it is *at this time*.
Paradoxically, such an adventuring in language, even as it is new,
merely renews our sense of a return to a fundamental ground of our
being. Duncan himself remains a generative guide:

> Often I Am Permitted to Return to a Meadow
>
> as if it were a scene made-up by the mind,
> that is not mine, but is a made place,
>
> that is mine, it is so near to the heart,
> an eternal pasture folded in all thought
>
> . . . .
>
> as if it were a given property of the mind
> that certain bounds hold against chaos,
>
> that is a place of first permission,
> everlasting omen of what is. (1993: 44)

Works Cited

John Ashbery. "Grand Galop," in *Self-Portrait in a Convex Mirror*. New York: Penguin, 1976.

Jake Berry. *Brambu Drezi*. A work in progress. Book One: Port Charlotte, FL: Runaway Spoon Press, 1993. Book Two: Berkeley: Pantograph Press, 1997.

Robert Duncan. "The Truth and Life of Myth" and "Towards an Open Universe," in *Fictive Certainties: Essays by Robert Duncan*. New York: New Directions, 1985.

———. *Selected Poems*. Edited by Robert J. Bertholf. New York: New Directions, 1993.

Jack Foley. *Exiles*. Berkeley: Pantograph Press, 1996.

Hank Lazer. *Doublespace: Poems 1971–1989*. New York: Segue, 1992.

———. *INTER(IR)RUPTIONS*. Mentor, Ohio: Generator Press, 1992.

———. *3 of 10: H's Journal, Negation, and Displayspace*. Tucson: Chax Press, 1996.

bpNichol. *The Martyrology*. A long poem begun in 1967 and continuing until Nichol's death in 1988. It includes *Books 1 & 2* (1972), *Books 3 & 4* (1976), *Book 5* (1982), *Book 6* (1987), *gifts: Books 7 &* (1990), and *Ad Sanctos: Book 9* (1992). Toronto: Coach House Press.

Ron Silliman. *The Alphabet*. A work in progress, which includes *ABC* (Tuumba, 1983); *Demo to Ink* (Chax Press, 1992); *Jones* (Generator Press, 1993); *Lit* (Potes & Poets Press, 1987); *Manifest* (Zasterle Press, 1990); *N/O* (Roof Books, 1994); *Paradise* (Burning Deck, 1985); *Toner* (Potes & Poets Press, 1992); *Xing* (Meow Press, 1996); *What* (The Figures, 1988). [Note: *The Alphabet* is now complete and is forthcoming from the University of Alabama Press in 2008.]

Louis Zukofsky. *"A"*. Berkeley: University of California Press, 1978.

Louis Zukofsky. "Mantis" in *All: The Collected Shorter Poems, 1923–1964*. New York: New Directions, 1965.

Force, Vector, Pressure: The Phenomena of that Relationship (An Interview with Chris Mansel)

1. What is the earliest tender moment you experienced, and how did it change you?

The problem, of course, is with what we remember, or, what, to serve present purposes, we claim to remember. I can't say that I have some particular intense first memory of tenderness. No doubt, like other infants, I must have early moments of tenderness—eating, caressing, fondling, eliminating, sucking, making eye contact, etc.

The earliest kinds of tenderness that I experienced that in some way might have been idiosyncratic or somehow personally defining would be associated with my grandparents. I grew up living close—often on the same block, sometimes within a few blocks—to all four of my grandparents. They were not quintessentially "sweet" grandparents—particularly my mother's parents, who were rather depressed, critical, and moderately paranoid. But they did spend a good bit of time with me; they indulged me; and, most importantly, since English was not their first language, I acquired some of their fascination with language. I learned, somewhat, to see and hear English through them. I remember them telling jokes—often turning on a simple pun. I remember their accents—their first languages were Russian and Yiddish. I remember their delight in humor—a complex quality of language acquisition. Especially from both sides of the family, I felt a deep respect of learning, of thinking, even a love of seemingly esoteric learning (for its own sake). I remember their pride in reading.

Eventually, they became the first important subject for my poetry—rather conventional brief or extended narratives telling elements of their history. These early poems can be found in the first half, Book One: Facts and Figures, of *Doublespace: Poems 1971–1989*

(New York: Segue, 1992). Having this desire—to tell *their* stories—proved to be very important, since from the outset my poetry was not particularly located in *self*-expression.

2. Should there be a specific role that spirituality should play in art?

Not really. I'd hate to be prescriptive—in regard to spirituality, or in regard to any important element in the making of poetry or art.

I suppose that what I have tried to do with my own exploration of poetry (and spirituality) is to be phenomenal. That is, to be truthful to the inconstant, shifting experience of spirituality—as a kind of force, or vector, or pressure, or presence (and disappearance), or immanence, or contiguous relationship. To be truthful to the phenomena of that relationship.

It seems to me that if one works at an adequately profound level of awareness of what's at stake in art-making, spirituality will already be adequately woven into the fabric of the making.

Over time, over many years of engaging in a mode of art-making, I think it's important to embody or represent the elusive and inconstant nature of the spiritual. As I've experienced it, it simply isn't something that's available on demand. That's part of why I'm suspicious of any kind of formulaic or axiomatic pronouncement about how spirituality "should" be present in art. Also, the nature and intensity of its location will be ever-changing. And like any other important or intense experience, the rhetoric or vocabulary of the spiritual may harden and become a merely repeated or second-hand, tired, received set of markers (that may actually stand in the way of a renewing experience).

3. Chogyam Trungpa said, "Buddhism will come to the West as a psychology." Do you think this is the case or has the true feeling of selflessness actually occurred in our culture?

Perhaps Buddhism will come—or has come—to the West as a psychology, or as a philosophy, or as poetry, or as a meditation discipline, or as a new hybrid sort of religion (as it has entered and met with our cultural conditions). The categories themselves blur. The particularities, the singularities of experience, come and go. That true feeling of selflessness itself comes and goes. As for the feeling of selflessness becoming a key value and revered accomplishment in our culture? Obviously not. The current war (in Iraq) shows how far away we are as a culture from anything like selflessness. It is a war based on arrogance—based on a narrow sense of "our" righteousness. Think how far the war expenditures could have gone toward ameliorating hunger, or poverty, or lousy education—here, in the US, or throughout the world. We have not—as a culture—learned how to give freely.

Clearly, though, Buddhism has arrived in the US—particularly in the western US (including Hawai'i). Purists may debate whether or not it is a "true" or "rigorous" Buddhism. So, again, the labels may be part of the problem. Something has arrived and developed—some collision and collusion, some generative interaction of Buddhism and elements of western culture. In the area of poetry, of course, there are many examples of the importance of Buddhist thinking in our writing—Gary Snyder, Norman Fischer, Jake Berry, Armand Schwerner, and many others. The writing of poetry itself can become a means—a site, a portal—for accessing and dwelling in (temporarily) that locale of selflessness. Certainly the language and its pre-existing specificities as well as the many traditions of writing are well beyond the doings of an individual "self." Consider too the wonderful (and at times frustrating) way that the best writing often is not a matter of will but of receptivity, of knowing when and what to listen to, of learning when and how to follow the suggestions of a few words that are given to one...

4. What do you feel is the anatomy of a poet? What makes some write, and others not?

I don't think there really is such a thing as "the anatomy of a poet"—other than the fairly obvious notion that a poet is someone with a particular fascination with words, someone who has experienced the peculiar depth and mystery of language (and its intimate relationship to human consciousness). As for what makes some write and others not—I think that it must remain a mystery. I tell myself—I try to learn it—that from appearances—say, looking at a

line of people in a restaurant or at a sporting event—I know nothing
about them. Poets may tend toward a certain seeming casualness (or
understated melancholy) of dress, but then there might be a Wallace
Stevens, or an Emily Dickinson, or there goes Dr. Williams. Or,
there goes John Coltrane, playing amazing sax in his coat and tie.

Plenty of people do dabble in poetry—and I think that's a good
thing. Why shouldn't art-making be an accessible activity? But the
more perplexing mystery is trying to determine who might persist
at the activity (and why). I remember from the first poetry writing
course I took in graduate school (at University of Virginia, taught
by a Robert Lowell disciple), we were nearly all students in our early
to mid-twenties. One student had, at age 21, published poems in
Poetry magazine, and the teacher seemed to worship this student. A
few years later, this person was no longer writing poetry. I think back
to that class of fifteen students. Who writes today has nothing to do
with the quality of writing done then (thirty some years ago). I'm
not even sure that the cliché is true: if you enjoy it, you'll continue.
Or that the severe version of the cliché is true: when asked by a
young poet, "should I continue to write poetry?," Auden supposedly
replied, "if you *can* quit, do." It's not as simple or clear-cut as either
of these extremes suggest.

Personally, I am enamored of poets who have some stubborn,
self-taught, non-institutional streak. But persistence—especially
for those who receive little or no recognition for many years—is a
tricky thing. An enemy of persistence: self-pity, a quality that often
seizes the poet (as a kind of prolonged adolescent agony for recognition or approval).

For me—and I did not publish a first book of poetry until I
was 42 years old—the persistence comes from the fact that when I
write certain poems, I am able to enter a space (like Robert Duncan's
"Often I am permitted to return to a meadow") that has a palpable
intensification to it, an emotional and intellectual power (simultaneously) that is addictive, that is a supreme pleasure, that feels like a
temporary participation in something quite splendid (even if painful). I feel it as a full and best use of my being, so I continue to seek
out that place, as a writer, but also most definitely as a reader too.

5. Could grace ever be achieved through a sudden impulse as opposed to re-writes and revision?

I think that grace can *only* be achieved through a sudden impulse—being and living within the intensified present of the moment of composition. Yes, a great deal of practice—writing, revising, reading, studying, thinking—may go into the developing of the skills and resources and concentration that may be of use in that moment of composition, but the achievement (or, perhaps more accurately, the experience) of grace will inevitably occur suddenly.

Such a conclusion, though, does not mean that all of our efforts in writing are wonderful. There is, of course, an absolute mode of revision—"yes" or "no"—that allows us to throw out poems that are not especially good. And I have had plenty of experience re-writing and revising poems, sometimes with beneficial results. But for the most part, I find it very difficult to re-enter the space or field of the poem after much time has elapsed. Eventually, the highly specific integrity of that moment—including the peculiar rhythms and sounds that one heard at that moment—gets lost. Perhaps over the span of several days, I am able to tinker with some individual word choices, make some deletions, and occasionally make some substantial changes. But for the most part, the poem itself is an embodiment of a highly specific (usually brief) duration of consciousness—its concentration, its intensification, its specific music (i.e., the music of that specific thinking).

I was relieved a couple of months ago to hear Robert Creeley, in an informal discussion, articulating a remarkably similar view. Such a viewpoint aligns poetic composition with jazz improvisation—an informed composition in the present. It does not necessarily mean that "first thought best thought" always turns out to be the case, but it does mean that the present—the specific duration of composition—will be honored to the utmost, the poem, among other things, being a record of attentive dwelling in that specific duration of time.

6. Where do you suppose the self-destructiveness trait comes from that occurs in so many writers?

From frustration, as a consequence of marginalization, and from succumbing to a dangerous set of culturally romanticized stereotypes. First, the frustration and marginalization routes. A writer, particularly a poet, places himself in an odd position in relation to dominant cultural value. A poet decides to value certain kinds of somewhat aimless, impractical, non-money-making activities, and he decides to make room and time in his life for these activities. Furthermore, he's apt to be pursuing a rather elusive mode of language—not necessarily the direct, communicative, "useful," commercially manipulative kind of language skill that society readily appreciates and rewards (in advertising, in journalism, and in other modes of persuasive and/or manipulative writing). So, what he's doing with his time is aberrant—hard to explain. And yet, if he is really engaged in a serious and profound relationship to poetry, he *does* have certain sporadic validating experiences—a sense of connection to a longstanding human enterprise of considerable wisdom, joy, and pleasure. The self-destructiveness may arise as a gesture of anger and frustration, arising from a sense that one's primary life activity is not appreciated or understood or respected. The self-destructiveness becomes an act oddly complicit with that ignoring and marginalizing by the society at large, while it is also a somewhat desperate call for attention and significance.

Society at large—at least here in the US—establishes an interestingly ambivalent role toward the poet/artist. Most of the time, it's business as usual: scorn, neglect, derision, lack of value. But then there is the flip-side: a compensatory romantic larger-than-life version (preferably made for the movies) of The Artist. This Artist is one who is—big surprise—too sensitive and volatile for this world. It is, in my opinion, a very dangerous and seductive model, particularly dangerous for the artist/poet who buys into it. This intuitive, somewhat childish artist figure—who can't help himself, who has to pursue the truth of his art at all costs (including family, personal health, etc.)—is exactly what the society at large needs to comfort itself. That is, some reassurance that being an artist is a big mistake, though a grand enough mistake—entertaining enough—that we can witness the story every couple of years in a big Hollywood production. And then we can return the rest of our days to ignoring such individuals in our midst.

For the artist/poet, the self-destructiveness can be conformation to this cultural stereotype of the "crazy" artist. Since it's already a bit crazy (in practical, capitalist America) to use your intelligence to pursue something like poetry, why not go all the way and become that "odd" figure as in the cinematic cliché? The result is an infantilizing identity: the artist/poet as intuitive creature severed from a penetrating cultural and practical intelligence. Personally, I find it hard enough to work with the nature and complexity of making poetry. No need to pursue additional clichéd personal drama (and self-destructiveness) just to make the story conform to a movie script. The real drama is one that can barely be seen: an internal drama, a drama of consciousness, the drama of wrestling with the issues, questions, and realizations of making the poem. You don't see those moments dramatized in the movies. You see the scenes of drunken abuse; you don't see the scenes of someone sitting in a chair, staring out the window, writing down three words.

Reflections on *The Wisdom Anthology of North American Buddhist Poetry*

Often our most productive thinking begins with a fortuitous error. When I first came across the title for Andrew Schelling's book, *The Wisdom Anthology of North American Buddhist Poetry*, I had no idea that the publishing company for the book was Wisdom Publications. My mistake allowed me—during the time lag between when I ordered the book and when the book arrived—to begin some sustained thinking about what might constitute "wisdom" today. Such an old and seemingly sentimental term! A concept and a label that hearkens back to a naïve (non-academic, unprofessional) mode of reading. I knew Schelling's work well enough to assume that the anthology itself would *not* be a set of oh little grasshopper fortune cookie proverbs and that it would include a significant selection of experimental, innovative poetry. So, my mistake-based thinking continued. Do we still read poetry—perhaps covertly, perhaps not in a way that we wear on our sleeves nor in our critical prose—as a quest for "wisdom"? Is such a language credible; is the term subject to rescue? More on that later...

—————

Many of our best projects are well-served by delays and deferrals. This anthology has been steeped for at least twenty years. That is smart. It is also a project, as Schelling realizes, that can not be completed with any sense of finality or definiteness.[1] Like the best projects, it must remain a work-in-progress, an open-ended anthology subject to revision and reconsideration. The end of his Preface hints at the inevitable specificity and partial nature of the anthology:

---

1 "Funny that no sooner did the anthology appear than I began to see many who could have also entered. More and more I realize writing, and its accessory acts like editing, are actually preliminary explorations, not summations at all." Andrew Schelling, e-mail to Hank Lazer, August 10, 2005.

"There is an old Zen phrase from the tea ceremony: *Ichi go, ichi e.* 'One chance, one meeting,' or 'this moment, just now'" (xvii).[2]

When Andrew first conceived of the anthology many years ago, he knew that at that time the book inevitably would have become the record of one particular generation: "From what I was reading in those days—the early 1980s—the major drawback [in making such an anthology] seemed to be that only a single generation of poets had written into their books poetry that resulted from adherence to Buddhist ideas. These were of course poets who had emerged in the post-World War II era, mostly the Beats" (xiii). Andrew sensed that a more amorphous, complex, variegated Buddhist poetry was beginning to take root. The new anthology represents the emergence of that multi-faceted Buddhist poetry.

———

Schelling's Introduction generously informs and guides readers—from those who have little familiarity with Buddhism's history in North America to those with quite a bit of background knowledge, from those who are quite comfortable reading a range of contemporary poetry to those who have a more fearful, timid relationship to the genre (particularly the more innovative versions of it). Schelling writes his own version of the confluent history of Buddhism and recent American poetry:

> There occurred a landmark event in May, 1987, which one day will get properly written into the annals of Buddhism, and come to be seen as one of the legendary gatherings that gave impetus to a specifically American form of Buddhist thought. Zoketsu Norman Fischer, a practice director at Green Gulch Farms Zen Center (about forty minutes by car up the winding coastal highway from San Francisco) put together a weekend retreat at which poets could talk to one another about meditation and poetry. He called the Green

---

2   Unless otherwise noted, all page numbers in parentheses refer to Andrew Schelling (ed.), *The Wisdom Anthology of North American Buddhist Poetry* (Boston: Wisdom Publications, 2005).

Gulch gathering "The Poetics of Emptiness," and opened it
to the public. (xiii)

I concur with Schelling's historical narrative. Norman Fischer's event
and Fischer's own work (as poet and Zen practitioner) define a place
for many important intersections: of experimental writing (Language
writing; Bay Area writing) and new versions of the spiritual; Jewish
and Buddhist practices; poetry and translation. Schelling notes
as well an important earlier anthology project: Kent Johnson and
Craig Paulenich's *Beneath a Single Moon: Buddhism in Contemporary
American Poetry* (1991), a collection of work by "a delightfully rag-
tag group of forty-five poets" (xiv). While Gary Snyder's introduction to that anthology was crucial, so too was the living presence
of two major poets of the time: Allen Ginsberg and John Cage. As
Schelling observes, "one can't overstate the impact Ginsberg and
Cage had on bringing Buddhist practice and thought into authentic
discussions of modern poetry. Their influence compelled not only
poets but academic critics and book reviewers to recognize Buddhist
ideas as central to an American poetry" (xiv).

As for the present moment, Schelling notes how pervasive
and ubiquitous Buddhist publications, sites, books, and journals
have become:

> ...suddenly Buddhism, Daoism, yoga, martial arts, and
> other practices from Asia seem naturalized to this continent.
> Grocery stores sell *Tricyle, Shambhala Sun, Buddha-dharma,
> Yoga Journal* and similar periodicals. But I'm also thinking
> of the emergence of a generation of young poets who have
> come to Buddhism not as something exotic, rather as a gra-
> dation they grew up with. (xv)

Schelling's historical narrative and his anthology make me wonder,
"why Buddhism?" What makes Buddhism in particular such a congenial and generative form of spiritual experience for a wide range of
contemporary American poets?

For a few days, I thought that the title for this essay would be "How Buddhist Is It?" Drawn toward the humor of the title and its play on Walter Abish's *How German Is It?*, I had begun to locate something crucial to Schelling's book (even if this initial stab at a title was eventually to be discarded). The complexity and indeterminacy of the object, subject, identity, and taxonomy of his book are among its prime virtues. The range of writing comfortably and unselfconsciously admitted into this anthology suggests, by contrast, how many other anthologies (regardless of their ostensible purpose) are severely segregated anthologies (into rigidly defined aesthetic or professional camps or tribes). Since Buddhism itself is so hard to define—particularly its fundamental beliefs—Schelling from the very beginning seeks out a fair and representative variety of poetry that will suggest the many ways that Buddhism can, has, and will inflect, alter, determine, inform, and enrich contemporary North American poetry. The result is one of the most excitingly democratic anthologies of recent times—though this result was never part of the project. Thus the anthology itself becomes a definitively Buddhist labor?

What makes a poem a "Buddhist" poem? Reference to a Buddhist text or term? A kind of thinking? A particular mode of attention to particulars? Deliberately, and wisely, Schelling's anthology does not answer this initial question—a question that cannot be answered, except through a reading of the poems, a consideration of what might be construed as a Buddhist poem. It—the Buddhist element—is not something that is added to a poem; it is not a separable element; it is not a seasoning added to a steamed vegetable. What then is it? How do you know it's there? Why this poem and not that poem, why this poet and not that poet?

Various strands and lineages, explicit and implicit, abound in Schelling's anthology. One key element that he delineates involves magical elements of sound or other language endeavors that stray from common uses of language to convey information. In Buddhist writing there is a considerable range

> From brief instructional aphorisms, goads to meditation, ceremonial changes, mealtime prayers, and benedictions, to the sort of uncrackable kernels of language that serve as magic spells and spiritual formulae (later formalized into mantra and dharani). Among contemporary poets the influence of these types of verse is most observable when you turn to the use of meaningless or non-sensical (call them *magical*) linguistic techniques brought to bear on the poetry. Here you can find the use of spells and chants built on seed syllables, or phrases of psycho-spiritual power meant to conjure (or instill) non-ordinary states of mind. Other possible directions influenced by religious or mystical texts include the direct violation of syntax and grammar. In these gestures, language is put forth not to tell stories or convey information but to render the mind susceptible to a supernatural or spiritual effect. (2)

Schelling concludes that such poetry *moves* us: "Poetry actually carries or transports you. The next question is where, and that's a tricky one" (3).

Schelling's attention to this "magical" or nonsensical strand exposes both the most cogent overlaps with contemporary innovative poetry and, at the same time, the site of an anxiety or difference. Yes, a short-circuiting of customary modes of meaning-making is a comfortable praxis in contemporary innovative poetry (of the past thirty years, but truly of a much greater duration as well). So, too, is a resistance to a constrained sense of language as principally a conveyor of information. But when Schelling refers to the magical power of language, the spiritual effects of language, and the ability to conjure non-ordinary states of mind, the overlapping assumptions may also become the site of skepticism and anxiety.

Schelling notes, "A belief many times documented among archaic or tribal traditions holds that hidden forces—deities, animal powers, protective spirits—can be called up through sounds made by the human voice" (4). As an anthropological or ethnographic con-

clusion, particularly when applied to a culture or a verbal tradition
with some remoteness, one might remain quite comfortable with
such an observation. But as a contemporary practice, the stakes, the
identifications, and the beliefs involved change. Perhaps the complexity of a present practice of magical powers is best illustrated by
the writings/performances of Jerome Rothenberg, a poet who defines
himself in intensely secular terms, but whose writings (especially his
anthologizings) are deeply involved in the shamanic and the magical.

For Schelling, as for Rothenberg, Dada and Surrealism provide a
bridge for European and North American poetries into the magical
elements of Buddhism and other practices:

> Dada and Surrealism had brought a politics of the non-ra-
> tional into poetry, seeing the modern nation-state as depen-
> dent on banishing patterns of thought and speech that didn't
> conform to a narrow sense of the human as an economic
> animal. Surrealists used a host of techniques to provoke a
> revolution that would open human consciousness to alter-
> nate realities: dream imagery, automatic writing, and col-
> laborative writing practices[.]… Performers among the Dada
> crowd and other groups influenced by contact with folklore
> and tribal traditions made poems out of sheer sound (the
> Futurists called them *zaum* poems). You could say that these
> explorations prepared the North American ground. (5)

They prepared the North American ground for a generative and
profoundly multi-faceted relationship to Buddhist texts and practices. But within contemporary experimental poetry, one might
also identify—perhaps too schematically, perhaps in too binary a
manner—a resistance and a skepticism. It would be easy to overstate such a difference. One would not expect an affirmation of
transcendental experience or spiritual transformation or magical
transport to non-ordinary consciousness in the writings or poetics of
Charles Bernstein, Bob Perelman, Ron Silliman, or Barrett Watten.
There is a long-standing critique within experimentalism—consider
the disagreements between Charles Olson and Robert Duncan over
such matters—of the allegedly sentimental and romantic excesses of
a poetry of inwardness and a poetry of spirit.

But what makes Schelling's Buddhist anthology a more welcoming home for a wide range of interesting poetry is that Buddhist thinking too is radically and decisively indeterminate. If we return to Schelling's question—transport to where?—Buddhism too refuses the task of definition and refuses to offer an answer.

～

My own passion over the past few years has been to read and think through what I'm beginning to understand as a series of overlapping radical indeterminacies. Before returning to a more direct, sustained consideration of the poetics and poems of Schelling's anthology, I propose a detour. The precise indeterminacy of Buddhism—as a kind of spirituality and a poetic practice—perhaps may best be understood through an indirect approach.

In Derrida's late writing, a faith defended against faithfulness, or a spiritual experience that exists apart from religious determinisms emerges: "Derrida differentiates the 'determinable' faiths, which are always dangerous, in order to differentiate their triumphalism from faith 'itself,' the *indeterminate* faith and open-ended hope in what is coming, in the incoming of the *tout autre*, the passion for which is what deconstruction is all about, what deconstruction 'is'" (C, 47– 48).[3] "How Buddhist Is It?" makes little sense as a lens through which to view Schelling's anthology, except as a kind of ironic question that itself suggests that a prime virtue of Buddhism is that it is without object, without essential beliefs, without a recitable or knowable dogma. How Buddhist Is It? can be answered by a process, by a movement, but not by a destination or a certified subject matter. Similarly, "it is no business of deconstruction, indeed it goes against the grain of deconstruction—to specify some *determinable* faith, to specify what faith is faith in, to calm the storm or arrest the play in which faith takes shape by proposing a determinate object of faith" (C, 64).

An axiom for Derrida's later writing might be: "Deconstruction means to be the delimitation of totalization in all its forms" (C, 126). I am tempted to say that the same axiom may apply equally

3   C = John D. Caputo, *The Prayers and Tears of Jacques Derrida: Religion without Religion* (Bloomington: Indiana University Press, 1997).

well to Buddhism, to mystical Judaism, and to innovative poetry.
What each strives to preserve in its resistance to totalization, its refusal of finality, its insistence upon a perpetually active and ongoing
hermeneutics, its passionate engagement with thinking as ever open
at one end, is the preservation of an ever-changing phenomenology
of spiritual experience. Or, as Caputo concludes about "deconstruction" (where, as I think it, "deconstruction" becomes a counter or a
term subject to substitution with the aforementioned off-rhyming
cognates), we are "able to see how deconstruction is a certain way of
putting something that is *also* religious, but over which the religions
do not have exclusive rights or hegemonic power, a way of freeing
something religious from the religions" (190).

The phrase "a way of freeing something religious from the religions" might also serve as a brief description for an American poet-
ics/spiritual lineage from Emerson through Thoreau and Whitman
and Dickinson, on to Robert Duncan, Ronald Johnson, and on to
Donald Revell, Harryette Mullen, Norman Fischer, and many others.

⸺〰⸺

In Schelling's history, "Two thousand years ago, when Buddhist
practice entered China (already a great and ancient civilization) and
encountered Daoist and Confucian ideas, it generated an unprecedented flowering of culture. Some think this set off the greatest
unfolding of poetry in world history" (13). One telling of American
literary history might suggest a similar road map, with the first great
wave of Eastern texts in translation being the spark and the collision
at the heart of the American Renaissance, a collision and collusion
that reaches a new flowering in Schelling's current anthology. Or, as
Schelling wonders (after tracing the remarkable range of translations
of Eastern texts by American poets over the past fifty years), "At this
point could one imagine our own poetry without the influence of Tu
Fu, Li Po, Su Tung-p'o, Li Ch'ing-chao, and Wang Wei? If I open a
current poetry magazine, I hear Li Po but rarely John Dryden" (17).

Ezra Pound's translations can be said to jump start the modern
era of translation of Chinese poetry. Though Pound's name and
deeds figure prominently in this history of an American encounter
with Chinese poetry, as Schelling notes, translation more generally

conceived than Pound's specific contribution plays a key role in the erratic entry of Chinese and other Asian poetries into a generative relationship with American poetry. Schelling points to dulling effects of many poor, florid, convoluted Tennysonian translations of key texts (such as the *Theragatha* and *Therigatha*, as well as most classical Sanskrit poetry) (2). Schelling cites Pound's *Cathay* (1915) as constituting a turning point in the quality and generativity of translations. Schelling's emphasis is on a process of translation, initiated by Pound, that makes Eastern poetries sound and feel contemporary:

> What Pound actually did was to change American poetry forever by introducing tones of voice and ways of writing that seemed waiting to arrive. More modestly, he ushered in a century-long practice of American poets translating the master poets of Buddhist and Daoist China, and of course getting their translations into the hands of readers. Pound's work from the Chinese introduced a clarity or directness of expression suited to the twentieth century. (14)

Schelling notes that in the wake of Pound's translations, many other fine translations followed "from the British poet Arthur Waley, the American Witter Bynner, and with terrific influence on Americans after the Second World, from Kenneth Rexroth" (15), a wave of poet-translators that Schelling traces (in his own anthology) to the more recent work of Gary Snyder, Sam Hamill, Mike O'Connor, Arthur Sze, Eliot Weinberger, and Shin Yu Pai (17).[4]

---

4 While Schelling's anthology provides a generous guide to "Translations of Buddhist Poetry from Asia" (388–393), there is one radically innovative book of translations which casts a very different light on the implicit goal of transparent, immediate, "contemporary" translation as the goal of such work. I am thinking of Yunte Huang's *SHI: A Radical Reading of Chinese Poetry* (New York: Roof Books, 1997). Huang's book presents a crucial reconsideration of the premises of translation and offers multiple translations of several classic poems from China. The result is a radical re-orientation which Charles Bernstein (in a back cover blurb for *SHI*) describes as transforming "our sense of 'Chineseness' by replacing the Orientalized scenic and stylistic tropes of traditional translations with multilevel encounters with the Chinese language."

Schelling's history can re-enforce an oversimplification through an almost formulaic equation of Eastern poetry (and, by extension, Eastern consciousness) with directness of perception. The American-made story of Eastern poetry as the essence of directness (and of an egoless and harmonic relationship to nature) is most pronounced in our estimation of the Japanese haiku form. As Schelling notes, one characteristic of haiku "is its near universal identification with Zen practice and the cultivation of present-moment awareness. The other is that it is surely the best-known and most practiced form of poetry on the planet today" (20).

But the Pound/Imagism railway express that tracks into the present and that still has considerable momentum departed from a rather unusual (and not exactly as advertised) station. Yunte Huang's *Transpacific Displacement: Ethnography, Translation, and Intertextual Travel in Twentieth-Century American Literature* presents a well-researched chapter on Pound which delineates the imaginary and invented nature of Pound's "Chinese poetry." Huang reminds us that Pound "never stepped on Asian soil, although he had a lifelong craving for Confucian culture, and he was an avid traveler. His earliest encounter with the Far East came from his frequent visits to the British Museum in London and from his reading various books on Chinese literature" (65).[5] Huang concludes, "From the Chinese legends to the Japanese interpretation, to Fenollosa's reinterpretation and re-creation, and to Pound's editing and his intertextual transposition that gave birth to his Imagistic poems was not a simple process of forgery, but a complex process of remaking culture" (92).

Huang's critique of Pound's imagined Chinese poetry of the direct, immediate image is worth noting:

> There is one aspect of the Chinese that Pound and most of his followers have either refused to recognize or simply blocked out of their imagination: The Chinese are not always a people "close to nature" when it comes to linguistic practice. Indeed, the Chinese have fashioned a textual tradition that cherishes scrupulous, at times even seemingly

5 Yunte Huang, *Transpacific Displacement: Ethnography, Translation, and Intertextual Travel in Twentieth-Century American Literature* (Berkeley: University of California Press, 2002).

tedious, annotation as a companion to their "close-to-na-
ture" poetry. To make it worse, the poetry and its intimate
companion are very often printed neck to neck on the
page, with poetry lines being ruthlessly interrupted by the
annotation. (76)

It is important, I think, to remain skeptical of an American imagining of another culture's written immediacy. So, too, while not wax-
ing nostalgic for a florid Victorian mode of translation, we should
retain some skepticism about an often unquestioned desire for a
contemporary, easy-to-read translated poem (in the mainstream
American poetic mode of the transparent scenic variety).

But there is another version of immediacy that Schelling identifies and which is quite different from the haiku-imagistic ideal.
Schelling points to a range of activities—calligraphy, painting, the tea
ceremony, martial arts, flower arrangement—that have been linked to
Zen practice. On calligraphy specifically, Schelling observes,

> In China, Ch'an/Zen approaches to calligraphy had long
> maintained that the character of a man—his level of individ-
> ual realization—could be observed in the *ch'i* or life-energy
> that moved through his brush and left an imprint of its pas-
> sage in ink on the rice paper. The same Zen insight suggests
> to American poets that the practice of writing poems is not
> so much to make a thing (let alone to secure prizes, awards,
> or grants) as it is to trace the way the mind moves. (20)

It is this notion of the poem as a location for the immediacy (and
grace) of a mind's movement that I find most appealing. Though
his work is not included in Schelling's anthology, the best example
of such a poetics in action is Robert Creeley's poetry. As Charles
Bernstein (in a recent memorial essay) summarizes, "Creeley's first
principle is that you find out what you have to say in the process of
saying it: poetry becomes a way of making not representing" (194).[6]

6 All references are to Charles Bernstein, "Hero of the Local: Robert

Whereas the Pound-imagism-haiku ideal proposes a transparency
of language and the poem as a site for transmission of a principally
visual experience, Creeley insists that *"poetry is not made of ideas but
words"* (194). As such, the words are not subordinated to the representation of a prior scene or experience, nor are the words of the
poem a vehicle for the indirect or direct expression of an idea. As
John Cage liked to say, "I have nothing to say, and I am saying it."
For Creeley, the fact and infinitely variable particularity of the poem
(and of the line breaks and infinitely variable pauses and cadences
of the poem) point toward a real time improvisational opportunity,
very much like the momentary, concentrated act of the calligrapher
in Schelling's example:

> ...a poem is not a summary of something thought but an
> arc of thinking. This is the temporal dimension of poetry, in
> which words move in time; in this sense, poetry is allied not
> to the visual arts but music and film. (194)

That is when the poems of Schelling's anthology are most exciting: when there is a fresh approach to the poem as a location for the
manifestation of the mind's movement in time. As Bernstein summarizes: "For Creeley, a poem is the fact of its own activity: it exists
in itself and for itself so that we can relate to it not just as 'expression'
but as enactment" (195).

———

To his credit, Schelling includes many poets and poems in his
anthology that do have that quality of (innovative) enactment.
Schelling wonders,

> What of the poems here that offer something new or un-
> precedented for Buddhist art? The ones through which you
> can't trace impulses or origins to earlier Asiatic models?
> These perhaps should fire our passion the most. Such po-

ems introduce a decidedly indigenous flavor to American Buddhism. (23)

That is my own preference in the anthology: for new forms, for unexpected "Buddhist" poems, for perhaps unprecedented ways of enacting an intersection of poetry and Buddhism. Specifically, I am most drawn to "something new" in the selections by Will Alexander, Norman Fischer, Robert Kelly, Michael McClure, Harryette Mullen, Hoa Nguyen, Shin Yu Pai, Dale Pendell, Leslie Scalapino, Andrew Schelling, and Cecilia Vicuña.

For me, one of the great pleasures of Schelling's anthology is encountering many poems and poets unfamiliar to me. My own reading habits in poetry lean toward the contemporary and the experimental. Another joy of reading Schelling's anthology is taking unexpected pleasure in work by more conventional poets. As I've suggested several times in these notes, it is the amorphous nature of what constitutes "Buddhism" (or evidence of Buddhism in the poem) that inadvertently provides Schelling the opportunity to create an excitingly democratic and wide-ranging anthology.

My own anthology within the anthology—my personal favorites—includes Diane di Prima's "Tassajara, Early 1970's" and "I Fail as a Dharma Teacher," Norman Fischer's "I've Changed" and "Poetry's a Way Not a Subject," Sam Hamill's "What the Water Knows," Jane Hirshfield's "Lighthouse," "Studying Wu Wei, Muir Beach," "After Long Silence," and "Why Boddhidharma Went to Howard Johnson's," Michael McClure's "Fourteen," Hoa Nguyen's "Shred," "Captive and Able," "Dark," and "[Roll in Your Skull Gone Green]," Shin Yu Pai's "Yes Yoko Ono," Dale Pendell's "Amrta: The Neuropharmacology of Nirvana," Miriam Sagan's "Contentment," Andrew Schelling's "Haibun Flycatcher" and "Hymns for the Perfection of Wisdom in Paradise," Gary Snyder's "Waiting for a Ride," Arthur Sze's "Thermodynamics," Chase Twichell's "Marijuana" and "The Quality of Striving," Cecilia Vicuña's extraordinary "Fables of the Beginning and Remains of the Origin," and Eliot Weinberger's "Wind." Occasionally, there are poems of tired conventionality and the manipulative poetic MSG that urges the reader to say and feel "wow," poems that lean too heavily on clichéd Buddhist postures: "Reply to T'ao Ch'ien," "Against Certainty," and

"My Listener." On balance, though, Schelling has done an extraordinary job of picking a range of poets and poems full of surprises and discoveries. Equally noteworthy—a nearly miraculous achievement—he has created a site where these varied poets and poems are at home. Perhaps that is possible because, as Norman Fischer puts it, "Poetry is a way not a subject" (86).

Inadvertently, I have been speaking about poetry and poets as if such a pursuit were simply and unequivocally consistent with Buddhist practice. But as Schelling points out, "poets have always regarded poetry as a Way, a path towards realization, though in Buddhist circles arguments have flown both for and against poetry" (21). Thus, Plato was not the only one a long while ago to develop an anxiety about the effects of poems and poets. If, as I've been suggesting, Buddhist practice fosters an affinity for the non-totalizable, the same might be said for most of the poetry in Schelling's anthology. Poetry, regarded as a Way, bears an off-rhyming relationship—a similarity with differences—to Buddhist practice. As Schelling describes it:

> The Way of Poetry became seen as a *practice* in and of itself.
> Moreover poetry draws a certain kind of practitioner—as
> Basho saw it—who is not exactly a priest, not exactly a
> layperson, but something other. The poet in his or her
> devotion to language and experience tries to realize the
> Unconditioned. From the Daoist perspective, such a practi-
> tioner approaches the realm of the "perfectly useless." (21)

If the practice of poetry does involve "a path towards realization," one might reasonably ask, "realization of what?" I would suggest that it is a realization of the oblique present tense grace of the experience of poetic practice itself. Call such a practice a fully attentive playful uselessness which constitutes an enactment and enhancement of essential human qualities.

⸻

But what of my initial question, based on a misunderstanding of the word "wisdom" in the book's title? In some ways, to ask the question—do we still read poetry as part of a search for wisdom—puts us in proximity to an embarrassing and often repressed question, repressed as naïve or amateurish by those of us who over the years have become professionalized and disciplined and serious about poetry: why do we read poetry? I doubt that the answer (or an answer) really veers much from the accustomed course: for pleasure and instruction. What has changed, I believe, is the way we describe and experience that pleasure and instruction. The nature of the pleasure and instruction has, I believe, changed radically.

Do we read for wisdom? Yes, but of a rather indefinite sort. I read, in part, for a kind of exploratory experience: to see and hear how others have explored the resources and possibilities of living and thinking in language. A far cry perhaps from a notion of wisdom as a beautifully stated fortune cookie message. I really do not read for that kind of wisdom—though it occurs at times, and can be a pleasure. And as I've suggested throughout these reflections on Schelling's anthology, an indefinite sort of wisdom is a major virtue of his anthology and of Buddhist thinking generally: they resist totalization; they resist fixating on a definable object or a catechism or dogma, aside from a belief in the value of a lucid, attentive, alert open-endedness.

Our sense of what "wisdom" means has shifted. It is no longer the moment of sudden clarification that Robert Frost avowed: "The figure a poem makes. It begins in delight and ends in wisdom" (18).[7] But even by Frost's time and in his thinking, a certain skepticism and limitation had entered into the conception of "wisdom": "It [the figure a poem makes] begins in delight, it inclines to the impulse, it assumes direction with the first line laid down, it runs a course of lucky events, and ends in a clarification of life—not necessarily a great clarification, such as sects and cults are founded on, but in a

7 Robert Frost, "The Figure a Poem Makes," in *Selected Prose of Robert Frost*, edited by Hyde Cox and Edward Connery Lathem (New York: Holt, Rinehart and Winston, 1966).

momentary stay against confusion" (18). Not an enduring solution
or dogma; no basis for a religion; at best, a momentary experience.

Today, we are not so inclined to think of the poem as something
that fights against a surrounding confusion but rather as a complex
instance of an elusively complex dialectical play of order and disorder.
If the poem tends toward "wisdom"—particularly wisdom linked to
clarification—it is not a wisdom that occurs only at the end of the
poem. It is not a concluding statement that unifies or brings into a
thematic order all the verbal exploration that precedes it.

If contemporary poems offer a kind of clarification, then that
clarification must be reconceived as a momentary intensely engaging
encounter with the infinitely variable particularity of the poem itself
(rather than the reception of a "message" or a concluding "point" or
thematized epiphany that pulls it all together). By the particularity of
the poem itself I mean the poem in all its contingency—down to the
line breaks, the oddly particular (this once) form of the poem as an
inseparable instance and enactment of a momentary wisdom. I mean
what Creeley describes as the arc of thinking. It is not a conclusive
wisdom; it is an exemplary wisdom that beckons forth more activity
and that calls for more thinking and conversing. It is a kind of cho-
reography for the page—an instance of grace or of graceful movement. Admittedly, that graceful movement may initially be called
ugly or jarring, though "beauty is beauty even when it is irritating
and stimulating not only when it is accepted and classic."[8]

Why call such a reading experience "wisdom," particularly when
the term has such a quaint, nostalgic feel to it? In part, I do so out
of trust for the fortuitous error of my initial misperception (thinking "wisdom" to be a decisive word in Schelling's title rather than the
name of the publishing company). But more importantly, I would
ask that we keep that word in mind as a reminder of what's at stake
in reading—what we stake when we devote a substantial portion of
our lives to reading and writing poetry.

As one gets older, the desert island game becomes less fanciful
and more exactly pertinent: if you knew you were going to be
stranded on a desert island, and you could only take three books

---

8 Gertrude Stein, "Composition as Explanation," in *A Stein Reader*,
edited by Ulla Dydo (Evanston: Northwestern University Press, 1993), p.
497.

with you, which three books would you pick? Those of us who have many demands on our time play the game in a less definite way every morning and every day. Increasingly, the mad rush to read and read and see what's new and read it all gives way to a deliberate return to those books, poets, poems that matter most to us. Perhaps fortunately, it is not at all easy to figure out which books these are. That's why we look at our bookshelves and have trouble each morning deciding what to read and why. I wish that the climate for critical prose writing in our time encouraged greater consideration of how and why these few key books matter to us. It is not an easy thing to discuss truthfully.

Hank Lazer has published 13 books of poetry, including *The New Spirit* (Singing Horse, 2005), *Elegies & Vacations* (Salt, 2004), and *Days* (Lavender Ink, 2002). He has given poetry readings and talks in the United States, Canada, China, Spain, France, and the Canary Islands. Lazer's poetry has been nominated for the 2005 Pulitzer Prize. With Charles Bernstein, he edits the Modern and Contemporary Poetics Series for the University of Alabama Press. His two-volume collection of essays, *Opposing Poetries,* was published by Northwestern University Press (1996). For the past twelve years, his essays on innovative poetry, new modes of lyricism, and representations of spiritual experience have appeared in a variety of journals, including *Facture, The Boston Review, Jacket, American Poetry Review,* and *Talisman*. Hank Lazer is a Professor of English at the University of Alabama where he is also an administrator serving as Associate Provost for Academic Affairs.